About This Book

D0491847

Why is this topic important?

A lot of instructional content is uninspiring or worse. And learning content delivered over the Internet or corporate networks is too often dreadfully dull, depersonalized, one-dimensional, generic, force-fed, lockstep, and prepackaged, with meaningless activities and assessments. (Say how you really feel, Patti). We can and must do better than that.

What can you achieve with this book?

Many books recommend teaching and learning strategies based on current learning research and theory but provide few examples of how to apply these in the real world. This book shows you concrete examples of people making learning more inspiring and more engaging every day, in all kinds of settings, all over the world.

In this book you will find valuable ideas that you can adopt or adapt in your own instructional materials to make them more engaging and more worthwhile for learning. These ideas will let you peek over the shoulders of some of the world's most creative instructors, instructional designers and developers, trainers, media developers, and others in order to spark creative ideas of your own.

How is this book organized?

I organized this book into five chapters:

1. Ideas for the Design and Development Process
2. Ideas for Supporting Learners and Learning
3. Ideas for Synchronous and Social Learning
4. Ideas for Self-Paced Learning
5. Ideas for Media and Authoring

Each section contains numerous individual ideas related to the section topic, and most ideas contain screen captures and other information about the idea that will help you adopt or adapt it.

What's New in Volume 2?

Well, duh, the ideas are different from those in the first volume! But it's interesting to note that there are a lot of synchronous and interpersonal activities ideas (Chapter 3) in the new volume related to all of the new social media tools and web applications we now have at our disposal that we didn't have when the first volume was written. Not sure which social media and web applications to use and how to use them? You'll know more after reading this book!

This volume of the book also has a whole lot of creative media ideas (Chapter 5) for you to explore and use. Producing media is much easier than it was when the last volume was published, and that means that you can make your materials look better and more engaging, even if you aren't a graphic artist or multimedia developer.

And there are also many great ideas related to the design and development process (Chapter 1), learning support (Chapter 2), and asynchronous and self-paced learning (Chapter 4). Whether you are an instructor, instructional designer or developer, trainer, or media developer, there are a lot of ideas in this volume to help you build better technology-based and assisted courses.

In addition, I've put more effort into providing a greater number of screenshots so you can really see more of the ideas in action. A picture really is worth a thousand words.

About Pfeiffer

Pfeiffer serves the professional development and hands-on resource needs of training and human resource practitioners and gives them products to do their jobs better. We deliver proven ideas and solutions from experts in HR development and HR management, and we offer effective and customizable tools to improve workplace performance. From novice to seasoned professional, Pfeiffer is the source you can trust to make yourself and your organization more successful.

Essential Knowledge Pfeiffer produces insightful, practical, and comprehensive materials on topics that matter the most to training and HR professionals. Our Essential Knowledge resources translate the expertise of seasoned professionals into practical, how-to guidance on critical workplace issues and problems. These resources are supported by case studies, worksheets, and job aids and are frequently supplemented with CD-ROMs, websites, and other means of making the content easier to read, understand, and use.

Essential Tools Pfeiffer's Essential Tools resources save time and expense by offering proven, ready-to-use materials—including exercises, activities, games, instruments, and assessments—for use during a training or team-learning event. These resources are frequently offered in looseleaf or CD-ROM format to facilitate copying and customization of the material.

Pfeiffer also recognizes the remarkable power of new technologies in expanding the reach and effectiveness of training. While e-hype has often created whizbang solutions in search of a problem, we are dedicated to bringing convenience and enhancements to proven training solutions. All our e-tools comply with rigorous functionality standards. The most appropriate technology wrapped around essential content yields the perfect solution for today's on-the-go trainers and human resource professionals.

Pfeiffer
www.pfeiffer.com

Essential resources for training and HR professionals

The **Online Learning Idea Book**

Volume 2

Proven Ways to Enhance Technology-Based and Blended Learning

PATTI SHANK, EDITOR

Showcasing great ideas contributed by the world's most creative instructors, instructional designers and developers, trainers, media developers, and others

Pfeiffer
A Wiley Imprint
www.pfeiffer.com

Published by Pfeiffer
An Imprint of Wiley
989 Market Street, San Francisco, CA 94103-1741
www.pfeiffer.com

Library of Congress Cataloging-in-Publication Data

Previously catalogued as: The online learning idea book: 95 proven ways to enhance technology-based and blended learning / Patti Shank, editor.

   p. cm.

   ISBN 978-0-787-98168-6 (pbk.)

   ISBN 978-1-118-09368-9; ISBN 978-1-118-09367-2; ISBN 978-1-118-09369-6

1. Internet in education.   2. Computer-assisted instruction.   3. Blended learning.   I. Title.

   LB1028.5 .O499 2007

   371.33/44678 22   2007000640

Acquiring Editor: Matthew Davis
Director of Development: Kathleen Dolan Davies
Production Editor: Dawn Kilgore
Editor: Rebecca Taff
Editorial Assistant: Michael Zelenko
Manufacturing Supervisor: Becky Morgan

Printed in the United States of America
Printing   10 9 8 7 6 5 4 3 2 1

CONTENTS

LIST OF FIGURES AND EXHIBITS

Figures

Exhibits

ACKNOWLEDGMENTS

This book exists because of the contributors who were willing to share their good ideas with me (and you!) and no doubt share their ideas every day with those around them. This book only exists because of their creativity and willingness to share. These are the kinds of folks who make the world a better place to live and work, and I'm so glad that our paths have crossed.

Writing books takes a lot of time and energy so I'm extremely grateful to the folks who make this possible for me. My husband, Greg, puts up with occasional (ha!) crankiness after I spend (far) too much time at my computer. He listens to my bandwidth gripes and computer woes. He's proud of what I do, and that makes me smile more often than he knows. My children, Jess and Andy, both good writers, inspire me to improve my craft (and not embarrass them).

I want to thank my clients, who often need simplicity and clarity as I help them navigate the rutted road and myriad decisions that arise when designing good instruction. I know that their need for simplicity and clarity makes me a better thinker about what I do, and that makes me a better writer.

And thanks to you for buying this book. I'm grateful for the comments you send my way and post online. You also help me improve my craft, and for that I'm most grateful.

Appreciation also goes to Redd, Minnie, and Cleo (my cats) for being such great workmates.

PREFACE

Ideas are like rabbits. You get a couple, learn how to handle them, and pretty soon you have a dozen.

—*John Steinbeck (American writer)*

The ideas in this book are terrific, if I do say so myself (and I do!). But even better than that, they are adaptable, so that you can make them work with different content, using different tools, and in different contexts. So the value of each idea goes beyond the idea itself. Each idea will likely spark additional ideas in your mind as you read them and think about how you can implement them in your world. I suggest that you write ideas that pop into your head as you read each idea in the margins before they run off, as good ideas are likely to do.

This book grew out of the success of the first volume, which grew out of my feeling that the good ideas that people who build online instruction have would be helpful to others who build online instruction. The first volume of the book started out as just an idea, and I am extremely grateful that Matt Davis, the acquiring editor I work with at Pfeiffer, thought it should come to fruition. I didn't know whether people would share their ideas to make the book possible, but because there are so many great people in this field, I thought many of them would. And they did.

And they did yet again for this second volume! My heartfelt thanks go out to those who shared these ideas so that you and I could become better at what we do!

It's easy to get in a rut, do everything the same way, over and over. But it gets boring. And if we are bored, learners are likely to be bored as well. So jump in and see what's here that you can use. I'm guessing that you'll find a lot!

Patti Shank
June 2011

INTRODUCTION

The widespread use of computer networks, especially the Internet, made even greater uses of technology for learning inevitable. The Internet and computer networks have specific affordances for learning that folks who were openly skeptical only a few years ago are beginning to adopt, including the ability to, for example:

- Share documents, help, and resources across time and space,

- Provide widely available and ongoing (rather than time-limited) instruction and support,

- Increase access to learning, and

- Augment classroom-based learning with additional tools and resources.

These same networks bring junk mail, pop-up ads, viruses, information overload, and information of dubious (or worse) value and, too often, boring, unengaging online instruction. It shouldn't be this way.

Learning takes time, contact with and input from others, realistic activities, and support. Many people build instructional materials, online and offline, that are engaging and enjoyable, and you'll see many examples of these in this book. Many of these ideas are quite fast and easy to adopt or adapt, which is a good thing, because almost no one has unlimited time and resources. And they are likely to prompt some great new ideas of your own (that we hope you'll share).

Purpose

The purpose of this book is to showcase proven ideas from some of the world's most creative instructors, instructional designers and developers, trainers, media developers, and others that can be adopted or adapted to make learning more fun and engaging. They are meant to spark creativity, improve your skills, and improve the instruction that you build.

Audience

If you picked up this book, chances are you are involved with using technology for learning in one way or another. This book will give you many dozens of ideas that can improve what you are doing or considering doing.

You may be someone who teaches online or creates instructional content. Or a multimedia developer. Or the head of distance learning. Or someone who occasionally puts something online for classroom-based learners to use in or out of class. Or someone who never uses technology but wonders how he might.

Perhaps you want to put instructional materials online and need some good ideas. You might want to develop a course to sell or to provide free tips on your favorite topic. You may have been putting courses online for a while and find yourself doing the same thing over and over. Perhaps you do professional development with teachers or faculty and want to give them some new ways to engage their students (many of the ideas can be adapted for classroom learning as well). You might be an online learner who wants to give your online instructor ideas on how to make the course more interesting (you might want to wait until grades are posted before you do this) or an instructional designer who wants to augment her skills.

You may work in K-12, higher education, corporate training, professional development, or do training as an adjunct to other duties. If you use or want to use technology for learning, this book is for you, filled with ideas that some of the world's most creative instructors, trainers, and instructional designers are willing to share.

How the Book Is Organized

The book has five chapters:

1. Ideas for the Design and Development Process
2. Ideas for Supporting Learners and Learning
3. Ideas for Ideas for Synchronous and Social Learning
4. Ideas for Self-Paced Learning
5. Ideas for Media and Authoring

Each chapter contains numerous individual ideas related to the topic. Each idea stands alone, but you will find that many ideas would work well together.

How Each Idea Is Presented

Most ideas contains screen captures and other information about the idea that will help you adopt or adapt it. Individual ideas are presented in the following format:

The Big Idea

What

A short description of the idea, so you'll know if you want to read it.

Why

A brief explanation of why the idea is valuable.

Use It!

How

A more detailed description of the idea, how it was implemented, and tips for using it.

Adopt or Adapt

A few ideas to help you start thinking about how to adapt the idea.

Attribution

The originators of the idea, their affiliation, location, and contact information.

Each idea was submitted by the person(s) listed in the Attribution section. Many submitted their own ideas, and some submitted them on behalf of a team of colleagues. These are their ideas, not mine (except for the ideas I submitted). I wrote the final write-up of each idea (the text you see in this book). Some of the words are from the original submission but, as editor, I took great liberties with wording, sequencing, titles, selecting screen captures, and adding or deleting content. Musings in the Adopt or Adapt portion of each idea are often my own. I changed spelling to American English (for consistency only) and attempted to make the voice somewhat consistent as well. I hope I represented each idea well.

How to Use This Book

Individual Use

I designed this book to be read in any order because each idea stands on its own. Open to any idea and read. Or skim for screen captures that intrigue you. It's that easy. If you are looking for ideas on a specific topic, find the chapter that most closely matches that topic and skim through the ideas. Take notes in the margins. This is important: Many ideas could have been placed in more than one section, so skim the rest of the book, too.

Group Use

One great use for a book of ideas is to use the ideas as jumping-off points for learning and new ideas. Brainstorming and discussion of ideas by interested groups of people can produce spectacular energy and results.

Instructional Design Courses

Use the ideas to enhance discussions of creativity, design, selecting instructional strategies, navigation, media and graphics, and other important instructional design topics. Discuss the applicability of various ideas to a variety of projects. Consider how the ideas could be implemented differently in classroom, blended, and online learning. Discuss how the ideas embody current research and thinking about learning. Use the ideas to brainstorm new ideas. Implement some of the ideas and evaluate the results.

Multimedia Authoring Courses

Determine alternate ways to implement the ideas. Build out and enhance the ideas and evaluate the results. Discuss the authoring and programming implications of the ideas and consider other methods for achieving similar results.

Teaching Methods Courses

Use the ideas as a springboard for considering the role of creativity in teaching. Discuss how to use the ideas in classroom and online teaching. Analyze the skills needed to implement the ideas. Consider how the ideas embody current research and thinking about learning. Use the ideas to brainstorm new ideas.

Faculty Workshops

Discuss the rationale for using these ideas. Brainstorm how to use the ideas in different content areas and how to implement them. Share the results of implementing the ideas. Have a contest to see who has the most creative adaptation and implementation. Give the book as a reward for creative online teaching!

Authoring Tool–Specific Groups

Discuss the development implications for implementing each idea and brainstorm effective approaches using specific authoring tools. Use new ideas to brainstorm. Develop a way to share new ideas with members of the group.

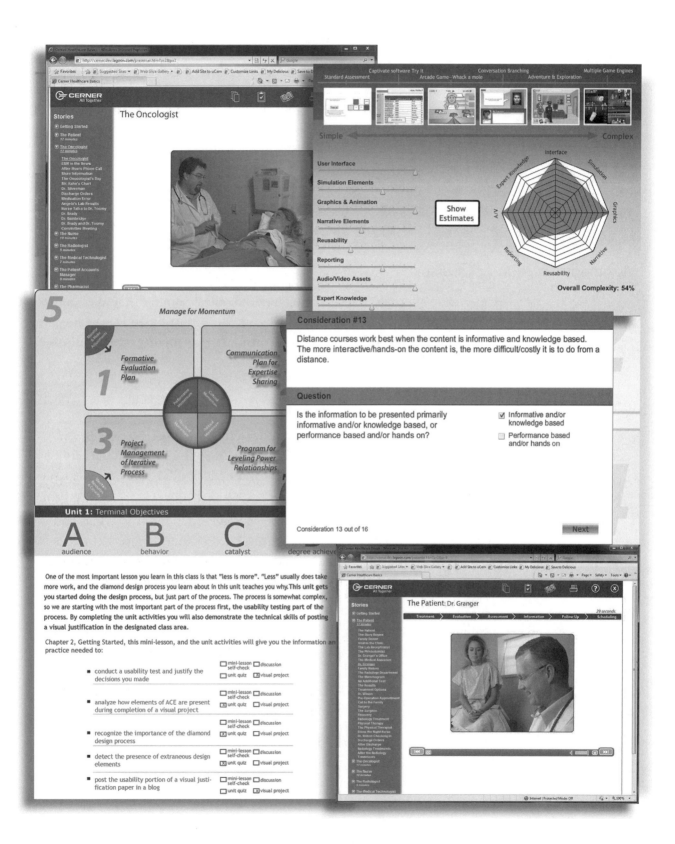

CHAPTER 1

Ideas for the Design and Development Process

This chapter emphasizes ideas that can improve the design and development process, which can make building online and technology-enhanced learning easier and less frustrating for all involved. Typically, building online and technology-enhanced learning involves numerous people (subject-matter expert, designer, developer, graphic artist, and so forth) and it's easy to miscommunicate or do other things that necessitate rework (no fun!). The ideas in this chapter make these processes more efficient and effective in order to reduce wasted effort and improve results.

I'm a strong proponent of good processes and communication and find they save sanity and resources. In the long run, it is extremely worthwhile to spend time and effort building (and updating as needed) good processes with stakeholders, gaining consensus on how they will be used, and helping people to become proficient with them.

Aligning Objectives

The Big Idea

What

This idea shows how using a simple process to write and align instructional objectives will help assure that strategies, assessments, and information presentation are on target and aligned with instructional objectives.

Why

Following the color-coded ABCD chart shown in Figure 1.1 helps you keep your objectives in mind while planning instructional elements. If you are working with people who are not used to instructional design, this may also make the process of writing objectives more meaningful to them.

Use It!

How

Writing meaningful objectives is easier when you follow an ABCD approach: **A**udience, **B**ehavior, **C**atalyst, **D**egree achieved.

The letter "A" stands for audience. Ask: Who is your learner? What about your learner is important for you to think about while you are designing? For example, if your learners are adults, you may not want to use lesson examples and graphics geared toward a teenage audience. And if they include novices, it will be important to explain terms that may not be familiar to them.

The letter "B" stands for behavior. Ask: At the end of the lesson what do you want the learner (the "a"udience) to do, think, or feel? Thinking and feeling are not directly observable, so you need to describe how you want the learner to think or feel and then translate those descriptions into something the learner does that reflects the thinking or feeling. For example, if you want the learners to simply notice something, you

Figure 1.1. ABCD Example for One Lesson

Unit 1: Terminal Objectives

A	B	C	D
audience	behavior	catalyst	degree achieved

One of the most important lesson you learn in this class is that "less is more". "Less" usually does take more work, and the diamond design process you learn about in this unit teaches you why. This unit gets you started doing the design process, but just part of the process. The process is somewhat complex, so we are starting with the most important part of the process first, the usability testing part of the process. By completing the unit activities you will also demonstrate the technical skills of posting a visual justification in the designated class area.

Chapter 2, Getting Started, this mini-lesson, and the unit activities will give you the information and practice needed to:

- conduct a usability test and justify the decisions you made

  ☐ mini-lesson self-check ☐ discussion
  ☐ unit quiz ☒ visual project

- analyze how elements of ACE are present during completion of a visual project

  ☐ mini-lesson self-check ☐ discussion
  ☒ unit quiz ☐ visual project

- recognize the importance of the diamond design process

  ☐ mini-lesson self-check ☐ discussion
  ☒ unit quiz ☐ visual project

- detect the presence of extraneous design elements

  ☐ mini-lesson self-check ☐ discussion
  ☒ unit quiz ☐ visual project

- post the usability portion of a visual justi-fication paper in a blog

  ☐ mini-lesson self-check ☐ discussion
  ☐ unit quiz ☒ visual project

Source: Linda Lohr

describe how they notice. Do they label what they notice, or do you want them to make a statement about what they notice? Feelings are the hardest type of objectives to write because feelings are related to, but different from, thinking. Feelings involve judgment, emotion, values. Words that describe feelings include "prefers" and "models." Writing a feeling objective requires that you describe what "prefers" looks like. If, for example, your objective is to instill a value, such as a value for healthy eating, then your objective describes what healthy eating looks like. You might write a "feeling" objective related to healthy eating as, "The learner selects dark green vegetables."

When you write out the B statements, begin each one with a verb that describes intended learner actions, feelings, or thoughts. The B statements in Figure 1.1 start with these words "conduct, analyze, recognize, and detect." Avoid the verb "understands" because it is not specific enough and it is too "squishy" to measure.

The letter "C" stands for the learning catalyst. Think of C as your instructional strategy for these behaviors. The strategy is how you plan to grab the learner's attention so that the "B" things can occur. The catalysts in Figure 1.1. refer to chapters, mini-lessons, and unit activities. The catalysts are those things that you do to spark learning or interaction.

The letter "D" stands for degree of achievement. Here you identify how you assess whether the listed behavior occurred. Self-check questions, quizzes, discussions, and projects are used to assess whether the behavior is present. To make sure that you match assessments to behaviors, create a checklist next to each "B" statement, as you see in Figure 1.1. If your B statement does not have any of the items checked, you probably need to go back and create a new C (catalyst) or B (identified behavior). The example shown is for a higher education lesson, but a similar approach could be used for online training content. In this case, the assessment elements might include quiz questions (multiple choice, drag and drop, etc.), branched scenario, a tweet response, or something else.

When you are done, look them over. Are all critical behaviors listed? Are there adequate catalysts for these behaviors to occur? Are they the right type? Do the assessment methods align with the behaviors to be assessed? Do you have a balance of assessment methods? The list of "D" items that you create also tells you about the catalysts used. You should see how the "C" items (such as the mini-lesson and quiz) become more specific when you describe how these items will be assessed.

Writing objectives is a back and forth process. You will find that you may jump around trying to get the B, C, and D actions aligned. Using the strategies listed should get you off to a good start.

Technologies used: document

Adopt or Adapt

This idea can be adapted for any content. Although those who regularly design instruction may not feel that they need to follow this type of process, doing so is likely to result in courses where the content, activities, and assessments are better aligned.

Attribution

Submitted by Linda Lohr, professor, University of Northern Colorado, Greeley, Colorado, USA

Contact: linda.lohr@unco.edu

Linda Lohr is a professor at The University of Northern Colorado, where she teaches instructional design. She is the author of *Creating Graphics for Learning and Performance* and has illustrated a children's book. Linda is currently co-authoring an instructional design textbook to support teaching and learning visually.

From Topics to Tasks

The Big Idea

What

This idea provides a simple format that is useful for developing a very high-level design based on tasks rather than topics. This is especially useful at the initiation of an online learning course, when analyzing how to put existing content into an online learning format or when deciding what content needs to be developed from scratch.

Why

Topic-based instruction often doesn't "connect" well to learners' worlds. Topics seem to float outside of the real world, but real-world tasks are inherently meaningful because they are directly associated with the things that learners do.

Use It!

How

When working with subject-matter experts (SMEs) or other stakeholders, one of the first orders of business is to determine what the instruction should "cover." Instruction is almost never able to "cover" everything, and this is especially true with self-paced online instruction. These modules often need to be as concise as possible.

In order to build instructional modules that are concise *and* relevant, Shank uses a short form to analyze the *most important* elements that need to be included. She shares the following form (one example is filled in).

Module: Paid Leave Procedures

A. Topic	B. Real-world task (what the learner does in the real world)	C. Challenges of doing this task	D. Resources used for completing this task	E. How the completion is assessed in the real world
1. Paid leave requests	Complete paid leave request	Determine whether paid leave is available Determine type of paid leave	Pay stub HR intranet Supervisor	Supervisor has adequate and accurate information to approve or reject request
2.				
3.				

Shank starts with topics, because that is a familiar starting place for most SMEs. Then she asks for the things that learners *do* in the real world related to this topic. (Real-world tasks are what the module centers around, but topics are listed to help subject-matter experts get to these tasks.) For each task, the SME then provides information about the challenges of doing each task, the resources used when doing the task, and how the completion of the task is assessed in the real world.

Designers design modules around the *tasks* that learners do, rather than around topics, in order to be relevant and to concentrate on the key things that learners need (especially critical when conciseness is important). The challenges and resources inform the most critical activities and interactions. And the real-world assessments inform the online assessments.

This very high-level design step is a starting place, and more information is obviously filled in after this first step. The importance of this first step, though, is to help shift the focus from topics to tasks and gain critical information to inform next steps.

Technologies used: documents or forms

Adopt or Adapt

Although this idea is primarily used to start the module design process for self-paced online learning, it could be adapted for use in synchronous and higher education online courses because the same elements are needed. Learners are generally more engaged in courses that focus on the tasks they are involved in, so using this approach across the board can be valuable.

Attribution

Submitted by Patti Shank, president, Learning Peaks LLC, Denver, Colorado, USA

Contact: patti@learningpeaks.com or www.learningpeaks.com

Two people have had a major impact on this idea: Joanna C. Dunlap, associate professor and faculty fellow for teaching, University of Colorado–Denver, and Dave Ferguson, The Strathlorne Group, Washington, D.C.

Patti Shank is the president of Learning Peaks LLC, an internationally recognized instructional design consulting firm that provides learning and performance consulting and training and performance support solutions. She is listed in *Who's Who in Instructional Technology* and is an often-requested speaker at training and instructional technology conferences. Patti is quoted frequently in training publications and is the co-author of *Making Sense of Online Learning*, editor of *The Online Learning Idea Book*, co-editor of *The e-Learning Handbook*, and co-author of *Essential Articulate Studio '09*.

Online? Yes, No, Maybe So

The Big Idea

What

This idea provides a decision tool used to analyze whether an online approach makes sense for instructional content for a given instructional situation.

Figure 1.2. Introduction Screen

Welcome to the CL&PD distance learning course decision aid

This decision tool is designed to help you determine whether your course content is suitable for delivering in Sandia's distance learning environment. At this point in time, we are just focusing on the remote site delivery options of videoconferencing or videostreaming.

Prior to making this decision, it is important that you know your target audience and have a solid understanding of the course content.

Each course should be considered individually as to its suitability to be offered via distance learning.

A distance learning program works well when the following four elements are in place:
- Consistent, effective means of transmitting and receiving information (Operational Criteria),
- A motivated group of learners (Participant Criteria),
- A motivated instructor/trainer (Instructor Criteria), and
- Effective training materials appropriate for the distance learning application (Instructional Design Criteria).

The following tool covers the criteria that should be considered when determining whether a course is suitable for distance learning.

Source: Elsa Glassman and Peter Heald

Why

Online learning is not suited for all types of learning or for all instructional situations. This online interactive decision aid is used to help stakeholders assess whether putting their training content online makes sense.

Figure 1.3. Question Screen

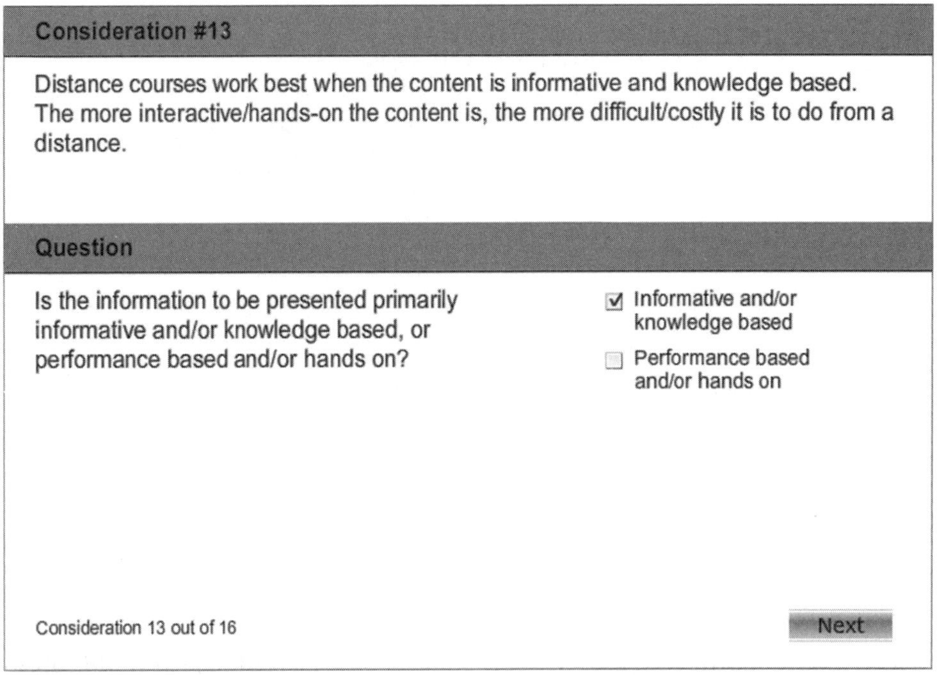

Consideration #13
Distance courses work best when the content is informative and knowledge based. The more interactive/hands-on the content is, the more difficult/costly it is to do from a distance.
Question

Is the information to be presented primarily informative and/or knowledge based, or performance based and/or hands on?

☑ Informative and/or knowledge based

☐ Performance based and/or hands on

Consideration 13 out of 16   Next

Source: Elsa Glassman and Peter Heald

Figure 1.4. Results Screen

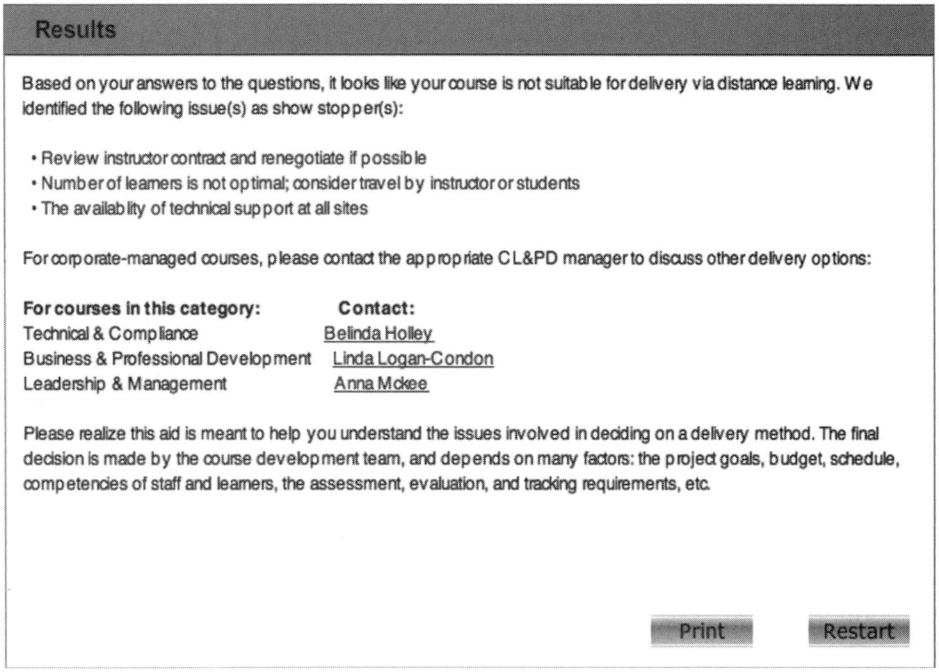

Results

Based on your answers to the questions, it looks like your course is not suitable for delivery via distance learning. We identified the following issue(s) as show stopper(s):

- Review instructor contract and renegotiate if possible
- Number of learners is not optimal; consider travel by instructor or students
- The availability of technical support at all sites

For corporate-managed courses, please contact the appropriate CL&PD manager to discuss other delivery options:

For courses in this category:	Contact:
Technical & Compliance	Belinda Holley
Business & Professional Development	Linda Logan-Condon
Leadership & Management	Anna Mckee

Please realize this aid is meant to help you understand the issues involved in deciding on a delivery method. The final decision is made by the course development team, and depends on many factors: the project goals, budget, schedule, competencies of staff and learners, the assessment, evaluation, and tracking requirements, etc.

[Print]   [Restart]

Source: Elsa Glassman and Peter Heald

Use It!

How

Glassman and Heald created the web-based decision aids shown in Figures 1.2, 1.3, and 1.4 to communicate major decision-making criteria and thereby help non-experts determine whether it makes sense to proceed with putting instructional content online.

Glassman and Heald found that using this aid improves the appropriateness of requests for service from their online learning services team, which helps the team operate more efficiently. It reduces the amount of time the team spends on initial scoping meetings to determine whether a given project is suitable for online delivery.

The text for the entire tool is provided below.

Online Instruction Decision Aid: Is Web-Based Appropriate?

Planning Document

Instructions: This aid will help you begin to determine whether your course content is suitable for online training. To best use this tool, you need to know who your audience will be and have a solid understanding of your content.

Fifteen considerations for putting a course online are listed, followed by a question that will help you assess your content in regard to that consideration. Read the consideration, then answer the question *with a single best answer*. At the end of the questions, you will add up the numbers next to your answers and gain some feedback about how suitable your content is for web-based delivery.

Issue/Question	Criteria	Rating	Consideration
1. How many organizations are impacted by this training?	One Multiple Lab-wide	0 2 3	As your content needs to reach more learners across more organizations, classroom-based training becomes more costly and difficult, while the cost and effort for online instruction stay the same.
2. Where are the learners located?	All at one location At both NM and CA Include remote sites	0 2 3	Online instruction can go across the world as easily and it can go next door. With classroom-based instruction, the more spread out the learners, the more difficult it is to reach them all.
3. Is the content better suited for collaborative/team or individual learning?	Collaborative/team Individual	−2 3	While it is possible to have collaborative learning via an online course, typically these types of interactions are better suited for classroom-based learning.
4. Do the learners have adequate computer skills/web literacy?	Yes No	1 −3	If the learners do not have the computer skills they need to use and interact with computers, being successful with online instruction is more difficult.

(continued)

Issue/Question	Criteria	Rating	Consideration
5. How frequently will there be changes to the course content?	No changes anticipated Plan to update yearly May need to update several times a year	0 1 2	Updates to content can be immediately incorporated into an online course and thereby be immediately accessible to learners.
6. Is there a need to allow learners to move at their own pace through the content?	Yes No	3 0	Classroom instruction has to move with the "average" learner, which leaves slower learners behind and frustrates faster learners. Online learning allows everyone to move at his or her own pace.
7. How important is it for the content to be available immediately or all the time?	Critical Somewhat important Not critical	3 2 0	Unlike instructors, online training never sleeps and can be available at any time and anywhere.
8. What type of skill is being taught?	Knowledge/awareness Procedural Interpersonal Hands-on/performing	3 2 1 –1	Online instruction works best when the content is informative and knowledge-based. The more interactive/hands-on the content is, the more difficult/costly it is to do online.

Issue/Question	Criteria	Rating	Consideration
9. How important is guaranteed consistency of content and/or presentation?	Critical Somewhat important Not important	3 2 0	Instructors' presentations can change slightly from day to day. With online instruction, every learner has the same presentation, which can be very important when dealing with compliance content.
10. What type of access to, or feedback from, the subject-matter expert does the learner need to be successful?	Immediate Delayed None	−3 0 1	Even though the course is available 24/7, it does not mean that a subject-matter expert will be. Learners can email questions, or post messages on course-related discussion boards, but if your content requires immediate feedback from an expert, online training might not be the best tool.
11. What is the availability of qualified instructors for this course?	Very limited Somewhat limited Not an issue	3 2 0	Good and knowledgeable instructors can be hard to come by. Once online training is built, it is available to as many learners as need it.

(*continued*)

Issue/Question	Criteria	Rating	Consideration
12. Do your learners have access to Sandia's restricted network (SRN)?	None have access Some have access Most have access All have access	-3 -2 2 3	Our courses require access to Sandia's restricted network (SRN), so if access is not available, online instruction may not be the best option.
13. Is there a need for automatic test scoring and tracking answers to questions?	Critical Somewhat important Not necessary	3 2 0	Online instruction can track how every single learner answered every single question and automatically compile reports.
14. Are there any resources that the learners need access to that cannot be put online?	Yes No	-3 2	If you have resources that learners will need that are not able to be accessed online (e.g., URLs, printed material, examples, subject-matter experts), this could be an issue to using online instruction.
15. How many learners a month need this training?	Fewer than 5 Between 5 and 25 More then 25	3 1 2	Holding a face-to-face class for a couple of learners per month can be costly and inefficient and can also be a logistical nightmare. Online training is scalable and can reach as many learners as you have, all for the same costs.

Add up the numbers next to your answers.

Scoring

- Less than 20: Reconsider putting instruction online.

- Between 20 and 30: Online training delivery may not be the only (nor best) option.

- Greater than 30: Online training delivery is probably a good fit.

- It is important to remember that this aid is meant to help you begin to understand the issues involved in deciding on a delivery method and that the final decision depends on many factors. You also need to take into account the project goals, budget, schedule, competencies and skills of staff and learners, the assessment, evaluation, and tracking requirements, as well as other factors.

Technologies used: HTML and Flash

Adopt or Adapt

This idea can be adapted for your own situation. For example, your department may want to add other criteria (such as having a desktop computer or experience with taking online courses) or change the values associated with each answer (each answer was weighted between 0 and 3). It can also be adapted to provide decision criteria for other common decisions, such as when to include multimedia elements or whether a synchronous or asynchronous approach makes the most sense.

Attribution

Submitted by Elsa Glassman, corporate online learning and e-learning services team lead, and Peter Heald, multimedia developer on e-learning services team, Sandia National Labs, Albuquerque, New Mexico, USA

Contact: ejglass@sandia.gov and pheald@sandia.gov

Also involved: Jared Pearce, e-learning services team member, and Leslie Gardner, e-learning services team member, Sandia National Labs

Elsa Glassman, a Certified Performance Technologist, has more than thirty years of experience applying her expertise to programs in public education, telecommunication, financial services, and government. In response to a need for more effective and efficient ways to deliver training across the labs, she launched a campaign for e-learning. As a corporate change agent, she founded the Corporate Online Learning Team to leverage organizational expertise in online learning, led a multidisciplinary team to put Sandia's first corporate course online, and was instrumental in creating and implementing corporate online learning standards. Since 1997, she has served as Sandia's e-learning services team lead.

Peter Heald holds a master's degree in instructional technology, with an emphasis in adaptive learning systems and game-based learning. He has worked in the field of e-learning for twelve years, designing, developing, and implementing interactive multimedia-based training. Highly experienced in all technical aspects of multimedia, he is accomplished in Flash programming, streaming video and audio production, LMS conductivity, and the design and programming of interactivity. Peter is currently a multimedia developer on the e-learning services team at Sandia National Labs.

Idea Title: Complexity Analysis

The Big Idea

What

Having a discussion about the desired complexity level for a finished project at the beginning of an online learning project can bring clarity to elements of the project that typically may add cost, time, and resources. Aleckson's Interactivity Calculator (Figure 1.5) is a tool that can be used to anchor this discussion.

Why

Knowing what level of complexity is needed and desired up-front helps all stakeholders understand the cost/time/resource implications of more complex projects. It can also jump-start a critical discussion about the elements that will add the most instructional value.

Use It!

How

Stakeholders often do not understand the implications of additional complexity. Designers and developers need a way of communicating with stakeholders about the investment necessary to achieve more complex and higher levels of learner engagement. Defining the components and the cost, time, and resources that go along with them can improve decisions made, increase collaboration, and lead to increased budget, time, or resource allocations (or stakeholder acceptance of less complexity and reduced budget, time, or resource allocations).

The U.S. Army uses a five-level system to help their design and development teams describe the level of investment that is needed for a particular online learning project. The following is an estimate/adaptation of these five levels.

- *Level One:* "Page-turner" materials
- *Level Two:* Drag-and-drop, sequencing, and similar types of Flash activities every five pages

Figure 1.5. Interactivity Calculator

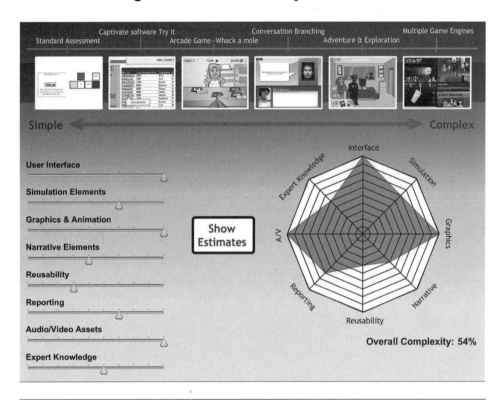

Source: Jon Aleckson

- *Level Three:* Adaptive features and branching depending on learner choices

- *Level Four:* Exploratory features combining multiple types of complex learning activities

- *Level Five:* Complex simulation or serious games such as a flight simulator

Aleckson's team found that, in order to define the effort it takes to create more complex online instructional materials, they needed to analyze each component that increased complexity. They created the Interactivity Calculator for this purpose.

The components that are analyzed using the Interactivity Calculator include:

1. *User Interface:* A complex user interface increases complexity and may require additional graphics and development resources.

2. *Simulation Elements:* Simulations require context (story, background, graphics, etc.) and this typically results in additional writing, graphics, and programming efforts.

3. *Graphics and Animation:* Adding characters, backgrounds, or animation requires more graphic design and programming effort.

4. *Narrative Elements:* Writing dialog requires specialized writing effort, and narration may involve voice-over talent and multiple retakes.

5. *Reusability:* Items designed for reuse may require additional design and programming effort.

6. *Reporting:* The need for more complex data and reports requires additional programming effort.

7. *Audio/Video Assets:* Adding audio and video requires specialized skills and equipment and typically requires multiple retakes.

8. *Expert Knowledge:* The more complex the instruction, the more time is typically needed from subject-matter experts and programmers.

Each of these components can be more or less complex. More complexity in multiple components ups the complexity of the project as a whole. All increases in complexity in each component may impact complexity in other components and impact costs, resources needed, and time.

Technologies used: web programming

Adopt or Adapt

Consider using Aleckson's Interactivity Calculator or developing one of your own (based on the components that are typically manipulated in your projects) and using it at the front end of a project to help stakeholders see the connection between each of these elements and cost, time, and resources needed. Your calculator doesn't have to be web-based. A paper model may work just as well.

Attribution

Submitted by Jon Aleckson, CEO, Web Courseworks, Ltd., Madison, Wisconsin, USA

Contact: jonaleckson@webcourseworks.com or www.webcourseworks.com/blog

Jon Aleckson has managed e-media development for over thirty years and is conducting his doctoral research on increasing collaboration with experts to enhance online learning and professional development programs for the Credit Union National Association, McDonald's Corporation, the World Anti-Doping Agency, and the Children's Hospital of Wisconsin. His company, Web Courseworks, Ltd., creates all types of online learning from self-paced tutorials to online games. Jon is an annual session speaker at the eLearning Guild's Learning Solutions Conference, ASTD, and the American Society of Association Executives. Jon writes a blog called Managing eLearning that can be found at www.webcourseworks.com/blog.

Frustration Reduction Checklist

The Big Idea

What

Online learning has numerous benefits, but it's easy to forget that there are challenges for learners for learning online as well. We should reduce as many of these challenges as possible. A checklist for reducing the typical frustrations of online learning is provided in this idea.

Why

If we don't take steps to reduce frustrations, it's harder to learn. Bad idea.

Use It!

How

It's hard to learn when the materials learners have to use, access to the materials, or learning processes get in the way of learning. To remind her of common frustrations that learners face when using online instruction, Shank created a frustration reduction checklist that she uses when evaluating her own or others' online instruction.

Shank shares the following checklist. All of the items may not be applicable in all online learning situations.

Checklist for Online Learning

Elements	Y/N	Suggested Fix(es) if N
Minimum hardware and software requirements are listed.		
Learner can self-assess that needed technologies are working.		
Technical support is provided prior to and during event.		
Clear and concise "getting started" information is provided.		
Learner expectations are listed.		
Clear instructions are provided.		
Exemplars for expected deliverables are provided.		
Navigation is intuitive and easy to use.		
Persistent navigation is provided for frequently used items/pages.		
Screens are uncluttered.		
Text transcript of narration is available.		
Navigation shows where learner is.		
Organization of materials is clear and consistent.		
Frequently printed materials are available in printable format.		
No competing or extraneous media are used.		
All media works as expected.		
All links work as expected.		
Callouts and annotations are used to focus learner attention as needed on complex screens.		
Conventions (such as buttons and links) act as expected.		

Shank recommends the following when using the checklist:

- Consider having people who didn't design or build the materials test them because those familiar with the program cannot easily judge whether the materials are frustrating (since they understand them because of their familiarity).

- Give testers a list of tasks to do (for example, "Find the assignment that is due after Unit 2") and see whether they can do them without getting lost. If they get lost, the navigation isn't intuitive and should be fixed.

- Watch the faces of people testing the program. If testers look frustrated or you have to explain what to do, it's frustrating and requires a fix.

- Delete and add your own elements to the checklist.

Technologies used: document

Adopt or Adapt

This idea could be adapted for all kinds of online materials, from information on a company intranet to instructional materials. The elements can be adapted for synchronous, asynchronous, and higher education online courses.

Attribution

Submitted by Patti Shank, president, Learning Peaks LLC, Denver, Colorado, USA

Contact: patti@learningpeaks.com or www.learningpeaks.com

Patti Shank is the president of Learning Peaks LLC, an internationally recognized instructional design consulting firm that provides learning and performance consulting and training and performance support solutions. She is listed in *Who's Who in Instructional Technology* and is an often-requested speaker at training and instructional technology conferences. Patti is quoted frequently in training publications and is the co-author of *Making Sense of Online Learning,* editor of *The Online Learning Idea Book,* co-editor of *The e-Learning Handbook,* and co-author of *Essential Articulate Studio '09.*

Better Collaboration with Your Subject-Matter Expert

The Big Idea

What

Creating highly interactive online learning activities, tutorials, games, or simulations requires a team effort. This requires an engaged subject-matter expert (SME), who wants to provide the right information and add to the team, rather than simply provide a content dump.

Why

Having an engaged and enthusiastic SME improves the quality of the final deliverable. This requires two-way communication and expertise-sharing, because the SME needs to understand enough about the design and development process to provide what is needed and the team needs appropriate insights about the content in order to make the content engaging and worthwhile.

Use It!

How

When developing complex online content, such as branched scenarios, games, and simulations, collaboration among the team members is truly critical since tacit knowledge (knowledge that is difficult to articulate and cannot easily be codified into simple rules) needs to be programmed into the content and activities. This requires the SME to share situational decision-making knowledge such as frequently encountered attitudes that need to be overcome for success. Figure 1.6 shows Aleckson's model overlaid on Bacharach's.

Aleckson's Five Factors for Good Collaboration (adapted from Bacharach, 2006) follow:

1. Project management

2. Expertise-sharing

3. Formative evaluation

4. Power Leveling

5. Project momentum

1. Project management. Developing online learning is typically an iterative process and, if it is not well managed, it can easily lead to communication problems and unnecessary work and rework. Make sure that there is a seasoned team leader who assembles the right people and manages resources,

Figure 1.6. Five Factors for Good Collaboration Overlaid on Bacharach's Momentum Model

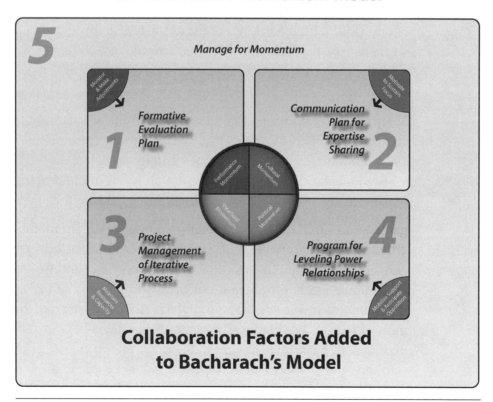

Source: www.webcourseworks.com/showcase/game-calculator, Web Courseworks

tasks, and interdependencies. Aleckson recommends the Agile software development method as an appropriate process for online learning development. "Well managed" means providing clear expectations, communicating schedules and deadlines, and keeping everyone in the loop. A well-managed process respects the SMEs' (and everyone else's) time.

Aleckson especially recommends two project management tools that improve communication and coordination:

- A collaborative project site to hold files, schedules, meeting notes, and communications

- Synchronous communication tools such as web conferencing so face-to-face time can be used as needed

2. Expertise sharing. Design and development teams often expect the SME to be willing to learn about their processes. But does the team also demonstrate a high level of interest in the SME's content area and work? To share expertise both ways, SMEs must understand team roles and expertise and team members have to understand the SME's content and work.

3. Formative evaluation. To increase your team's reputation for quality and to appropriately involve your SME, make a commitment to formative evaluation (evaluation that finds and fixes weaknesses) so quality is assessed on an ongoing basis while the project is under development. Make sure the SME is involved in user testing because this increases his or her commitment to quality and improves understanding of learners' needs.

4. Power leveling. Creating an environment that empowers the team and encourages creativity makes collaboration more fun and fruitful. Promote professional development that positions your team members as experts. Equip the team with tools and templates that make the day-to-day work more efficient. Consider how to upgrade the status of your staff and department, including changes to the office environment and business cards and use of titles like lead game designer or information designer versus the traditional instructional designer title. This, in turn, helps SMEs realize that they are dealing with competent experts in the field of interactive information design.

5. Project momentum. SMEs sometimes complain that projects are stuck. Nothing is more frustrating to an SME than to put forth a ton of effort and not see that effort result in forward movement. Paying attention to the first four factors helps the team move forward and complete the task at hand.

Technologies used: project site and collaboration/communication tools

Adopt or Adapt

These factors can impact online learning projects of *all* kinds, so consider how they might be attended to for your own situation.

References

Agile Development Manifesto: http://agilemanifesto.org/

Bacharach, S.B. (2006). *Keep them on your side: Leading and managing for momentum.* Avon, MA: Platinum Press.

Attribution

Submitted by Jon Aleckson, CEO, Web Courseworks, Ltd., Madison, Wisconsin, USA

Contact: jonaleckson@webcourseworks.com or www.webcourseworks.com/blog

Jon Aleckson has managed e-media development for over thirty years and is conducting his doctoral research on increasing collaboration with experts to enhance online learning and professional development programs for the Credit Union National Association, McDonald's Corporation, the World Anti-Doping Agency, and the Children's Hospital of Wisconsin. His company, Web Courseworks, Ltd., creates all types of online learning from self-paced tutorials to online games. Jon is an annual session speaker at the eLearning Guild's Learning Solutions Conference, ASTD, and the American Society of Association Executives. Jon writes a blog called Managing eLearning that can be found at www.webcourse works.com/blog.

Multiple-Choice Question Checklist

The Big Idea

What

This checklist will help you check the quality of your multiple-choice questions.

Why

Multiple-choice questions seem easy to write but are often poorly written. A checklist can help those who write these questions edit and fix problematic multiple-choice questions before they "go live."

Use It!

How

Multiple-choice questions are frequently used in tests because they are easy to score electronically and question writers think they are easy to write. Even though they may *seem* simple to write, they are typically fraught with problems. Poorly written questions cause problems for learners and make it difficult for question writers to make appropriate inferences from test results.

Shank built the Multiple-Choice Question Checklist on the next page to analyze multiple-choice questions. She suggests that multiple raters (such as instructional designers and content experts) use the checklist to uncover likely problems prior to "going live."

Multiple-Choice Question Checklist

Multiple-Choice Question	Y/N	Fixes Needed
Are multiple-choice questions an appropriate way to measure each learning objective (that multiple-choice questions are being used to assess)?		
Does the percentage of questions for each learning objective match the relative priority of the objective?		
Does the question require the same depth of thinking as the corresponding learning objective?		
Does the question measure more than recall of factual information?		
Is irrelevant or superfluous information eliminated from the question?		
Are irrelevant or superfluous images eliminated from the question?		
Does the question have a single, unambiguously correct answer (or more than one single correct answer for a *select all that apply* question)?		
Is *select all that apply* added to questions with more than one correct answer?		
Are negatives (**not**, DO NOT, etc.) avoided or made to stand out?		
Was the question content adequately covered in the instruction?		
Are the directions clear?		
Is all language clear and non-ambiguous?		
Are the spelling and grammar correct?		
Is the wording at an appropriate reading level?		
Does the question contain enough information from which to choose the correct answer or answers?		
Are *all* distractor answers plausible?		
Are only as many distractors as are plausible used?		

Technologies used: document

Adopt or Adapt

This idea can be used to evaluate any multiple-choice questions. It can be adapted by adding or deleting questions. An online form may be a useful way to obtain evaluations of questions from multiple raters.

Attribution

Submitted by Patti Shank, president, Learning Peaks LLC, Denver, Colorado, USA

Contact: patti@learningpeaks.com or www.learningpeaks.com

Patti Shank is the president of Learning Peaks LLC, an internationally recognized instructional design consulting firm that provides learning and performance consulting and training and performance support solutions. She is listed in *Who's Who in Instructional Technology* and is an often-requested speaker at training and instructional technology conferences. Patti is quoted frequently in training publications and is the co-author of *Making Sense of Online Learning*, editor of *The Online Learning Idea Book*, co-editor of *The e-Learning Handbook*, and co-author of *Essential Articulate Studio '09*.

Story-Based Learning v2

The Big Idea

What

> This idea follows the process of making changes to an existing self-paced story-based instructional module and describes lessons learned from the experience.

Figure 1.7. Healthcare Industry Basics Course

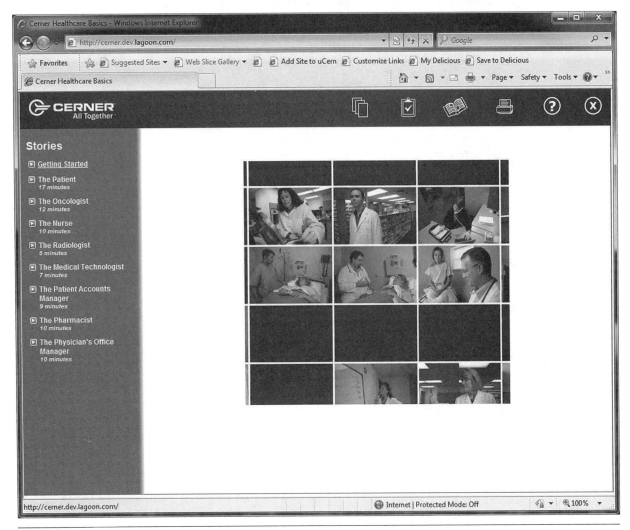

Source: Cerner Corporation, www.cerner.com

Why

> Stories are a powerful and engaging way to learn. Improving existing stories improves instruction. Learning from others' redesign experiences can improve the design of your instruction.

Figure 1.8. Scenario: Dr. Toomey, Patient

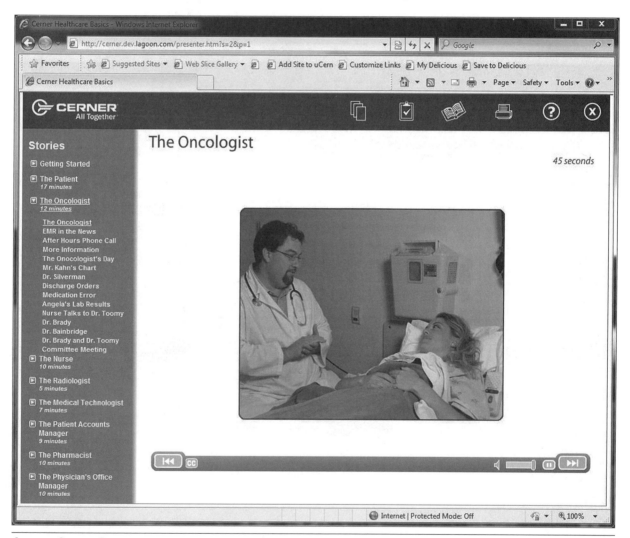

Source: Cerner Corporation, www.cerner.com

Use It!

How

Stories are used in this module to help people new to a field better understand what it takes to succeed. This includes key terminology, important facts, key concepts, rules and procedures, people and roles, and guiding

Figure 1.9. Scenario: Nurse, Patient

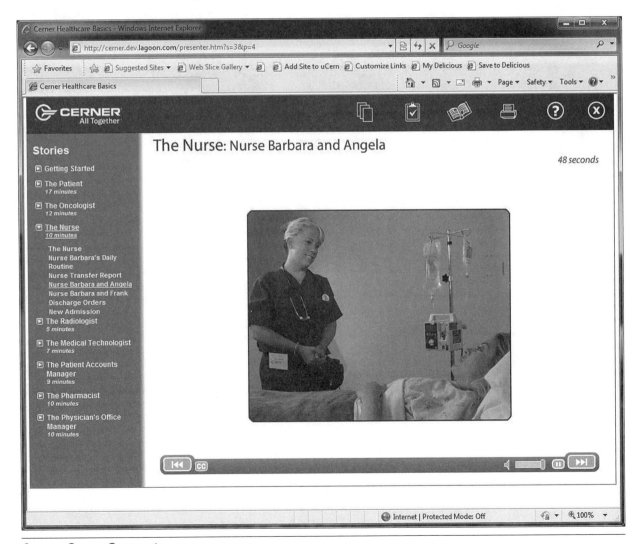

Source: Cerner Corporation, www.cerner.com

Figure 1.10. Scenario: A Second Opinion

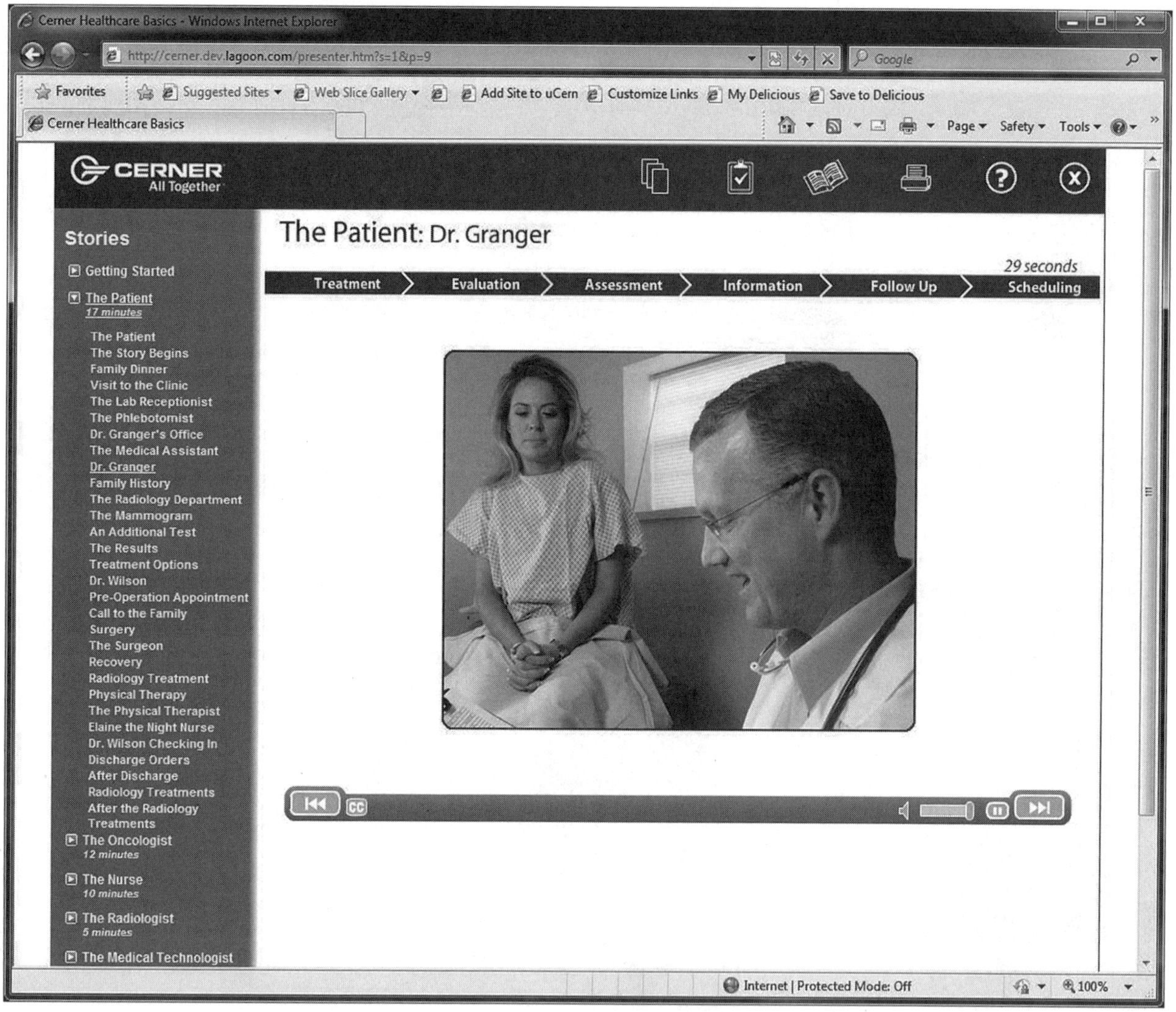

Source: Cerner Corporation, www.cerner.com

principles. The initial version of this story (described in Volume 1) contains a main character, supporting characters, dramatic conflicts, and emotional content. In that version, the learner follows a patient, nurse, oncologist, radiologist, medical technologist, pharmacist, patient accounts manager, and physician office manager through a series of scenarios. In

Figure 1.11. Scenario: Patient Care

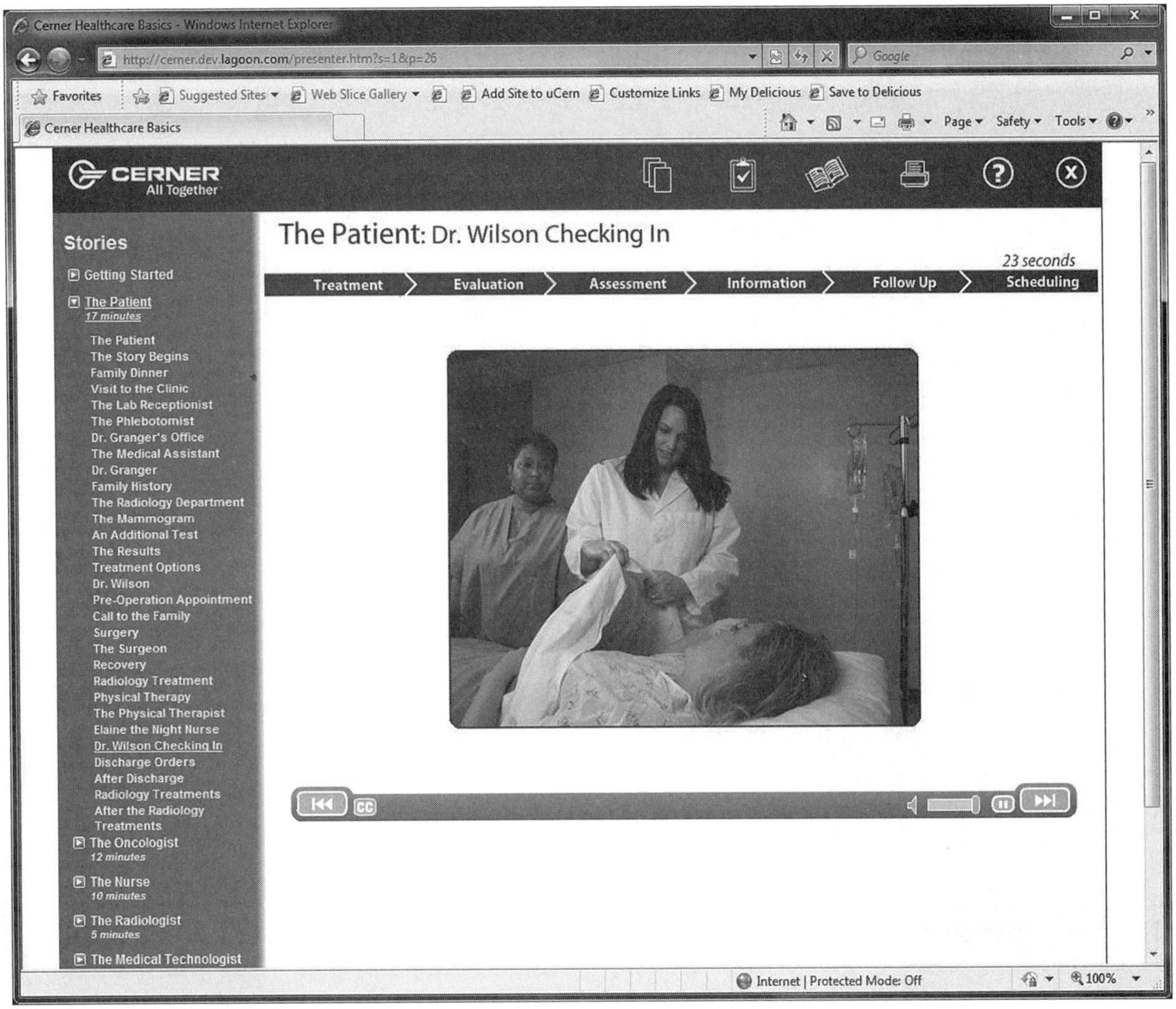

Source: Cerner Corporation, www.cerner.com

the patient scenario, for example, the learner follows the main character, Terry, who has been diagnosed with cancer, and watches how Terry interacts with a primary care physician, an oncologist, a nurse, and other clinicians.

The same story is then retold from other perspectives, including a nurse and an oncologist. The aim of these scenarios is to introduce the learner to healthcare terminology and processes, key players and tasks, key drivers, and healthcare regulatory and government agencies affecting each role, department, or process. (See Figures 1.7 through 1.11.)

The initial version of the instruction focused on the perspectives of physicians, nurses, and patients regarding the diagnosis and treatment of breast cancer. The story described the patient's experience with healthcare professionals in diagnosing, treating, and recovering from the unexpected illness. The experience of the patient introduced learners to various clinicians and doctors who worked with the patient over time.

In the second version of this instructional module, the instructional design team connected the storylines to the performance workflows that supported the various doctors' and clinicians' efforts to treat the patient. Connecting the various performance workflows to the doctors', nurses', and patient's experience introduces additional depth and creates a foundation for deeper learning as learners advance in their professional careers.

Smith shares some of the lessons learned as the team improved the initial version of the module:

- The first version storyline was written by an instructional designer. In the second version, a professional script writer was hired to write the dialog so that it was more realistic, flowing, and cohesive.

- When building the first version, members of the team expressed concerns about overloading learners. Experience showed, however, that learners can keep track of multiple storylines and disconnects within the storyline.

- The images in the first version were taken in an office building that was made to look like a patient's home and hospital environment. Feedback showed that the environment detracted from the story. In the second version, images came from a hospital, clinic, doctor's office, patient's home, and other locations that were more realistic and more associated with the storylines. Images were shot in a wing of a hospital that was being remodeled, using equipment after hours, and using unused sections of doctors' offices. Feedback showed that learners better bought into the storyline when these real locations were used.

- In the second version, green screen technology was proposed to speed up the time required to shoot images and place the story's characters in specific environments. But this technology was too costly and the location-based image shoots made better financial sense.

Technologies used: Flash, content development engine

Adopt or Adapt

This idea provides multiple "ah-ha's" about updating an existing instructional module that can be used when considering a redesign of existing instruction, such as what additional talent may be needed, which locations are best for video or photos, and the assumptions about learners that need to be tested. It also shows the value in rethinking how courses are designed and developed to improve them, especially as new information and insights are gained.

Attribution

Submitted by Stephen Smith, instructional designer and performance consultant, Sole Proprietor, Lenexa, Kansas, USA

Contact: SteveSmith@gmail.com

Others involved: Shawn Foley, manager, Healthcare Professions Education, Cerner Corporation; Miles Coleman, learning architect, Cerner Corporation; and Robert Campbell, chief learning officer, Cerner Corporation

Stephen Smith is a learning strategy consultant. His interests include designing impactful learning experiences, aligning those experiences with individual and organizational growth, and extending the boundaries of meaningful instructional technology use.

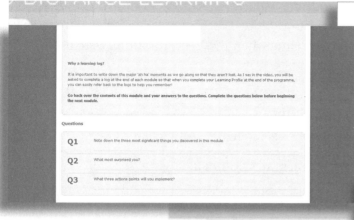

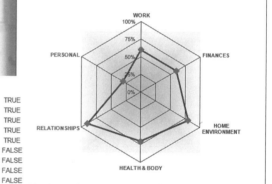
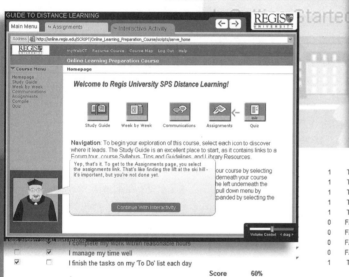
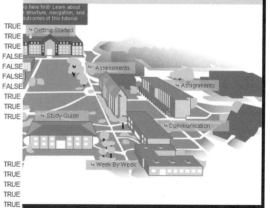

Ideas for Supporting Learners and Learning

This chapter highlights ideas that make learning easier or that support learners during the learning process. Organizations too often pour myriad resources into building instruction without assessing what support learners need to be successful. Learners who aren't supported are often less successful and less persistent, so support can be quite essential. We can dramatically improve results by adequately supporting learners and learning!

Survival Skills

The Big Idea

What

This idea provides practical guidelines that can be offered to online learners to help them cope with the challenges of being online learners. It is primarily aimed at online higher education students but could be adapted for others.

Why

New online learners often come with apprehensions about the technology and about whether they can really learn this way. The truth is, being successful in an online class requires some unique strategies, and these strategies may not be obvious. And because learner problems tend to become instructor problems, sharing these strategies may save headaches for both!

Use It!

How

Barber shares a list of tips with online learners in her courses so they can enjoy greater success. The list provides numerous strategies for coping with the challenges of taking online classes and completing online degree programs. Here are the tips Barber shares with online learners:

Tips for Online Learners

Scheduling Tips

1. If you are taking more than one online class, I recommend that you gather the syllabus/calendar for each class at the beginning of each semester and transfer the dates to a master calendar that includes all important things like synchronous course times, assignment due dates, exam dates, and so forth, for all classes.

2. Look over this master calendar at least at the beginning of each week and determine what needs to be done that week to make progress on upcoming items.

3. Cross off each item or assignment once it is completed. It is rewarding to be able to look back and see everything that has been accomplished!

Habits Tips

1. Review your personal life and work life and plan the days and times to be devoted to online coursework. If the class were being taken in a face-to-face format, an attendance schedule would have to be followed. Creating a personal attendance schedule (time to spend on coursework) requires self-discipline but is needed to succeed.

2. Recognize that some sacrifices will likely need to be made. But remember that this is short-term pain for long-term gain!

3. Rearranging your typical habits and lifestyle may be needed. For instance, those who normally stay up late may find it hard to have enough energy at the end of the day for coursework. You may find it easier to study if you go to bed earlier and then get up very early, before others in the household are awake, to work on coursework.

4. I encourage you to work on coursework on weekends, but don't give up all of your weekend time to study or work on assignments. To stay with this long term, you have to spend some time doing the things you really enjoy doing, including spending time with loved ones and friends.

5. If there are certain people or situations that cause unnecessary stress, do what you can to avoid those people and situations. You'll need your energy level to remain high to keep on track with your work, life, and studies.

6. Don't sweat the small stuff. Make that your mantra.

Getting Help and Support Tips

1. Before emailing the instructor with questions about an assignment or project, reread the instructions first. Most instructors spend a great deal of time to make sure that instructions are clear and concise. If the answers you need aren't there, see whether someone has already asked this question in the discussion forum.

(*continued*)

2. On the other hand, don't be so self-sufficient that you feel like you're all alone. Becoming isolated from classmates and the instructor is a mistake. Use the class discussion board to post questions or use the course email to communicate with other learners, the instructor, a distance education advisor, or coordinator.

3. Take advantage of online or face-to-face orientations. These orientations can increase your comfort level and skill with course technologies quickly.

4. Use learner technical support for help with (inevitable) technology glitches. First determine (if you can), whether technology issues are due to your computer or they are due to the course platform.

Preparing for the Unexpected Tips

1. There are times when unexpected crises will impact your coursework. I recommend that you try to keep ahead of schedule and *assume* that there will be things that get in the way of doing coursework or meeting deadlines from time to time.

2. Don't assume instructors will allow late work due to personal issues. And those who do are unlikely to deal with this pleasantly more than once. So if you are late, be prepared to have points taken off.

3. It can be helpful to print out assignment information, lecture notes, and so forth, for when you cannot access a computer. This way, you can do coursework at times when you cannot be at a computer (when waiting for a doctor's appointment or at your children's sports games).

4. Be prepared for Internet failure or course system down time. That means never wait until the last minute to do the work. And realize that you *need* a reliable computer and access to be successful.
   If you have computer problems, have them fixed.

5. Pay attention to campus-wide announcements about times that the course system will be off-line and unavailable. If learners are given ample notice of these down times, instructors are unlikely to accept late assignments or allow learners to make up missed work.

These tips will help you experience greater success and satisfaction!

Technologies used: electronic document

Adopt or Adapt

These tips could be adapted for use in a variety of online learning situations. For example, a set of tips could be provided to learners in both asynchronous and synchronous online training courses. They could be adapted with tips for being successful in learning certain types of content, such as physics or leadership skills.

Tips like these could be provided in electronic or print documents or they could be posted on a web page or a course page.

Attribution

Submitted by Susan Barber, distance education instructor/coordinator, Stephen F. Austin State University, Nacogdoches, Texas, USA

Contact: sbarber@sfasu.edu or www.sfasu.edu/education/departments/elementary/areasofstudy/ec-6dist.asp

Susan Barber has been teaching online courses for six years and serves as program coordinator for Stephen F. Austin State University's EC-6 Distance Education Program for students to earn a bachelor of science in interdisciplinary studies and earn Texas state teaching certification for grades pre-kindergarten through sixth grade.

Rules of Engagement

The Big Idea

What

Group activities can be hindered by poor group communication and unequal sharing of obligations. These activities can be enhanced by having teams develop a "Rules of Engagement" team contract.

Why

A team contract helps groups determine how they will work together to achieve the desired results and documents commitments to each other.

Use It!

How

Involving learners in group projects is a popular instructional strategy in online courses because:

- Group work can help counter the isolation some online learners can feel because they are physically removed from the institution, their peers, and their instructor.

- Exposing learners to multiple perspectives can open their eyes to diverse ideas.

- Learners can achieve higher results with support.

- The quality of individual learner work can be enhanced through collaboration.

- Group projects can help instructors manage their workload because, instead of evaluating twenty-five individual learner projects, they may instead evaluate five group projects.

But lack of adequate support for group projects may erode positive outcomes and lead to groups that are dysfunctional or learners who feel that the assessment process is inequitable. To minimize obstacles to effective group work, teams can establish a formal agreement describing how they will work together. A "Rules of Engagement" team contract may be especially important for learners who have had negative past experiences in which they had to cover for team members who did not contribute.

In the contract, each team specifies:

- Who will post deliverables?

- Who will lead the group during various projects?

- How will they communicate with each other? How often? Will they set interim deadlines?

- How will work be distributed?

- What is the preferred work style?

- What are the consequences for not getting work done?

- What are the known problems?

Some examples of team questions and team responses are shown in Figures 2.1 and 2.2.

Team members can use these with the Team Review Form (the next idea in this chapter) to assess each other's contributions to group projects.

Dunlap explains that this strategy addresses her need to make sure the learners (and she) have a chance to better realize the benefits of group projects by minimizing the problems associated with unstructured group activities. It also gives the learners responsibility for determining how they will work together and empowers them to establish their own rules and consequences.

Figure 2.1. Team Questions

Teamwork Questionnaire

Each team needs to respond collaboratively (which means all team members are in agreement with the response) to the following questions:

1. **Purpose of teams:** Define the role and purpose of your team (and the teamwork completed) during the course? What value does the team offer, if any?

2. **Individual learning goals vs. team requirements:** What are each team member's individual learning goals for the course, and how will the team make sure that everyone achieves those goals? (Teams need to be responsible for every team members' learning, not just completing products together.)

3. **Project leadership:** Who will provide leadership during each phase of the project? Will leadership rotate? What are leaders responsible for (e.g., Does a leader need to fill in the gaps if other team members do not follow through? Does a leader need to send reminders to team members regarding products and timelines?)?

4. **Independent and/or collaborative work:** Do members of your team prefer to work on their own? If so, how will they coordinate their individual contributions so that they "go together" in both form and style? Or, do members of your team prefer to work collaboratively, perhaps in joint work sessions during which work can be coordinated?

5. **Weekly communication patterns and format:** Discuss the issue of asynchronous vs. synchronous -- strength, weakness, reason for both -- as part of this process so you have a plan of action for working together. Will you communicate asynchronously or set up a synchronous time each week to connect?

6. **Workload:** What agreements has your team developed regarding workload? Will team members assume equal portions of the work each week, or do you anticipate contributions varying over the semester? If the latter, how will you ensure that this is fair?

7. **Review and feedback:** What expectations have been established regarding thoughtful, regular critique of team members' work? How will you provide feedback when you feel someone's work needs to be revised? When you are receiving feedback, how can you remain open to new ways of thinking and doing?

8. **Addressing problems:** How will your team communicate about problems that emerge, and develop solutions? (Unanticipated emergent problems; Work not done on time/not what was agreed to/not of sufficient quality or quantity; Meetings are missed; etc.)

9. **Commitment to quality:** Describe the commitment team members are making and the quality of work you are aiming for.

10. **Evaluating process:** How and when will you evaluate your team process/collaboration in terms of what is working, not working, needs adjustment, and so on?

11. **How, when, and why to ask for mediation:** Specifically define under what conditions you will ask for mediation from Dave and Joni?

Source: Joanna Dunlap

Figure 2.2. Team Responses

Team E Agreement

1. Will you have a leader who keeps the team on track during team assignments?

After a preliminary review of the projects, Team E has decided that it is best to have a different team leader for each of the weeks that have a team assignment. The team leader will be assigned a week in advance based on personal schedules at that time.

2. How do you prefer to work?

After reviewing individual work schedules, we have decided to assign a team leader a week in advance so that he/she can organize and assign tasks to be completed by the weekend before the due date. This will provide an adequate amount of time for completion and review by our teammates. The team leader will assign a preliminary due data prior to the actual due date for all to adhere. This offers flexibility to each team member to work on his/her task, yet hold him/her accountabele to successful completion of his or her tassk by the due date.

3. Do you agree to provide timelym substantive feedback?

We all agree that it is importan to provide feedback that is positive. This benefits the team and provides open communication. It is important to critique constructively...the team wants to create superior product.

4. How will you handle a team member who does not do what he/she has agreed to do?

The team is comprised of professionals and we expect if an individual has a problem (technical or personal) hindering him or her from performin the assigned task, the team will be notified ASAP so the team can assist in the completion of that task. The team may advise, inform, break the task into smaller and more manageable parts, or assign to another team member. The team leader will be th focal poin for managing these activities. At that point the team will also negotiat how the team member's assignment score should be aggected.

Source: Joanna Dunlap

Adapt or Adapt

This idea is perfect for classroom-based, blended, and online courses that utilize group work and could also be used in non-instructional group situations, such as committees or project teams.

Attribution

Submitted by Joanna C. Dunlap, associate professor and faculty fellow for teaching, University of Colorado–Denver, Denver, Colorado, USA

Contact: joni.dunlap@ucdenver.edu

Joanna C. Dunlap is an associate professor of instructional design and technology at the University of Colorado–Denver. An award-winning educator, her teaching and research interests focus on the use of sociocultural approaches to enhance adult learners' development and experience in post-secondary settings. For over fifteen years, she has directed, designed, delivered, and facilitated distance and e-learning educational opportunities for a variety of audiences. Joni is also the university's assistant director for teaching effectiveness, working through the Center for Faculty Development to help online and on-campus faculty enhance their teaching practice.

Team Review Form

The Big Idea

What

Group results are hindered when team members do not fulfill their obligations. A Team Review Form provides information to help team members know where they stand in meeting team commitments, which can improve group process and results.

Why

A Team Review Form allows learners to provide feedback to each other about how well they are meeting commitments.

Use It!

How

Learners use the Team Review Form (Figure 2.3) to assess each group member's contributions (including their own contributions) on group projects.

Team reviews can have ramifications, such as grade reductions for individuals who receive less than a certain number of points from other team members. This empowers learners to have a say in the point distribution on group projects. This review process also functions as an incentive for all group members to fulfill their obligations (see the previous Rules of Engagement contract idea for a way to document agreed-on obligations). The review process also provides the instructor with helpful insight and data for giving feedback and support to individual group members and the group as a whole:

1. The Team Review Form summarizes the project work and the content of private group discussions.

2. It alerts the instructor to specific group and group member problems. This allows the instructor to address the issues quickly and efficiently.

Figure 2.3. Team Review Form

For each item, select the score you believe best reflects that person's efforts and contributions.

If the person:

- Always demonstrates the quality, you would give a score of 5.
- Frequently demonstrates the quality, you would give a score of 4.
- Sometimes demonstrates the quality, you would give a score of 3.
- Seldom demonstrates the quality, you would give a score of 2.
- Never demonstrates the quality, you would give a score of 1.

Your Name:					
Team Member Reviewed:					
1. Is willing to frequently share ideas and resources.	5	4	3	2	1
2. Accepts responsibilities for tasks determined by the group.	5	4	3	2	1
3. Respects differences of opinions and backgrounds.	5	4	3	2	1
4. Is willing to negotiate and make compromises.	5	4	3	2	1
5. Provides leadership and support by taking an active role in initiating ideas and actions.	5	4	3	2	1
6. Respects decisions of others.	5	4	3	2	1
7. Provides positive feedback of team members' accomplishments.	5	4	3	2	1
8. Is willing to work with others for the purpose of group success.	5	4	3	2	1
9. Online communication is friendly in tone.	5	4	3	2	1
10. Keeps in close contact with team members for the purpose of maintaining team cohesion and collaboration.	5	4	3	2	1
11. Produces high quality work.	5	4	3	2	1
12. Meets team deadlines.	5	4	3	2	1
13. Comments (Please provide your teammate with positive and constructive feedback.):					

Source: Joanna Dunlap

Often, when given the means and opportunity, learners provide thoughtful and detailed feedback to group members and are honest about their own contributions. Plus, these reviews provide the instructor with useful comments to be included in feedback to individual learners. Dunlap explains that this strategy addresses her need to make sure the learners (and Dunlap) have a chance to better realize the benefits of group projects.

Technologies used: web form

Adapt or Adapt

This tool would work well for classroom-based, blended, and online courses that utilize group work and could also be used in non-instructional group situations, such as committees or project teams.

Attribution

Submitted by Joanna C. Dunlap, associate professor and faculty fellow for teaching, University of Colorado–Denver, Denver, Colorado, USA

Contact: joni.dunlap@ucdenver.edu

Joanna C. Dunlap is an associate professor of instructional design and technology at the University of Colorado–Denver. An award-winning educator, her teaching and research interests focus on the use of sociocultural approaches to enhance adult learners' development and experience in post-secondary settings. For over fifteen years, she has directed, designed, delivered, and facilitated distance and e-learning educational opportunities for a variety of audiences. Joni is also the university's assistant director for teaching effectiveness, working through the Center for Faculty Development to help online and on-campus faculty enhance their teaching practice.

Motivation Matters

The Big Idea

What

This idea from Kate Cobb provides a worksheet that learners complete before an ongoing coaching or training series to document their goals and reasons for and against proceeding.

Why

By asking the learners to thoughtfully consider the change they want to see happen and to rate their motivation on a scale of 1 to 10, learners are cognizant of the forces at play that can assist them or hold them back and more focused on the effort that will be involved.

Use It!

How

Before learners enter Cobb's coaching program, they complete a Motivation Matters Balance Sheet (shown on the next page). It is intended to

- Capture learners' motivation at a point at which they are enthusiastic and eager

- Document the learners' goals, what may get in their way, and how much they want to make the desired changes (how much do they really want this?)

- Help learners recommit later in the coaching process when things are getting tough

- Provide a yardstick for measuring achievement of goals or changing them as the process continues

Cobb shares the Motivation Matters Balance Sheet she developed for this process.

Motivation Matters Balance Sheet

You're motivated by your goals NOW, but will this last throughout the coaching process? It's quite usual that once you get about halfway to your goals, you'll experience a dip in your motivation.

By completing this Motivation Matters Balance Sheet at the start of the journey, we will have something to go back to later if you waver. It's a little like insurance for when things get off track, when you are very busy with other things, and the coaching process begins to become too challenging.

It's important to complete a section for each goal that you have, so create a separate grid for each goal.

- Think about the reason to make the change you want.

- Think about the reasons NOT to make the change.

- Rate the importance of each of those reasons between 1 and 10 (1 being not important at all, 10 as important as possible).

Goal: _____

Reasons FOR Making the Desired Change	RATE	Reasons for NOT Making the Desired Change	RATE
_____	_____	_____	_____
_____	_____	_____	_____
_____	_____	_____	_____
_____	_____	_____	_____
_____	_____	_____	_____

Cobb says that this process works especially well for clients whose organization is expecting a return on investment from the process. Completing the process may point out how the learners' and the organization's goals may be at odds. If this is the case, the coach and learners will initially work on how to blend these goals. The process also points out people who have been "sent" for coaching and who may not yet buy into the need for coaching. If that is the case, that issue needs to be resolved before coaching commences through discussion between the coach and learner. If there is a clear disparity between what the organization wants and what the learner wants, the manager may also need to be involved.

Cobb provides the following recommendations for implementing this process:

- Ask learners to complete the form after they have established their initial goals for the process.

- Refer back to the sheet at the mid-program review point or when any milestones have been reached.

- Use it again at the end of the process as a review of progress.

Technologies used: email, online meeting tool, online forms, course management system

Adopt or Adapt

This idea can be adapted to fit a variety of coaching, mentoring, and learning situations. For example, if a learner is entering a difficult or time-intensive training program or going back to school to complete a degree program, it may be very helpful to begin the process with a worksheet much like the one shown in this idea and to have discussions about what is written with someone who will be with him or her throughout the journey (instructor, student advisor, supervisor, and so on). This process may be especially valuable when coaching, mentoring, or learning is occurring at a distance, as it may be harder to maintain motivation.

Attribution

Submitted by Kate Cobb, director, Blended Learning Zone, Cagnes sur Mer, France

Contact: kate@blendedlearningzone or www.blendedlearningzone.com

> Kate Cobb works with HR/L&D professionals who are seeking solutions to management learning issues by supporting them in the development and implementation of blended learning programs to move business objectives forward. She assists companies in designing learning strategies to develop true learning cultures. Cobb is also a coach working to empower women leaders, both face-to-face and online.

Virtual Campus

The Big Idea

What

Develop a virtual campus with amusing tutorials for distance learners to help them get off to a good start and feel connected to the actual campus.

Why

A virtual campus graphical interface with embedded tutorials helps distance learners "visit," connect, and get onboard.

Figure 2.4. Main Menu

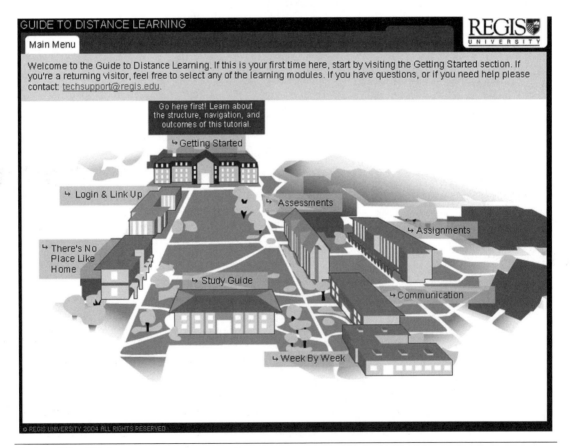

Source: Ellen Waterman

Figure 2.5. Guide

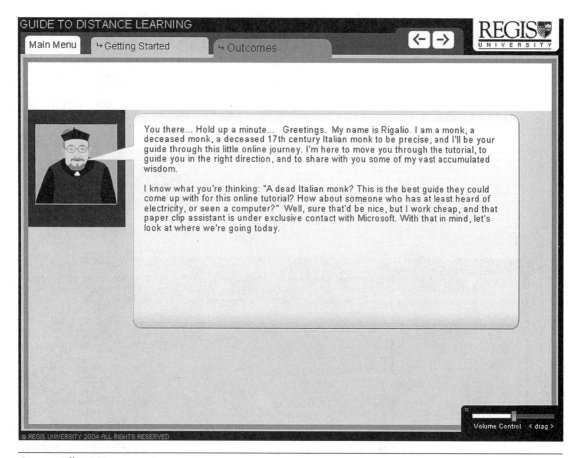

Source: Ellen Waterman

Use It!

How

Regis University's Distance Learning Team developed the Guide to Distance Learning tutorial shown in Figures 2.4 through 2.7 with a graphical interface of a virtual campus in order to prepare distance learners for a successful distance learning experience.

The main menu (Figure 2.4) shows numerous buildings, each of which corresponds to a module within this tutorial. The tutorial includes modules that help learners use the tutorial, discover how to get into

Figure 2.6. Assignments Overview

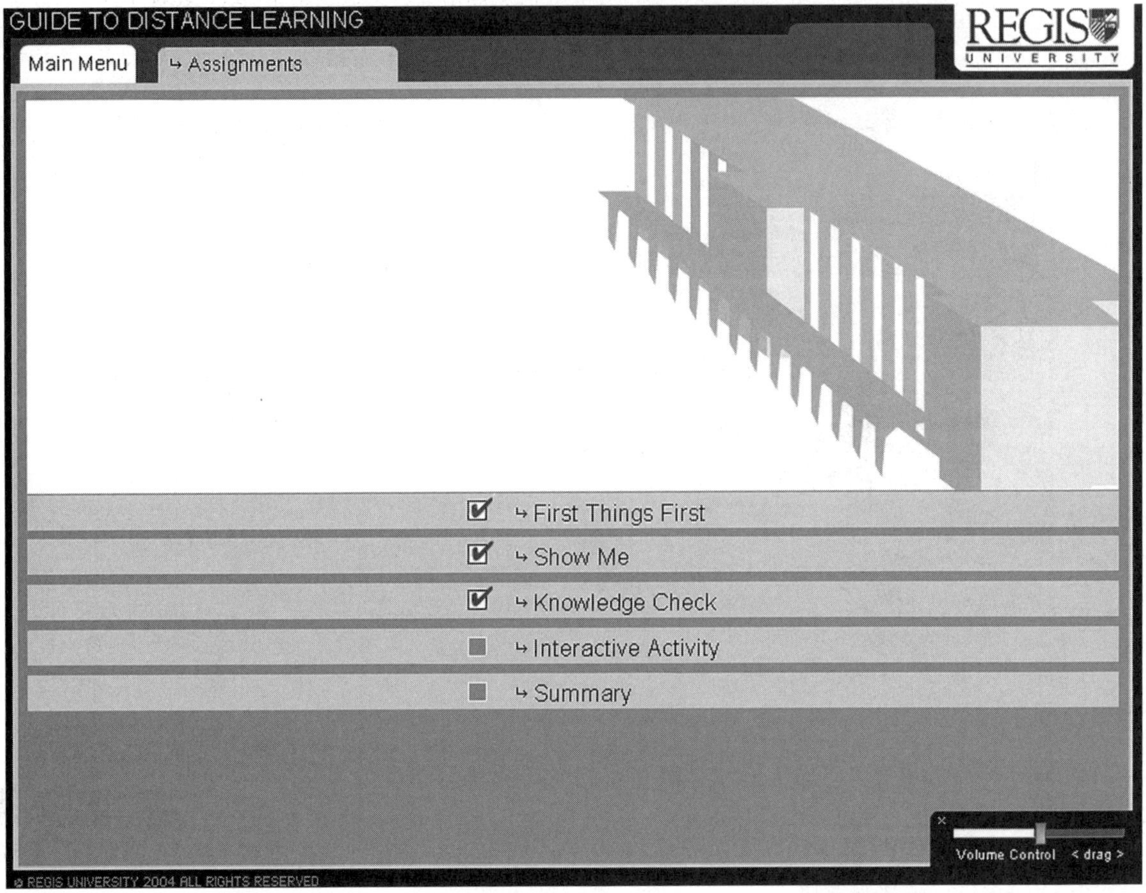

Source: Ellen Waterman

their online courses, find and use the course syllabus and other course resources, use course management system elements, complete and submit course assignments, and communicate with the instructor and other learners. When a learner places his or her mouse over any of the buildings, a description of that module is displayed. Click on any building and that modules starts with an overview. As each element in the module is completed, it is checked off.

The tutorial contains numerous interactive elements, including interactive demos of online course components and quiz questions with feedback. One humorous aspect of the tutorial is the guide, Rigalio, a deceased

Figure 2.7. Assignments Demo

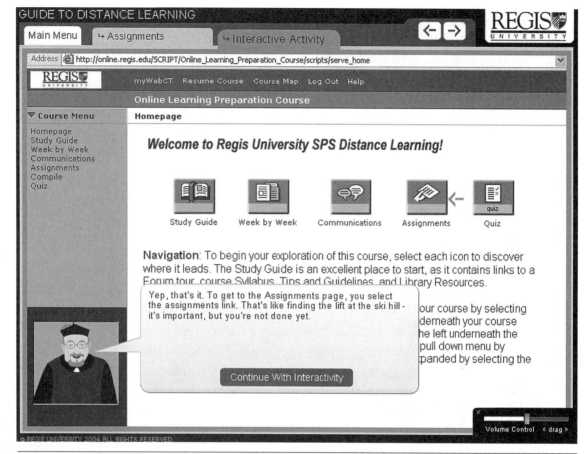

Source: Ellen Waterman

17th century Italian monk (Regis University is a Jesuit higher education institution). He speaks and provides feedback throughout the tutorial in a Brooklyn accent.

Technologies used: HTML and Flash

Adopt or Adapt

Providing support to new distance learners helps them become successful quickly. This idea can be adapted for introducing learners to any type of online program.

Attribution

Submitted by Ellen Waterman, associate dean, CPS Department of Learning Design, Regis University, Denver, Colorado, USA

Contact: ewaterma@regis.edu

Also involved: Maureen Hencmann, instructional designer, Regis University, School for Professional Studies, Denver, Colorado, USA; Kevin Himmel, director of performance consulting, Regis Learning Solutions, Golden, Colorado, USA; Alex Benedict, web developer, Regis University, School for Professional Studies, Denver, Colorado, USA; Blenda Crawford, faculty chair, communication, psychology and sociology, Regis University, School for Professional Studies, Denver, Colorado, USA; Fr. Don Highberger, undergraduate faculty, Regis University, School for Professional Studies, Denver, Colorado, USA

Ellen Waterman is associate dean for distance education at Regis University. Her group works with faculty to design and develop courses for online delivery and pedagogical guidelines and support models for students and faculty working in all technology enhanced delivery formats. She is a frequent presenter at conferences focused on best practices and teaching and learning with technology, and has been published internationally. She is an active member of the Association of Jesuit Colleges and Universities Deans of Adult and Continuing Education and is currently exploring using online learning for the international Jesuit Refugee Services initiative.

Read Me First!

The Big Idea

What

This idea is about preparing a Read Me First! document to provide learners with a roadmap through the course materials.

Why

Although course management systems such as Moodle and Blackboard are popular tools for hosting online higher education courses, to learners, the courses often look like a mass of unorganized files. Course management systems typically let instructors organize files by week, but that's about all the organization provided. And it's not enough for most learners to feel comfortable.

Use It!

How

A file named Read Me First! appears **first** on the list of the files for each unit (lesson/week/module) and provides learners with a roadmap through the files for that unit. A Read Me First! document is designed so learners can easily scan it and figure out how to go through the lesson materials.

Carliner suggests that the Read Me First! document specifically tell learners:

- The purpose of the lesson (briefly—in thirty-five words or fewer)

- Activities in the lesson—listed in the order in which learners should take them

- Names of each file used for performing each activity, such as the name of the file with a video lecture and the names of the files containing readings.

Ideally, the files appear in *the same order in which they're listed in the Read Me First! file* but, if not, learners have a means of figuring out which file to use first, second, and so on. In the sample Read Me First! file on the next page, the information is presented in a chart, so learners can easily scan it.

Read Me First! File

Read Me First!

Lesson Five: The Impact of Species Endangerment

This fifth lesson of the course describes the impact of species endangerment on habitats. It also explains how conservation efforts can slow down climate change or, when that is not feasible, mitigate the effects.

This Read-Me First! page provides a roadmap to the activities in this lesson—and which files on Moodle you use for each activity.

Activity	File Name(s)
1. Video introduction to the lesson	Welcome to Lesson Five file
2. Learning activity, in which you try out an activity that you can later use with your learners	Build-a-Rainforest Plant
3. Video debriefing of the learning activity	Debrief of Build-a-Rainforest Plant
4. Reading Guide Sheet, which lists the readings and suggestions to guide your reading	Reading Guide Sheet and Reading Reflection 5 files
5. Lecture, a recorded lecture that (a) debriefs the reading experience, (b) describes the science underlying the opening activity so teachers can feel comfortable teaching it (and learn a bit about a major issue, too!), and (c) deepens learning through additional learning activities, guest lectures, and other surprises	Lecture file
6. Contribute to the Discussion Board	Discussion Questions
7. Insights from a Wildlife Conservation Society scientist working in the field	Three Questions

Technologies used: electronic documents

Adopt or Adapt

This idea can be easily adapted for use in any content area. It could also be used to support learners in corporate online learning programs. For instance, for a hybrid (online/classroom) project management program, a Read Me First! document can be prepared to help learners know which elements are online (and where to find them), which elements are in a classroom (and when each event occurs), and in what order these items are to be completed.

Attribution

Submitted by Saul Carliner, associate professor of educational technology, Concordia University, Montreal, Quebec, Canada

Contact: saulcarliner@hotmail.com or http://saulcarliner.blogspot.com/

Saul Carliner is an associate professor of educational technology at Concordia University in Montreal. His research focuses on the design, development, and management of online learning and communication for the workplace. He has published seven books and written more than one hundred articles. A Certified Training and Development Professional, Saul serves on the board of the Canadian Society for Training and Development and is editor-in-chief of the IEEE *Transactions on Professional Communication*.

Pre-Work Verification

The Big Idea

What

This idea shows the use of a simple web form (Figure 2.8) to let learners verify that they have completed the required pre-work prior to a learning event. This form can also request important information about each of the learners so the instructors can be prepared to meet their needs.

Figure 2.8. Example of a Pre-Work Form

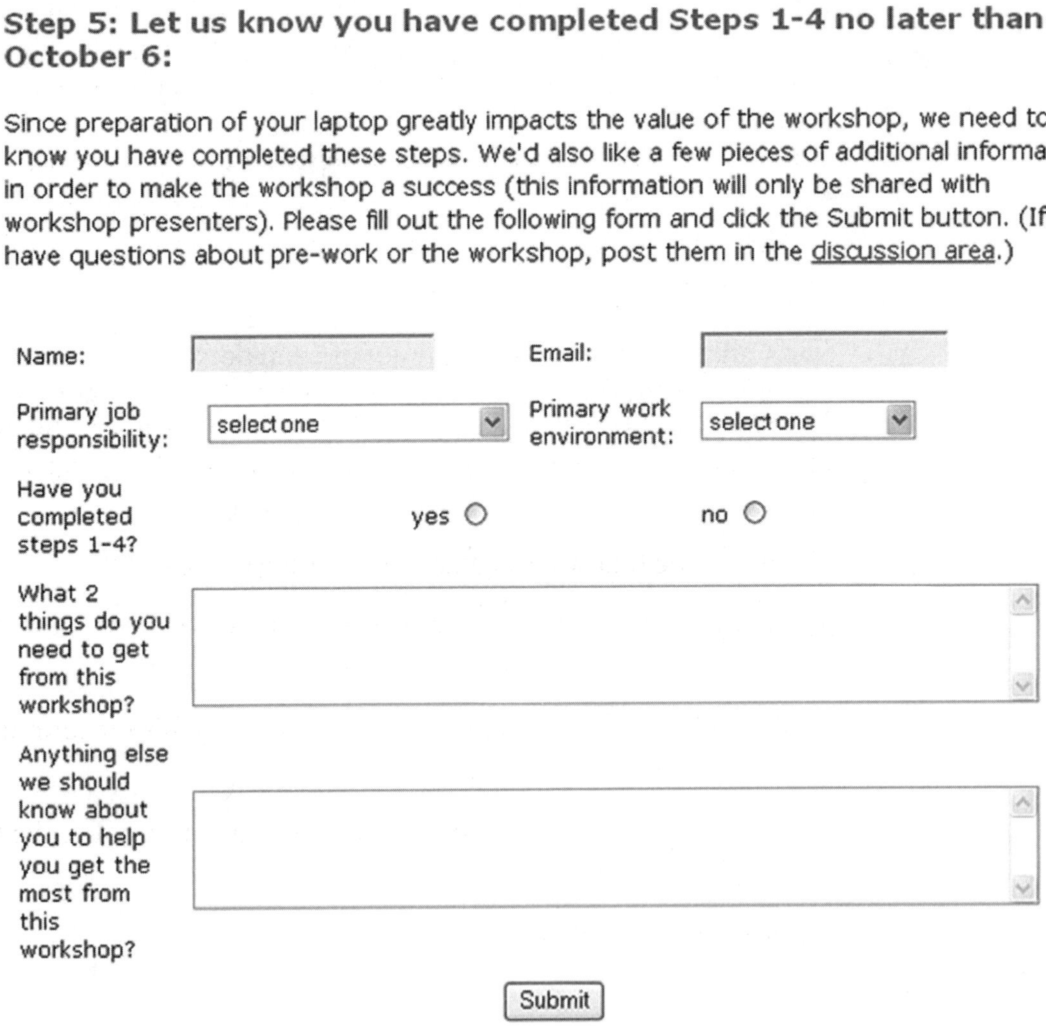

Step 5: Let us know you have completed Steps 1-4 no later than October 6:

Since preparation of your laptop greatly impacts the value of the workshop, we need to know you have completed these steps. We'd also like a few pieces of additional information in order to make the workshop a success (this information will only be shared with workshop presenters). Please fill out the following form and click the Submit button. (If you have questions about pre-work or the workshop, post them in the discussion area.)

Name: Email:

Primary job responsibility: select one   Primary work environment: select one

Have you completed steps 1-4?   yes ○   no ○

What 2 things do you need to get from this workshop?

Anything else we should know about you to help you get the most from this workshop?

Submit

Source: Patti Shank and Eric Replinger

Why

Confirming completion of pre-work helps learners to be more accountable and allows instructors to intervene as needed with those who have not completed the pre-work. Obtaining information about learners in advance helps instructors prepare to meet learner needs.

Use It!

How

Many workshops and learning events work better if learners have completed pre-work such as completing reading assignments, filling out questionnaires, checking to make sure that technical requirements are met, downloading applications, or gathering needed materials. It's hard to get learners to do the required pre-work, and that means that some learners arrive without being ready. This causes problems for those learners, of course, and often for other learners, if instructors or others need to take time away to help them.

In advance of learning events that require pre-work, Shank creates online forms that learners fill in to advise her of their pre-work status. Having learners fill in the form verifies that all pre-work is complete and also lets Shank know whether there are any problems she needs to help a learner with prior to the event.

Shank has the following suggestions for using this idea:

- Remind learners who have not yet completed the pre-work verification form prior to the due date.

- Consider offering a small prize for anyone who fills the form in *earlier* than the due date.

- Decide what you will do if some learners do not complete the form, despite reminders.

Technologies used: online forms

Adopt or Adapt

This could be adapted for any type of pre-work or follow-up for a classroom-based, blended, or online course. For example, this process would work well before instruction to commit to the steps needed to complete the instruction or to confirm pre-reading, and afterward to commit to follow-on activities or to confirm completion of action plan items. Other ways to accomplish these measures include emails, a discussion forum, or a Facebook page. A discussion forum or Facebook would allow others in the group to see all postings, which could be valuable for sharing concerns or ah-ha's.

Attribution

Submitted by Patti Shank, president, Learning Peaks LLC, Denver, Colorado, USA

Contact: patti@learningpeaks.com or www.learningpeaks.com

Also involved: Eric Replinger, Flambeau Productions, Inc., Centennial, Colorado, USA

Patti Shank is the president of Learning Peaks LLC, an internationally recognized instructional design consulting firm that provides learning and performance consulting and training and performance support solutions. She is listed in *Who's Who in Instructional Technology* and is an often-requested speaker at training and instructional technology conferences. Patti is quoted frequently in training publications and is the co-author of *Making Sense of Online Learning*, editor of *The Online Learning Idea Book*, co-editor of *The e-Learning Handbook*, and co-author of *Essential Articulate Studio '09*.

Accountability Check-In

The Big Idea

What

This idea presents an accountability process used with learners during self-paced study.

Why

This process helps the learner take responsibility for making progress and meeting self-study goals.

Use It!

How

Cobb suggests that a trainer, expert, or supervisor check with a learner who is engaged in self-study once a week (or on an agreed-on schedule) to see what work has been undertaken and what progress has been made toward self-study goals. A check-in prompts learner action and helps the trainer, expert, or supervisor who is communicating with the learner identify assistance needs. It can also identify learners who are moving faster than expected so that these learners can help with speeding up the process.

Cobb sends a prompt by email and follows receipt of the answer with an encouragement email, resources to help with any problems, answers, or pointers back to relevant sections of the learning program. Clients have told her that the process is good for motivational purposes and keeps the learning goals more alive in learners' minds. This may not be needed for short self-paced programs, but for longer programs or for programs that involve a series of courses, this type of accountability may be critical. An example is given on the next page.

Weekly Accountability Survey

Accountability is a great tool to help you make the shifts that you want. Not only are you making the commitment to yourself, but stating what you are going to do helps your subconscious set the wheels in motion toward your goals. By stating a clear goal you automatically begin to move toward it. The weekly accountability will help raise your awareness of where you are holding yourself back by not doing the very things that will move you forward.

I am 100 percent committed to your success and I will give you the support and encouragement needed with feedback, tips, or suggested resources when I receive this information from you each week.

Date:

> **How has this week been for you?**
>
> Good. I think that generally the week has seen me more organized with a bit more time.
>
> **What has been your biggest accomplishment?**
>
> Setting aside time to deal with emails
>
> **What has been your biggest challenge?**
>
> Setting aside time to deal with emails!! I haven't managed it every day.
>
> **What have you done regularly to increase your awareness of the changes you want?**
>
> Can't say I've done much regularly, but I've been much more aware of when I lose focus and get distracted from what I planned to do.
>
> **Have you been regularly visioning your goal? What does it feel like?**
>
> Yes, and it feels very good to see myself calm and in control of my work!!
>
> **If you could change anything, what would it be?**
>
> For things to move quicker and to see more results
>
> **Please summarize the past week in three or four lines.**
>
> I've been more aware of how I use my time and have tried to keep a structured To Do list each day, as well as set aside regular time to deal with emails and NOT keep

checking them all day long. I haven't always succeeded, but think the awareness of the situation generally helps me feel I am at last doing something about this issue!!

What are you committing to do next week?

Prioritizing work, keep my To Do list going, and having two periods a day ONLY (morning and after lunch) when I check and deal with emails!

Cobb explains that it is important that all parties agree to the process up-front. Some may need to be reminded that they agreed to this as part of the program.

Technologies used: email, online meeting tool, online forms, course management system

Adopt or Adapt

This idea can be adapted for a variety of learning situations. For example, if a learner is entering a difficult or time-intensive training program or going back to school to complete a degree program, it may be very helpful to set in motion an accountability process that creates an ongoing dialog between the learner and someone who is available to support him or her.

Attribution

Submitted by Kate Cobb, director, Blended Learning Zone, Cagnes sur Mer, France

Contact: kate@blendedlearningzone or www.blendedlearningzone.com

Kate Cobb works with HR/L&D professionals who are seeking solutions to management learning issues by supporting them in the development and implementation of blended learning programs to move business objectives forward. She assists companies in designing learning strategies to develop true learning cultures. Cobb is also a coach working to empower women leaders, both face-to-face and online.

My Personal Learning Network

The Big Idea

What

This idea shows the use of Twitter to create a personal learning network and grow relationships.

Why

There is a lot to learn in many domains, and things change rapidly. Using Twitter can provide bite-sized nuggets of information that help you stay on top of the things you are most interested in (personal and professional).

Use It!

How

Twitter allows Milstid to follow educators, trainers, writers, authors, and companies in order to keep her finger on the pulse of her industry as well as build professional relationships with the people and companies she "follows" and who follow her. She explains that she is introduced to many valuable resources such as articles, books, websites, collaboration opportunities (such as adding her ideas to this book!), and a multitude of concepts and perspectives in her field.

Milstid says that the best aspect of using Twitter as a learning tool is that she is able to learn from well-respected people in the industry. She finds that what she learns often reduces the time needed to solve an issue and is a great starting point for doing research.

To organize her tweets (maximum of 140 characters each), she uses Twitter's "Favorites" feature, which allows her to "bookmark" valuable tweets to revisit and refer back to later. Some samples are shown in Figures 2.9 and 2.10.

Discovery is a natural result of using Twitter. Milstid finds that a single tweet can often lead to a large amount of valuable information. For instance, a tweet about best practices for interaction in online learning can lead to additional tweets with examples of online learning interactions,

Figure 2.9. Example of Others' Tweets in Milstid's Favorites Collection

Home

Quinnovator RT @JamesMcLuckie: Q2. Define specific learning outcomes that can be used as measures. #lrnchat < agreed, but 'performance' outcomes!

2 minutes ago via TweetDeck

C4LPT Q2) Make sure they relate closely to the *performance* outcomes #lrnchat

3 minutes ago via web

Quinnovator Q2) set outcome metrics, and prototype, test, refine, until achieved (HT @jaycross) #lrnchat

4 minutes ago via TweetDeck

LearnNuggets RT @NunesMarketing: @Quinnovator Is there ONE LEARNING DESIGN that fits all? I cataloged 5 in my Masters < 5 designs? or styles? #lrnchat

4 minutes ago via TweetChat

Source: Lauren Milstid

Figure 2.10. Example of Milstid's Tweets

@SecondBananaLS Welcome aboard!

1:34 PM Sep 17th via TweetDeck in reply to SecondBananaLS

we finally submitted our course for #Articulate Guru Awards. what a feeling of accomplishment: http://bit.ly/cdV2FM

6:41 AM Aug 17th via TweetDeck

shortened version of my fav. sent from http://bit.ly/d5EBPW "leadership is learned through experimentation, observation, study, reflection."

2:30 PM Aug 16th via TweetDeck   🗑 Delete

Source: Lauren Milstid

quizzes, and games. A tweet about an effect built in an authoring tool can lead to tweets with links to screencasts of how to build the effect. A tweet about a recommended e-learning book can lead to more information about the author, tweets by the author, and following tweets by that author or even opportunities to connect with the author.

"Often," Milstid explains, "I will follow someone on Twitter after I hear about that person because of another tweet. I usually do some investigation of that person, product, or company, read the bio, look at the website, and read the most current tweets to get a feel for what the person writes about. I then decide whether to follow that person. If I decide to follow someone and later realize that the tweets are inapplicable, then I can simply stop following him or her."

Milstid says that the discovery process that takes place is infinite and non-linear, helping her continually grow professionally. She believes that proper Twitter etiquette requires a balance of collecting and sharing valuable knowledge, so she also feels an obligation to spread what she learns.

Technologies used: online web application (Twitter)

Adopt or Adapt

This is a bite-sized way to keep up with developments in any field. In addition to being used as a personal learning network, it's easy to see how this approach could be part of an assignment in a higher education course in order to get a handle on what is happening within a given domain. In addition, this approach could be used by experts inside a company to provide ongoing tips to others in the company. Milstid thinks you should start using Twitter, and I agree!

Attribution

Submitted by Lauren M. Milstid, course developer, St. Petersburg, Florida, USA

Contact: MilstidL@yahoo.com or www.linkedin.com/in/laurenmilstid

Lauren M. Milstid completed her master of science degree in instructional technology in May 2009 at Chestnut Hill College in Philadelphia, Pennsylvania. She wrote her thesis on learning through games and also worked as a graduate assistant, serving as a project manager for various instructional design projects. She is currently a course developer for a health and human services training organization in St. Petersburg, Florida, and is involved in all phases of the instructional design process. Her responsibilities include script writing, voice-overs, sound editing, graphics production, interaction design and development, and client and SME management.

Reading Guide

The Big Idea

What

This idea is a great way to encourage learners to pay adequate attention to required readings, gain the appropriate insights, and make connections across readings.

Why

If online lectures or webinar courses build on what's in the readings, then the instructor *really* needs to make sure that learners read and gain appropriate insights from them! That's why many online instructors require that learners answer questions about the readings on a discussion board—as a means of checking up, in addition to promoting thinking about the reading. But Carliner's reading of some of the research on discussion boards (for example, Bradley, Thom, Hayes, & Hay, 2008; Jeong & Frazier, 2008; & Palmer, Holt, & Bray, 2008) suggests that learners need far more direction to ensure that they're not merely posting, but critically thinking about what they read. Furthermore, other research (such as Sitzmann, Bell, Kraiger, & Kanar, 2010; Sitzmann , Ely, Brown, & Bauer, in press) suggests that even self-regulated adult learners can benefit from some help in thinking through course readings.

Use It!

How

Prepare a Reading Guide like the example on the next page that not only links learners to required and suggested readings, but also provides questions or other tools for focusing attention on important aspects of individual readings and for creating connections across readings.

Reading Guide

Writing Descriptions, Lesson 3

Before we continue our discussion of writing descriptions, it would be helpful if you could read about two topics.

Reading 1

The first reading is a page from the instructor's website that provides tips for writing reference entries. The source is http://saulcarliner.home.att.net/id/references.htm.

Use the following questions to guide you through the reading of these pages. Your teaching assistant might ask you to share your responses with your online discussion group.

Question	Your Answer
What is a reference entry?	
Which references do you use in your life? Based on the guidance in this reading, do you feel they are effective? Explain why you feel that way.	
Name at least five tips for effectively writing reference entries.	
What is a template?	
How do templates assist in the writing of reference entries?	

(*continued*)

Reading 2

The second reading provides tips for designing pages. Chapter 12 in the Markel text presents these tips.

Use the following questions to guide you through the reading of these pages. Your teaching assistant might ask you to share your responses with your online discussion group.

Question	Your Answer
What are the five purposes of effective page design?	
Describe in your own words the design principles of proximity, alignment, repetition, and contrast.	
Explain how each of the following affects page design: • Size • Paper • Bindings • Accessing tools (also known as retrievability aids)	
From the list of items about designing the page (such as layout, white space, and columns), which two seem most important to you? Why do you feel they're important?	
Choose any of the sample page designs in "Analyzing Some Page Designs." What is effective about the design of the sample you chose?	

Reading 3

The third reading provides tips for designing screens (web pages). Chapter 20 in the Markel text presents these tips.

Use the following questions to guide you through the reading of these pages. Your teaching assistant might ask you to share your responses with your online discussion group.

Question	Your Answer
How does the process of designing a website compare with the process for designing any other piece of educational communication? How is it similar? Different?	
Explain in your own words what the author means by each of the following: • Aim for simplicity. • Make the text easy to read and understand. • Create informative headers and footers. • Help visitors navigate the site. • Create clear, informative links. Avoid web clichés. • Include extra features your visitors might need.	
How should designs of websites be altered for persons with disabilities? For members of unique cultural groups?	
Describe the ethical issues that arise in using materials from other websites.	

Technologies used: electronic documents

Adopt or Adapt

This idea can easily be adapted for use in any content area. It could also be used to support learners in corporate online learning programs. For instance, for a hybrid (online/classroom) performance management program, a Reading Guide can help learners give appropriate attention to and get the most from pre-work, readings, or action plans.

References

Bradley, M.E., Thom, L.R., Hayes, J., & Hay, C. (2008). Ask and you will receive: How question type influences quantity and quality of online discussion. *British Journal of Educational Technology, 39*, 888–900.

Jong, A., & Frazier, S. (2008). How day of posting affects level of discourse in asynchronous discussions and computer-supported collaborative argumentation. *British Journal of Educational Technology, 39*, 875–887.

Palmer, S., Holt, D., & Bray, S. (2008). Does the discussion help? The impact of formally assessed online discussion on final student results. *British Journal of Educational Technology, 39*, 847–858.

Sitzmann, T., Bell, B.S., Kraiger, K., & Kanar, A.M. (2010, March). A multilevel analysis of the effect of prompting self-regulation in technology-delivered instruction. *Training and Development.*

Sitzmann, T., Ely, K., Brown, K.G., & Bauer, K. (in press). Self-assessment of knowledge: A cognitive learning or affective measure? *Academy of Management Learning & Education.*

Attribution

Submitted by Saul Carliner, associate professor of educational technology, Concordia University, Montreal, Quebec, Canada

Contact: saulcarliner@hotmail.com or http://saulcarliner.blogspot.com/

Saul Carliner is an associate professor of educational technology at Concordia University in Montreal. His research focuses on the design, development, and management of online learning and communication for the workplace. He has published seven books and written more than one hundred articles. A Certified Training and Development Professional, Saul serves on the board of the Canadian Society for Training and Development and is editor-in-chief of the IEEE *Transactions on Professional Communication.*

Combating the Free-Rider

The Big Idea

What

This idea provides some effective ways to deal with the "free-rider" (Kerr & Bruun, 1983; Roberts & McInnerney, 2007). This occurs when some learners working on group projects do little or no work, contributing almost nothing to the group and decreasing the group's ability to work together successfully.

Why

The benefits of group work are compelling, but many instructors fear that the challenges of dealing with group work and group members overshadow the benefits.

Use It!

How

"Free-riding" by learners in group projects can cause a number of problems, including damaging the morale and performance of the other members of the group, gaining unwarranted grades despite performing little or no work, and making it difficult for others to learn. In addition, free-riding tends to give rise to problems for the instructor, including dealing with the resentment of learners who *are* pulling their own weight or more and being seen as unfair when it comes to assigning grades.

One effective tool that may be used to combat these problems is monitoring and pressure from the instructor. Unfortunately, if this is the only method used, *constant* monitoring by the instructor may be needed. This can be time-consuming and stressful at best, particularly in an online environment, so other or additional solutions are generally needed.

One very effective solution is to employ a grading scheme that penalizes free-riders. For this to work effectively, the grading scheme must be made explicit at the start of the course and clearly understood by all learners. Grading schemes that penalize free-riders must provide learners with the ability to assess the contribution of individuals within their groups, and those assessments must impact individual grades for group projects. Learners must also realize that the instructor retains responsibility for final grades, but utilizes group member recommendations when deciding how to reward individual contributions on group projects.

One technique is to have learners within each group anonymously rate their fellow group members. The advantage of anonymity is that it allows learners to rate their fellow group members without the fear of bullying or repercussions.

Technologies such as online surveys or forms can be very useful in maintaining a workable group member assessment process. For example, it is valuable if learners can anonymously input, at the end of each group deliverable, a rating for each of their fellow group members on a fixed scale from 0 to +10.

One particularly simple and effective scale is one that ranges from −1 to +3. A rating of −1 indicates the group member was actually deleterious to the group (that is, the group would have performed better had the person not been in the group); 0 indicates that the group member's contributions were negligible or non-existent; +1 indicates a below-average contribution; +2 indicates an average contribution; and +3 indicates an above-average contribution.

The grade for the group as a whole is then modified for each individual within the group according to the average rating. This can either be applied subjectively by the instructor or objectively according to a fixed formula (which should be made explicit at the start). For example, if the overall group grade is adjudged at 50 percent, 75 percent, or whatever, then all group members can be awarded a grade according to the following formula:

$$IG = GG * IAR/2$$

where IG = Individual Grade, GG = Group Grade, IAR = Individual Average Rating

Thus, learners with an individual average rating of 2 will be awarded the grade for the group as a whole. Members with an average rating of 0 (or below) will be awarded 0, since their group members judged them as noncontributory (or even deleterious). There are, however, significant disadvantages to applying these formulae, such as awarding some learners 100 percent or more or reducing several learners to below a passing mark. A subjective method, where the instructor applies ratings with a significant degree of discretion, is often preferred.

Other variations are possible: for example, group members apportion a total number of points (say 100) according to the contributions of each group member.

A variety of technologies are useful for supporting this process (see the EZ Forms idea in Chapter 5 for one tool that can be used to implement this approach), including an exchange of emails between learners and the instructor.

Technologies used: various, including email and online forms

Adopt or Adapt

This idea can be used in higher education courses that utilize group work. It can also be adapted for use in team projects at work or in volunteer work in order to provide feedback to team members about their contributions. See Joanna Dunlap's Rules of Engagement and Team Review Form ideas early in this chapter for additional ideas to help with group projects.

References

Kerr, N.L., & Bruun, S.E. (1983). Dispensability of member effort and group motivation losses: Free-rider effects. *Journal of Personality and Social Psychology, 44,* 78–94.

Roberts, T.S., & McInnerney, J.M. (2007). Seven problems of online group learning (and their solutions). *Educational Technology & Society, 10*(4), 257–268.

Attribution

Submitted by Tim S. Roberts, senior lecturer, CQ University Australia, Bundaberg, Queensland, Australia

Contact: t.roberts@cqu.edu.au or http://fabie.cqu.edu.au/FCWViewer/staff.do?site=536&sid=ROBERTST

Tim S. Roberts is a senior lecturer in the faculty of arts, business, informatics, and education at the Bundaberg campus of CQ University, Australia. He has published more than thirty articles in refereed journals and conference proceedings and has edited four books on various aspects of online education, including collaborative and cooperative learning, self, peer, and group assessment, and the problems of plagiarism.

Learning Log

The Big Idea

What

This idea showcases a journal that is completed by learners at the end of each module in order to document their learning.

Why

The process helps learners recognize the personal benefits of the instruction. At the end, learners use the logs they have completed to pull together a big-picture view of how the program has benefited them.

Use It!

How

Online learners complete an online learning log at the end of each module, noting three things they've learned from the module that they can apply. The log is reviewed by the trainer and he or she can input comments for the learner. In addition, the entire set of comments by the learner and the trainer serves to inform a learning summary at the end of the module, reminding learners of important parts of the training and things they want to be sure to remember. The summary can also be sent to a learner's manager. Sample end-of-module and end-of-program logs are provided below. Some sample completed logs are shown in Figures 2.11 and 2.12, with sample question prompts and sample answers.

End-of-Module Learning Log

Note the three most important things you have learned in this module to aid your growth in the area of leadership communication.

1.

(continued)

2.

3.

Anything else that you want to record from this module?

Figure 2.11. Example of Online Learning Log

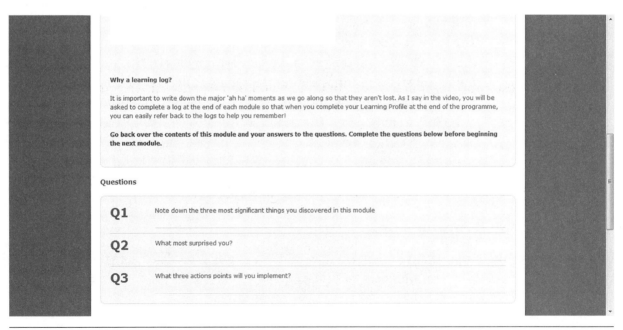

Why a learning log?

It is important to write down the major 'ah ha' moments as we go along so that they aren't lost. As I say in the video, you will be asked to complete a log at the end of each module so that when you complete your Learning Profile at the end of the programme, you can easily refer back to the logs to help you remember!

Go back over the contents of this module and your answers to the questions. Complete the questions below before beginning the next module.

Questions

Q1   Note down the three most significant things you discovered in this module

Q2   What most surprised you?

Q3   What three actions points will you implement?

Source: Kate Cobb

End-of-Program Learning Summary

Now that you have completed the course, please refer back to your Learning Logs and complete this Learning Summary.

Name:

1. The most important thing I have learned about leadership is

2. The most important thing I have learned about myself is

3. The most important thing I am going to put into practice is

4. The most important thing that I can do to help lead business efficiency is

5. The most important thing I need to find out more about is

Technologies used: email, online meeting tool, online forms, course management system

Figure 2.12. Example of Learning Profile

Source: Kate Cobb

Adopt or Adapt

This idea is designed for use at the conclusion of a learning module but can also be used at the end of a class or coaching session. If it is completed at the conclusion of a group training event, each learner may be asked to share an item from his or her Learning Summary as an action step. This idea could easily be adapted to use at the mid-point and end of a higher education course or at specific intervals during on-the-job training.

Attribution

Submitted by Kate Cobb, director, Blended Learning Zone, Cagnes sur Mer, France

Contact: kate@blendedlearningzone or www.blendedlearningzone.com

Kate Cobb works with HR/L&D professionals who are seeking solutions to management learning issues by supporting them in the development and implementation of blended learning programs to move business objectives forward. She assists companies in designing learning strategies to develop true learning cultures. Cobb is also a coach working to empower women leaders, both face-to-face and online.

Project Grading Checklist

The Big Idea
What

This idea shows creation and use of a project grading checklist, a scoring tool with criteria for evaluating a deliverable, which is provided to learners before they begin to work on a course project. In addition, it contains components that let learners assess and score their own work.

Why

Project grading checklists (aka rubrics) help learners understand what project elements are expected and how much each is worth. This allows them to check to make sure that everything is included or self-select to leave something out and sacrifice the points. Having learners score their own work and explain the rationale for their scores requires them to deeply consider the quality and completeness of their work.

Use It!
How

At the beginning of course projects (so learners know from day one what is expected), Chatfield provides learners with a project grading checklist that describes the criteria for completion of the project (using the same language learned in weekly instructional activities) and the points associated with each criterion. Learners can use the checklist both to guide their work and to determine when their projects are complete and whether they *really* are complete. Additionally, the checklist commonly brings to the forefront questions learners have about the project and any criteria that they don't understand. This alerts the instructor to areas that may need additional emphasis so that learners *can* fully complete the requirements of the project.

This idea came about because Chatfield taught an online web design course where the term-long project was the design and development of an eight-page website. While she was trying to grade the projects, she would spend a lot of time looking for the different components she expected to find (since in a website it could be in so many different places). So she decided to have learners *tell her* where she could find each component and explain how it met or did not meet the criteria. That way, she could spend more time assessing the quality of the overall website (and providing more targeted feedback) and not spend so much time searching for individual elements. Use of the checklist was a great success in that course and she now uses this strategy for every class she teaches that includes multi-week projects.

Chatfield has learners return the checklist document with comments about their work on each criterion. She says that the scoring and rationale for that scoring give her insights into what each person has learned. If they don't fully complete any criterion, she says that learners expect their final grade to be lower. "I find students are often tougher on themselves than I am," explains Chatfield.

She says that using this checklist is extremely helpful for learners as well. If a learner has not included a component, he or she typically acknowledges that points will be lost, sometimes explaining why and sometimes just acknowledging that he or she ran out of time. Learners rarely indicate that they didn't know how to do it or don't understand the criteria, because they could have received help along the way, which many do. Learner explanations help Chatfield provide project feedback specifically geared to what learners describe (such as insights and problems they have had), which she feels is quite valuable.

Some guidelines from Chatfield:

- Be as specific as possible, listing the individual criterion and the degree to which excellence is required.

- Make sure that the weekly instructional activities provide the basis for learners to complete all requirements. In Chatfield's courses, checklist criteria reflect homework or other course activities that have been completed prior to the project.

- Refer learners back to the checklist and where they learned how to complete each requirement as needed.

- Consider having multiple check-in points with learners so that they can self-assess how they are coming along toward completing the whole project.

Chatfield recently used a project grading checklist like the example below with a brand new e-commerce course she is teaching. The process helped learners think about the quality and extensiveness of their upcoming project very early on, and the resulting project work was higher in quality than expected.

Project Grading Checklist

Web Design Grade Checklist

Fill in all blank cells. Rename file with your actual last name.

Must be submitted with final project by due date to receive maximum points.

Your Name:		Your Site URL:	
Total Points Possible	Points You Believe You Earned	Criteria	Comments on WHAT You Did to Deserve Points and Description of WHERE (Name of Page) and HOW Used
18		Folder view and navigation view (screen shots required)	
32		Page count (8 minimum)	
5		Proper name of "home" page	
24		Site navigation system (no orphans or dead-ends)	
15		Balanced pages and good design throughout	
10		User-friendly site design—easy to get around; always know where you are	

(continued)

Total Points Possible	Points You Believe You Earned	Criteria	Comments on WHAT You Did to Deserve Points and Description of WHERE (Name of Page) and HOW Used
3		Unordered list/bullets (1 minimum)	
3		Ordered list/numbers (1 minimum)	
3		Nested list/list within list (1 minimum)	
9		External links (3 minimum)	
9		Internal links (besides navigation) (3 minimum)	
9		Named anchor links (bookmarks) (3 minimum)	
3		Email link (1 minimum)	
10		Background color or image, coordinated throughout site	
3		Text colors in BODY tag (page properties) or in external CSS (style) file—even if black	
3		Link colors in BODY tag (page properties) or in external CSS file	
12		Images (6 minimum) *Note:* For all images, you must be able to prove ownership and/or free-use permissions. Identify this within your site somewhere.	
3		Horizontal rule (1 minimum)	

10		Nice use of color in all aspects throughout	
12		Tables (1 minimum with at least 2 columns and 3 rows)	
6		Keywords and description in head tag of at least home page	
8		Image maps (hot spots) (1 minimum)	
10		Forms (at least one page)	
10		Search page with ability to search within site or all Internet	
230		**FINAL INSTALLMENT TOTAL POINTS**	

Technologies used: electronic document

Adopt or Adapt

This strategy is useful for any online or classroom-based project or assignment with numerous components that are both challenging to grade and complicated for learners to complete. A rubric could also be a useful tool to guide the development of large deliverables in training programs. For example, a group building a job aid could use a rubric and examples to guide their work.

The form used for this purpose could also be implemented with a survey tool inside a higher education course management system or a stand-alone web application such as SurveyMonkey or FormSite.

Attribution

Submitted by Kathleen Chatfield, senior instructional designer/affiliate faculty, Clark College, Vancouver, Washington, USA

Contact: kchatfield@clark.edu

Kathleen Chatfield is the senior instructional designer and an affiliate faculty member at Clark College in Vancouver, Washington. She has taught courses for seven other universities and community colleges. She has taught over 150 technology-enhanced community college and university credit-level courses in business, instructional design and technology, and education, most of which she developed. Chatfield is a certified online instructor.

Chatfield has a bachelor's degree in theology and cross-cultural communication from the Arizona College of the Bible and a master's degree in adult education from Oregon State University and is currently pursuing her doctorate in teacher leadership at Washington State University–Vancouver.

Life Web

The Big Idea

What

This idea helps learners think more deeply about areas of their lives that need attention.

Why

We know that learners' lives affect their performance in all areas but people who design instruction rarely pay attention to this fact, even though we know it affects learners' ability to encode and retain information. Self-reflection can benefit the learners' ability to focus and learn.

Use It!

How

In especially important instruction, it may be useful to have learners do some self-reflection in order to consider what's needed to be successful. Cobb developed an Excel-based tool that provides learners with a visual indication of areas of their lives that may need more attention. The tool consists of a checklist and a corresponding visual summary that shows the answers to learners questions (they just answered) visually. The learner fills out the checklist (Figure 2.13) and this populates the visualization tool (Figure 2.14). The resulting visual shows patterns that are less obvious in the checklist.

Cobb explains that this is a very useful tool to use with busy people who have difficulty managing their time and achieving an appropriate life balance. It is especially important for women who are juggling home and family demands as well as work. The visual summary shows which areas of life are being "ignored." Considering this information helps learners understand the risks they are taking when trying to add new items to their plates and may help them reassess, find resources, or reprioritize.

The process can be used in a coaching or training setting where self-awareness and work/life balance issues are crucial. The learner can use the tool ahead of time and the coach or trainer can debrief the experience in a face-to-face session by asking questions like "What surprised you?" "What pleased you?" "What changes do you feel are most needed?"

Technologies used: Excel

Figure 2.13. Balance Checklist

WORK

TRUE	FALSE			
☑	☐	My work stimulates me	1	TRUE
☑	☐	I am proud of what I do for a living	1	TRUE
☑	☐	I feel appreciated in my workplace	1	TRUE
☑	☐	I respect the people I work with	1	TRUE
☑	☐	I know where my career is heading	1	TRUE
☐	☑	I respond to calls and emails within 48 hours	0	FALSE
☐	☑	I don't let paperwork pile up	0	FALSE
☐	☑	I complete my work within reasonable hours	0	FALSE
☐	☑	I manage my time well	0	FALSE
☑	☐	I finish the tasks on my 'To Do' list each day	1	TRUE

Score   60%

FINANCES

TRUE	FALSE			
☑	☐	I am satisfied with my income	1	TRUE
☑	☐	I have a budget that I use	1	TRUE
☑	☐	I pay my bills on time	1	TRUE
☐	☑	I know how much I owe and when it will be paid off	0	FALSE
☐	☑	I have an active long-term financial plan	0	FALSE
☐	☑	I am able to reward myself without feeling guilty	0	FALSE
☐	☑	I use my credit card wisely	0	FALSE
☑	☐	I have a will	1	TRUE
☑	☐	My wallet is uncluttered	1	TRUE
☑	☐	All my payments are up to date	1	TRUE

Score   60%

HOME ENVIRONMENT

TRUE	FALSE			
☑	☐	I am happy with my home	1	TRUE
☑	☐	My home is generally clean and tidy	1	TRUE
☑	☐	I surround myself with things that I love	1	TRUE
☑	☐	I don't acquire clutter	1	TRUE
☑	☐	I recycle at home	1	TRUE

Source: Kate Cobb

Figure 2.14. Balance Visualization

	Score
WORK	60%
FINANCES	60%
HOME ENVIRONMENT	80%
HEALTH & BODY	70%
RELATIONSHIPS	90%
PERSONAL	30%

(0% is dissatisfied and 100% satisfied) for how satisfied you are with each aspect of your life.

The object of the exercise is to identify which areas you need to focus on to get the picture back into balance.

The centre of the web indicates you are "Totally Dissatisfied" and the rim displays "100% Satisfied".   Where do you fall on each of these?

The object is to get the dots equally spaced, and then to work on moving ALL the dots out together, improving all aspects of your life... keeping it all in balance.

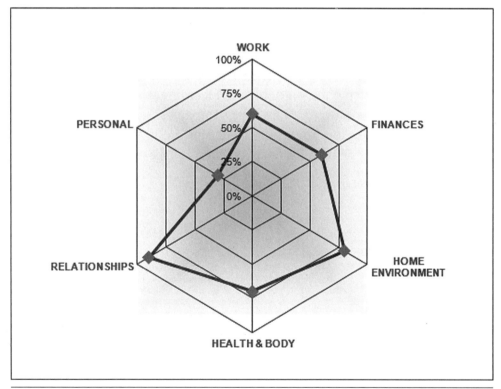

Source: Kate Cobb

Adopt or Adapt

This idea can be adapted with whatever topic areas and questions you desire. It can be modified for a web of leadership or a web of professional skill, for example. It can be used for discussions about readiness to take online courses to complete a degree or capacity to take on additional responsibility.

Attribution

Submitted by Kate Cobb, director, Blended Learning Zone, Cagnes sur Mer, France

Contact: kate@blendedlearningzone or www.blendedlearningzone.com

Kate Cobb works with HR/L&D professionals who are seeking solutions to management learning issues by supporting them in the development and implementation of blended learning programs to move business objectives forward. She assists companies in designing learning strategies to develop true learning cultures. Cobb is also a coach working to empower women leaders, both face-to-face and online.

Reminder Tips

The Big Idea

What

This idea involves sending tips to learners during an ongoing learning program.

Why

Tips provide a reminder of what a learner is learning in order to keep the content alive in the learner's mind. In addition, it shows learners that someone cares about their progress and, as a result, may augment motivation.

Use It!

How

Cobb sends tips to learners, like those in the example, on a schedule. Clients tell her that the tips help them remember to do the things they need to do to see the results they want! At the end of the program, she compiles all the tips into a Tips and Tricks document that is sent to learners for future reference.

Tips to Learners

Dear,

This message is intended to motivate and encourage you and keep you on track on short-term planning, so make sure you read it and **take action**! Here's a reminder of some tips for short-term planning:

- Spend five minutes at the beginning of the day BEFORE YOU DO ANYTHING ELSE planning that day.

- Approach your day with positive self-questioning (e.g., *What will make today successful? How will I better meet my client's needs today?*).

- Ensure your planning is related to your purpose (WHY I AM HERE).

- Spend five minutes at the end of the day reviewing what you achieved.

- Ask yourself: *What could be done better tomorrow?*

- Begin to form a plan for tomorrow!.

Cobb provides the following recommendations for implementing this process:

- Be consistent with the timing of your messages and tell learners ahead of time what to expect (weekly email? bi-monthly text?).

- Explain how long it should take to read the message. For example, "This message will take you about 2.5 minutes to read and will involve about 20 minutes of action."

Technologies used: Tips can be sent by email, Twitter, text message, or PDF documents sent to smart phones.

Adopt or Adapt

This idea can be adapted for use during or after any instruction. It could also be used at the end of coaching sessions as a reminder of what was discussed and agreed to. It might be especially valuable to use this during self-paced online learning so that learners feel like there is a "live" person who cares about their progress and to add another dimension to the experience. If learners feel unmotivated, this may tempt them to progress, especially if the tips also contain a hint of how unfinished parts of the course may benefit them.

Attribution

Submitted by Kate Cobb, director, Blended Learning Zone, Cagnes sur Mer, France

Contact: kate@blendedlearningzone or www.blendedlearningzone.com

Kate Cobb works with HR/L&D professionals who are seeking solutions to management learning issues by supporting them in the development and implementation of blended learning programs to move business objectives forward. She assists companies in designing learning strategies to develop true learning cultures. Cobb is also a coach working to empower women leaders, both face-to-face and online.

Celebrate

The Big Idea

What

This idea presents a way to help learners celebrate achievement.

Why

Celebrating achievement helps learners identify what they gained so that they can use this knowledge in other situations and can replicate their success.

Use It!

How

This idea is about taking the time to notice and reflect on achievement. It requires learners to reflect on their experience.

Cobb provides two examples (Figures 2.15 and 2.16) of how she has used this in her coaching practice and the results:

- Doris was determined to leave her job but wasn't very confident about finding another. By the end of the coaching process she had another job offer and the Celebrate process helped her realize that she has great determination and, if she uses these qualities in other situations of her life, she can achieve similar results.

- Paul didn't achieve all of his identified goals, but the Celebrate process helped him identify progress he had made in other areas that were as important as his initial goals.

This process can be used at the end of a training or coaching program or partway through to celebrate achievement before moving on to the next stage of the learning.

Figure 2.15. Celebrate Questions 1

Source: Kate Cobb

Figure 2.16. Celebrate Questions 2

The questions below will help YOU to reflect on what YOU have achieved over our time together.

1. Review all the strategies and significant actions you have taken to get to your goals (you might like to look back in The Coaching Room and all your notes to remind you of what's been happening!). What three things are you particularly proud of having achieved?

2. Where do you think you are now percentage-wise in relation to your goals? Are you 100% there?

3. What three main things have you learnt about yourself during the coaching programme?

4. What three things will you do differently in future because of this learning? How will

Source: Kate Cobb

Technologies used: email, online meeting tool, online forms, course management system

Adopt or Adapt

Finding ways to celebrate achievement is valuable in any coaching or instructional situation. It can be a formal process, as shown here, or more informal, such as having team members reflect on what they have achieved at the end of a milestone together. It may be worthwhile, as well, to determine what can be celebrated when desired goals were not fully met, such as lessons learned that will be valuable in the future.

Attribution

Submitted by Kate Cobb, director, Blended Learning Zone, Cagnes sur Mer, France

Contact: kate@blendedlearningzone or www.blendedlearningzone.com

Kate Cobb works with HR/L&D professionals who are seeking solutions to management learning issues by supporting them in the development and implementation of blended learning programs to move business objectives forward. She assists companies in designing learning strategies to develop true learning cultures. Cobb is also a coach working to empower women leaders, both face-to-face and online.

Installment Plan

The Big Idea
What

This idea presents creation and use of an installment plan for lengthy or term-long projects that include many facets.

Why

Many instructors have experienced learners panicked about projects that are due the next day but aren't nearly completed. With a weekly accountability plan, learners are much more likely to stay on top of a project and learn some critical project management skills as well.

Use It!
How

Many higher education courses include long projects. One example might be designing a website from scratch. The textbook and course activities teach individual aspects of creating a website (such as how to build hyperlinks or insert images), but rarely look at the whole site as a single, complex project, explaining where to start and how to go from one step to the next.

With an Installment Plan, the instructor develops a project management process like the one on the next page that learners use to go from the start of the project to the end, one week at a time. This scaffolding not only results in incremental and final success, but also illustrates and provides practice using a project management process that can be used for other projects too. Another, and even more significant, benefit is that the instructor can provide formative feedback on a timely basis, so each learner has the opportunity to revise his or her efforts while the project is underway and be successful despite going off track from time to time (normal in most projects).

The first installment is almost always the submission of a project topic or idea, and the last installment is almost always final submission of the project along with a project grading checklist (see Chatfield's Project Grading Checklist idea earlier in this chapter for more information). Chatfield also integrates group teamwork and peer feedback into this process, utilizing learning management discussion forums so each team can see the activity taking place in every other team. For example, if one of her courses has twenty-five learners, she creates five teams of five learners. Each learner provides feedback to others in his or her team along the way so that they all can learn from and help each other.

Installment Plan

Individual Website Project

This class will include an individual website project. It will involve the creation of a website with specific requirements (provided in a checklist at the end of this document).

Installment 1: Selecting a Topic for Your Site

You have until Thursday of Week 2 to finalize your idea and start your website project design. I strongly encourage you to create a "real" website . . . one for a business (the company you work for or a friend's business) . . . one for which you will have a real client.

There are a couple of cautions in doing this, however:

- You'll want to make sure that you can work on the project even if your client becomes unavailable to help you or contribute to the design and content.

- There will likely be course requirements that will not ultimately fit in this company's desired site. You may have to create a phony page or two purely to contain these requirements. These phony pages can be removed from your real site after you have completed the term and your project has been graded.

Your site requirements will include a minimum of eight pages, good navigation throughout, a clean look and balanced flow, appealing colors and design elements, and a minimum of six images.

You will be completing a journal while you complete the website. Your journal should look like the following (see instructions below). Insert your own information in place of the sample text from a previous student.

Installment and Link (When Necessary)	Your journal comments about progress so far. Be sure to specify what's new and where you included it.
Installment 1 (Idea/Topic)	I've been trying to come up with an interesting, yet educating topic. Something that not only others can learn from, but I can learn as well. I think my website will be on African American history. My grandfather will be my client, as he has an intense interest in the subject and belongs to an organization that is interested in it. My site will become the organization's website if they approve it upon its completion. My grandfather's organization has a wonderful library of books with many images and content that I can use. My grandfather and I will spend this next week going through some of the books and selecting relevant parts that I should include in the website. That will help me decide how many pages my site will have and the content for each. The other members of the organization will be able to provide feedback occasionally throughout the term about what they want, what they like and don't like, and what I should add, delete, or change. I'm really excited about working on this.

Installment 1

For this first installment, you'll create your journal document using MS Word. You'll use this document to record information about your website progress throughout the term. This week, your journal will include:

(continued)

- The topic your website will be about

- Who your client is and how you believe you will obtain information from him or her, including how available the person will be to provide you with information, feedback, and more data

- Why this subject is of interest to you

Submissions for Installment 1

Due Thursday, end of day—Your journal: Using the discussion board, attach your journal so it will be available to be viewed by your team members. Your journal must be in Word format and include your complete idea and topic as well as the details about who your client is and how he or she will contribute, work with, and provide feedback to you. Indicate why this subject is of interest to you.

Due Saturday, end of day—Your feedback: Return to the discussion board and open each journal submitted by your classmates, read their journal entries, and reply to each person's discussion message. Do not create a new thread. Your reply should supplement their information with ideas or suggestions that would contribute to their projects and not merely indicate that you like it or think it is a good idea.

Note: This document continues but is truncated to fit into this format.

Technologies used: electronic documents

Adopt or Adapt

This idea is useful for any project or assignment with multiple steps that is challenging to manage, tricky to monitor, or complicated for learners to thoroughly and accurately complete. It can be used for writing research papers, creating a historical event presentation, conducting a scientific experiment, or writing a computer program. It could also be used to track completion of milestones in an ongoing and lengthy training program such as a phlebotomy (blood drawing) skills, financial skills, or online learning authoring skills program that includes multiple courses.

The forms used for this purpose could also be implemented with a survey tool inside a higher education course management system or a stand-alone web application such as SurveyMonkey or FormSite.

Attribution

Submitted by Kathleen Chatfield, senior instructional designer/affiliate faculty, Clark College, Vancouver, Washington, USA

Contact: kchatfield@clark.edu

Kathleen Chatfield is the senior instructional designer and an affiliate faculty member at Clark College in Vancouver, Washington. She has taught courses for seven other universities and community colleges. She has taught over 150 technology-enhanced community college and university credit-level courses in business, instructional design and technology, and education, most of which she developed. Chatfield is a certified online instructor.

Chatfield has bachelor's degrees in theology and cross-cultural communications from the Arizona College of the Bible and a master's degree in adult education from Oregon State University and is currently pursuing her doctorate in teacher leadership at Washington State University–Vancouver.

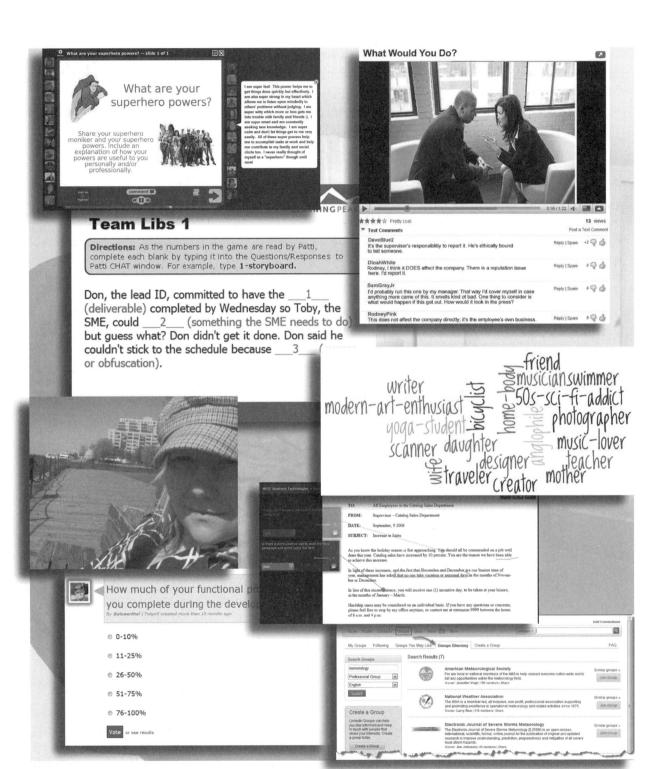

Ideas for Synchronous and Social Learning

Synchronous online learning is "live" during a specific time period. Learners typically use an online classroom application to "attend" and interact with other learners and one of more facilitators or instructors. You can also use other tools for synchronous online learning, such as chat, instant messaging, SMS (mobile texting), Twitter, and audio conferencing. Although synchronous online learning isn't as flexible for learners, because they are interacting live and therefore need to be available at the same time, as self-paced online learning, synchronous online learning can overcome some typical barriers, including motivation. As a result, using synchronous and self-paced learning (also known as asynchronous learning) together, in order to obtain the benefits while reducing the challenges of both approaches, is often a good plan!

Social learning implies collaboration with or support from others. This often involves use of social media such as Facebook, Twitter, and media-sharing sites such as YouTube (as well as others that you'll read about in this chapter). Social learning is not always synchronous, but synchronous learning should ideally be social (otherwise, why get everyone together at the same time?)! Social learning may involve synchronous technologies such as online classroom applications or Twitter or asynchronous technologies such as discussion forums, shared applications such as collaborative writing applications, or use of social media applications.

This chapter illustrates ideas for synchronous and social activities. They are together in this chapter because the *social* aspect is critical. If you are looking for ideas for synchronous and social learning, also review Chapter 5, Ideas for Media and Authoring, as many of those ideas may be valuable for synchronous and social learning as well.

Open House

The Big Idea

What

This idea shows how to use breakout rooms in an online classroom application (such as Connect, WebEx, or Elluminate) to host a virtual open house or "cracker barrel" session.

Why

This activity allows for smaller group interaction and more interaction with instructors/presenters during a larger group synchronous session.

Use It!

How

At a desired point in the online classroom course, separate breakout room areas are opened so learners can interact with other learners and the instructors/presenters. Separate breakout spaces are assigned to different topics or instructors/presenters.

Prior to having learners move into the breakout rooms, the facilitator explains the exercise as analogous to an open house, in which learners move from space to space to talk to different people. Learners can either select a topic or instructor/presenter (as with the cracker barrel example in Figure 3.1) or, alternatively, they can be assigned to rotate among specific rooms (as with the new hire orientation example in Figure 3.2).

Bozarth used this idea during a North Carolina Government Training Network online meeting. As shown in the cracker barrel example, she had four breakout rooms set up. Each presenter offered a fifteen-minute question-and-answer session in a room, and each of these was repeated three times. Participants chose three of the four sessions to attend. When

Figure 3.1. Cracker Barrel Breakout Sessions

Trainer Cracker Barrel

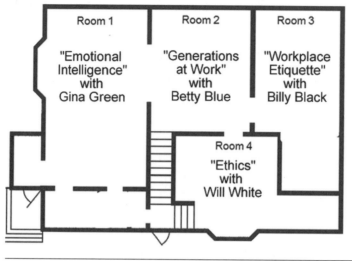

Source: Jane Bozarth

Figure 3.2. New Hire Orientation Example

New Hire Orientation

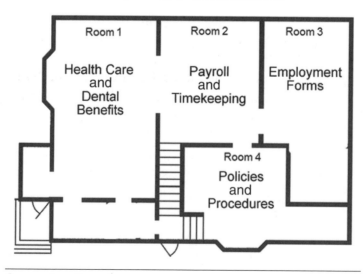

Source: Jane Bozarth

the activity ended, all the participants returned to the main room and voted on the topics they wanted more information about at future meetings. This was a very effective way to expose learners to new topics and instructors and identify the topics and instructors worth pursuing on a bigger scale.

Some of Bozarth's recommendations for making this work include:

1. Work in fifteen- to twenty-minute periods, where learners move from room to room and instructors/presenters remain in their assigned breakout rooms.

2. Allow learners to choose which events to attend. This mimics a "real" event.

3. No more than six people in one breakout room at one time.

4. Give a three-minute and one-minute warning before moving people from breakout rooms. This will give people time to wrap up conversations and keep the transition from being so abrupt.

Technologies used: online classroom application

Adopt or Adapt

This would work for any online classroom session in which learners would benefit from interacting more closely with different instructors/ presenters. Additional approaches could include "virtual tours" of an organization, with rooms hosted by department heads or expansion areas on a topic presented in a general session. For instance, a "Generations at Work" topic might offer breakout rooms hosted by a different representative: one by a Baby Boomer, one by a Gen X-er, and so forth, each offering his or her point of view on the workplace, on work ethics, and on approaches to work.

Attribution

Submitted by Jane Bozarth, author of *Better Than Bullet Points* and *Social Media for Trainers*, State of North Carolina's Human Resource Development Group, Raleigh, North Carolina, USA

Contact: info@bozarthzone.com or http://bozarthzone.blogspot.com

Jane Bozarth has been a training practitioner since 1989. She holds an M.Ed. in training and development and a doctorate in adult education. She is the author of several books: Pfeiffer's *e-Learning Solutions on a Shoestring; Better Than Bullet Points; From Analysis to Evaluation;* and new in 2010, *Social Media for Trainers.* Following a ten-year stint as a member of *Training* magazine's "In Print" book review team, she began writing *Learning Solutions* magazine's popular "Nuts and Bolts" column. She has received numerous awards, including a Live and Online Award and a *Training* magazine Editor's Pick Award.

Roll Call

The Big Idea

What

In online courses where learners interact with each other, getting-to-know-you exercises at the beginning of the course are common and fill an important role. Roll Call is a unique way for learners to begin to get to know each other.

Why

When learners interact with each other in online courses (during collaborative activities, discussions, etc.), it helps to establish connections. This is especially important for creating a sense that "real people" are out there taking the course with and learning alongside them. It also helps learners make connections between their own lives and those of their classmates. According to Borich (2007), learners appreciate a non-threatening opportunity to try out chat technologies, and they love learning trivia about fellow classmates.

Having learners post bios is a traditional way for them to exchange information. Here's something new (and fun!) to try instead of or in addition to that exercise. Figure 3.3 shows a portion of an actual activity as it was conducted in one of Abel's courses.

Use It!

How

This exercise involves a chat session that is held the first week of class. The instructor institutes a chat-based "roll call" using information gained from a survey sent to all learners on the first day of class. In addition to information she wants to know such as their majors, prior learning experiences, etc., Abel asks her students to share something unique about themselves that they would not mind the rest of the class knowing.

Figure 3.3. Roll Call Transcript

12:43 PM: **Carolyn Abel (Ins)**: Let's do a roll call. This will give you a chance to try out the chat equipment, too. When I type a sentence that DESCRIBES YOU, please type HERE.

12:44 PM: **Carolyn Abel (Ins)**: this person is....

12:45 PM: **Carolyn Abel (Ins)**: from Athens, and designed automated system for _____ Airlines

12:45 PM: **STUDENT A**: oh Im here

12:45 PM: **Carolyn Abel (Ins)**: great, you're quick

12:45 PM: **Carolyn Abel (Ins)**: next.. this person has a new 6 month old baby and is tired. ☺

12:45 PM: **Carolyn Abel (Ins)**: is that anyone?

12:46 PM: **STUDENT B**: i think it is me

12:46 PM: **STUDENT B**: i mean here

12:46 PM: **Carolyn Abel (Ins)**: Great! Thanks.

12:46 PM: **Carolyn Abel (Ins)**: next is a pastor from Nashville who rebuilds motors

12:46 PM: **STUDENT C**: I'm here.

12:46 PM: **Carolyn Abel (Ins)**: Thanks!

12:47 PM: **Carolyn Abel (Ins)**: Next is a person w an orange cat named Pumpkin from LA

12:47 PM: **Carolyn Abel (Ins)**: oops, don't see STUDENT D here today

12:47 PM: **Carolyn Abel (Ins)**: next is

12:47 PM: **Carolyn Abel (Ins)**: an administrative assistant who works with at risk high schools students

12:47 PM: **STUDENT E**: HERE!

12:47 PM: **Carolyn Abel (Ins)**: Hi!

12:48 PM: **Carolyn Abel (Ins)**: Next is someone from Michigan who teaches 7th grade TX history and is likes to sew

12:48 PM: **STUDENT F**: That me! I'm here.

12:48 PM: **Carolyn Abel (Ins)**: next is an artist from LA who likes teaching teens how to paint

12:48 PM: **STUDENT G**: hello everyone

12:49 PM: **Carolyn Abel (Ins)**: next is someone who is a science teacher and is getting married this year!

12:49 PM: **STUDENT H**: That must be me!

12:49 PM: **Carolyn Abel (Ins)**: yes!

Source: Carolyn Abel

Abel suggests that after receiving each learner's survey, the instructor should prepare a document with each learner's name and information about that learner that can easily be cut and pasted during the chat. For example:

A—New to TX from MICH, 23 yrs in Navy but never stationed on ship

B—Plays a mean trombone and loves music and video games

C—Getting married this JUNE and drives same car since age sixteen

D—Gets long distance award—currently living in Korea!

E—Adult probation officer and poet, expecting baby in 5 mos.

F—Expecting baby any time and has accounting degree and will teach math 4 to 8

G—Security consultant and football player and fan; this is his first chat!

H—Works at mental health facility and wants to teach KDGN. Has 3-yr-old

Technologies used: chat, surveys, online classroom application

Adopt or Adapt

This idea could be used with different technologies such as emails (instead of surveys) and Twitter/hash tags (instead of chat). It could also be used with true/false responses to statements or with statements from learner assignments.

Reference

Borich, G. D. (2007). *Effective teaching methods: Research-based practice.* Upper Saddle River, NJ: Pearson Education.

Attribution

Submitted by Carolyn Abel, professor, Stephen F. Austin State University, Nacogdoches, Texas, USA

Contact: www.sfasu.edu

Carolyn Abel is a full professor of education in the James I. Perkins College of Education at Stephen F. Austin State University, where she supervises teacher candidates in the Early Childhood Research Center, teaches graduate courses online, and conducts research on professional development for teachers. In April 2000, Dr. Abel won the department's Teaching Excellence award

Reenergizing Lectures with
Insert-Learner-Activity-Here Strategies

The Big Idea

What

This idea explores strategies that can be used to reenergize lectures delivered online in asynchronous and synchronous settings by incorporating active learning strategies—insert-learner-activity-here strategies—to encourage learner involvement and responsibility during online lectures.

Why

Lectures can be an efficient way of delivering content and sharing expertise, whether delivered in-person or online. However, let's face it, lectures can be boring under the best of circumstances unless the instructor is a dynamic speaker and good storyteller. Embedding insert-learner-activity-here strategies throughout an online lecture is a good way to enhance the learners' experiences and opportunities to process and reflect on the content. These strategies turn dull—albeit efficient—content-delivery events into more dynamic learning opportunities.

Use It!

How

Dunlap and Lowenthal suggest the following insert-learner-activity-here strategies to make typical online lectures more engaging learning experiences:

*   **Think-pair-share.** This strategy involves (1) asking learners a question about the content; (2) providing them time to individually answer the question; (3) asking them to confer with their peers regarding their answers to the question; and (4) asking them to reconsider their original responses to the question in light of their discussion with

peers. There are many variations on this strategy that can be used during asynchronous and synchronous online lectures, especially in terms of how to handle the "share" aspect. For example, using an online polling tool such as Polldaddy (http://polldaddy.com/) or Poll Everywhere (www.polleverywhere.com/) or form created in Google Docs, or even Twitter, the instructor can stop the lecture, pose a question to the learners, and collect learner responses in a dynamic way that can also be displayed for the group to see.

- **Interview.** Instead of listening to a lecture, learners can interview the instructor about the topic. This can be done asynchronously (using a threaded discussion forum) or synchronously (using a tool such as Connect, Elluminate, or Skype). For this strategy, the instructor can tell learners that during the interview they must collect all of the information they need on the topic to fulfill the requirements for writing an essay, completing a project, or preparing for an exam. Then learners working in teams (again, using a discussion forum, or Skype, or breakout rooms in an online classroom application such as Connect) work together to determine what three to five questions their teams need to ask in order to achieve the objective. This strategy encourages learners to reflect on what they already know, what they can find out via their text or other resources, and what they absolutely need to ask the lecturer. It also helps them construct good questions and prioritize needs.

- **Point-counterpoint.** A great lecture-enhancement strategy is to invite a colleague/guest lecturer to participate in a point-counterpoint discussion on an (often controversial) topic with the learners as the audience. This strategy allows learners to listen to two (or more, with a panel) practitioners/experts discuss and debate issues related to the topic. It helps learners recognize that there are differing perspectives on the issues and to see how colleagues grapple with those differing perspectives. Using online synchronous communication tools such as Connect, Elluminate, or Skype makes it very easy to invite colleagues from all over the world to participate in a point-counterpoint discussion.

- **Fishbowl.** Another strategy that works well is to select different groups of learners to participate with the instructor in a small group discussion, with the rest of the learners listening in and engaging in their own "back channel" discussion. Using a tool like Connect, for example, the instructor and small group of learners can use their webcams and microphones to engage in a small group discussion, while the rest of the learners use a text-based chat to carry on their own discussion based on what the small group is sharing. Twitter can also be used for the back channel chat.

- **Stump the instructor.** For this strategy, small groups of learners compete to see who can compose a question he or she thinks will stump the instructor as well as the rest of the class, and send it to the instructor (by email or by posting it to a form created in Google Docs (along with his or her name). Then the instructor can address each question. Learners have a certain amount of time to answer the questions themselves in writing (either as individuals or in their original small groups)—depending on how many questions there are—as the instructor works out her response. Using Connect, for example, each small group can work in its own breakout room and then bring its response forward to the large group either via a text-based chat pod or webcam/microphone. After each group shares responses and the professor shares her response, the large group can discuss similarities and discrepancies across responses and summarize and come to final conclusions. This strategy helps learners enhance their question construction, gives them some ownership over the questions, and can be a lot of fun.

- **Scavenger hunt.** This is a simple strategy to implement during a lecture. In advance of a prerecorded or synchronous lecture, instructors provide learners with a series of questions that can only be answered by attending to the online lecture. Learners turn in their answers to the instructor.

Technologies used: asynchronous threaded discussion forum; synchronous text chat and voice discussions using online classroom applications such as Connect, Elluminate, Skype (including text-based chat, webcams, microphones); polling tools; Google Docs; Twitter

Adopt or Adapt

These strategies can be used for lectures in secondary and post-secondary online courses, using both asynchronous and synchronous communication tools. They can also be used instead of conventional online training courses, webinars, and web conferences—anywhere in which a lecturer or presenter delivers content but wants to be more playful and encourage audience participation and responsibility. They could be easily adapted for traditional classroom training as well.

Attribution

Submitted by Joanna C. Dunlap, associate professor and faculty fellow for teaching, University of Colorado–Denver, Denver, Colorado, USA

Contact: joni.dunlap@ucdenver.edu

Also involved: Patrick R. Lowenthal, academic technology coordinator, University of Colorado–Denver: CU Online/School of Education and Human Development

Joanna C. Dunlap is an associate professor of instructional design and technology at the University of Colorado–Denver. An award-winning educator, her teaching and research interests focus on the use of sociocultural approaches to enhance adult learners' development and experience in post-secondary settings. For over fifteen years, she has directed, designed, delivered, and facilitated distance and e-learning educational opportunities for a variety of audiences. Joni is also the university's assistant director for teaching effectiveness, working through the Center for Faculty Development to help online and on-campus faculty enhance their teaching practice.

Group Formation

The Big Idea

What

In higher education online courses, it is common to have learners work collaboratively. But these learners often know little about each other and forming groups by self-selection, however desirable, is difficult. A simple and effective process to facilitate group formation based on common interests makes group formation easier and more fruitful.

Why

The process of forming groups can create problems for online instructors and learners, and this idea can reduce angst and improve group results as well as how learners feel about group work.

Use It!

How

In online courses, learners often start out knowing nothing about each other, so it's quite difficult to form groups. The process described here allows learners to find out enough about each other to form more meaningful groups. First, learners post information about themselves and then they use others' information to find commonalities and form groups.

Lawrence-Slater created this process to help learners form groups to collaboratively review journal articles. Figures 3.4 through 3.6 show examples from the activity. Learners post the topics they are most

Figure 3.4. Journal Group Formation Instructions

Journal Interests

As discussed in the <u>Subject Outline</u>, it is my preference that you create your own journal groups.

This page on the web-site is for you to publish your personal interests in the subject topic. These will then become the basis from which your journal groups can be created.

You should look through the entries and, when you find one which corresponds with your own interests, send an email to that person stating your interest in forming a group.

To help in searching for students from other classes, the Journal Interest entries are grouped as follows. Click for access to that class of students.

> NSW Regional University (<u>Undergraduate</u>)

> Singapore Open University (<u>Postgraduate</u>)

> Victorian Metropolitan University (<u>Postgraduate</u>)

Click <u>here</u> for guidelines on forming groups.

Source: Michael K. Lawrence-Slater

interested in so they can form groups with those who have common interests.

In this activity, learners post their information into forms (see the EZ Forms idea in Chapter 5). This could also be done using higher education course management system discussion forums or Facebook pages.

Figure 3.5. Journal Group Postings

See Yang (Ian)	Singapore Open University	MITM
	G'day Learning is an essential part of daily life. We learned when we worked on something. We accumulate knowledge without knowing. How can we share and impart individual knowledge among the members of an organization? Can we achieve this in a collaborative manner with the current technology. Can Information Technology (IT) helps in speeding up knowledge transfer. As a Project Manager, I am interested to share information with my staff located in 3 locations. Can IT further enhance the way we learn and work in order to complete a successful task. Knowledge is the key to commercial success. Thank you	
isee27@sin-open-u.edu.sg	Success through E-Learning in the Commercial World	

Kshitij Dave	Singapore Open University	MITM
	The New Economy has changed many aspects of business, including learning and teaching. To stay competitive, companies and employees must continue to learn and continue to discover innovative ideals. They must act upon information and share the knowledge among all in the company. Therefore a desirable framework, platform or a productive learning system for defining, monitoring, exchanging and communicating is necessary. I am particularly interested in the following areas from a commercial perspective. • **Community-based learning system for self-paced learning** With the improvement in PC's multi-media support, this way of learning is becoming more feasible than ever. It is a powerful training tool for companies that require to cross-train global employees constantly. • **Knowledge-based Management System for knowledge sharing** Such system is commonly used in support based industry such as software support. Its potential can be extended to education and it can be part of the learning system.	
horizon@yahoo.com.sg	Self-paced learning, Knowledge-based	

Source: Michael K. Lawrence-Slater

Figure 3.6. Final Journal Group

Journal Group 11			
Journal Title: e-Learning in Organisations			
Journal Topic			
Our team will look at the technologies available to IT managers when trying to achieve e-Learning objectives within organisations. We will discuss some of the technologies being utilised to contribute to the success of organisations. And conclude by looking at the issues associated with E-learning in organisations such as those that exist on a legal, political and economical level.			
Group Member's Name	**Email Address**	**Institution**	**Degree**
1 Chin Ho Hsien	chh3@pgrad.VicMetro.edu.au	Victorian Metro University	MIS
2 See Yang (Ian)	isee27@sin-open-u.edu.sg	Singapore Open University	MITM
3 Steve Williams	swill99@hotmail.com	NSW Regional University	B.Comm
4 Kshitij Dave	horizon@yahoo.com.sg	Singapore Open University	MITM
5 Ben Erickson	be0043@nsw-reg.edu.au	NSW Regional University	B.IT (Systems)

Source: Michael K. Lawrence-Slater

Adapt or Adapt

This idea can adapted easily in online or blended courses and could be adapted for classroom-based courses. Depending on the collaborative task, learners could post or share different types of information that would help with group formation for that task. This might be an effective way to find and select project team members as well.

Attribution

Submitted by: Michael K. Lawrence-Slater, Sydney, New South Wales, Australia

Contact: mklawrenceslater@gmail.com

Following a thirty-year career in the computer industry, Michael Lawrence-Slater was invited to join the teaching staff of the Faculty of Informatics at the University Wollongong. There, and later at the Universities of Melbourne and Sydney, his research focused on practical ways in which IT might be used to enhance student interactions where students were increasingly electing a hybrid mode of face-to-face and online in their learning. Although he is now retired from academia, Michael still maintains an interest in the use of IT in teaching and learning.

Better Connections with Online Learners

The Big Idea

What

This idea shows how to use social media to form better connections with online learners that can also extend into the larger community of practice.

Why

Social media applications such as Twitter, Facebook, and LinkedIn have affordances that higher education course management systems do not—namely, the ability to connect instructors and learners outside of class (and beyond the confines of a semester) as well as connect learners to a larger professional community of practice.

Use It!

How

Higher education course management systems are modeled after classrooms; while they support some learning activities (e.g., information and document sharing, online discussions, and online tests and quizzes), they are less capable or incapable of supporting others. For example, they currently cannot support the just-in-time, and sometimes playful, inter-actions that happen before and after class, during a break, and so forth. These out-of-the-classroom interactions have instructional value and can strengthen interpersonal relationships between and among instructors and learners. And higher education course management systems are by default closed systems—closed from the larger community of practice and also typically closed to learners except during the semester that the class is being held.

Intentional use of social media tools like Twitter, Facebook, or LinkedIn can establish and nurture connections that are difficult if not impossible to have in the confines of a higher education course management system. These social networking tools offer the ability to establish informal, free-flowing, just-in-time communication between and among learners and instructors as well as the larger professional community at large. These tools also offer additional ways of accessing instructors and learners, increased opportunities to learn to communicate in a concise manner, and the ability to maintain professional relationships once a course is over.

Lowenthal and Dunlap explain that the value instructors and learners get out of using social media will likely depend on how frequently they participate and how conscientious they about contributing value to the community. Samples from each author are shown in Figures 3.7 and 3.8. They recommend using the following steps for using social media tools like Twitter, Facebook, or LinkedIn in online courses.

Step 1. Identify a tool. Pick one tool. Lowenthal and Dunlap predominantly use Twitter, but they recommend finding out what social media tools learners are currently using as well as what social media tools are being used by their larger community of practice before deciding which tool will work best.

Step 2. Establish relevance. This is a critical step because if learners don't see the relevance, they will likely see the activity as just another thing to do. Lowenthal and Dunlap establish relevance by highlighting the importance of connecting with others. They recommend people, organizations, and publications for learners to follow (on Twitter). They don't require learners to participate in social media though. They feel that, while an instructor could grade participation, it is unlikely to be the best way to gain usage and relevance.

Figure 3.7. Twitter Activity

INTE 6710 ~ Creative Designs for Instructional Materials
Twitter (and/or Facebook) Invitation

As I keep mentioning, I think it is important for us to get to know each other -- and feel connected to each other -- so we can more fluidly and comfortably learn and work together through the course. The last few times I've taught this course, I invited students to follow me in **Twitter**. Not everyone took me up on the invitation, but about half of each group did. And, since then, we have been using Twitter (and occasionally Facebook too) to be in touch with each other. For more on Twitter, please check out an article written by Patrick Lowenthal and I that was recently published in Educause Quarterly (a follow-up to our *Tweeting the Night Away* article, published in the Journal of Information Systems Education):

Horton Hears a Tweet

Bottom line, I invite you to follow me in Twitter (and I will, of course, follow you...and you will follow each other). And, we can use it as a way to stay connected, share ideas, and ask and answer questions....in a more casual, flexible way then logging into the eCollege shell for all of our communication. [Note: Also, a few of our authors are on Twitter, so you can follow relevant professionals too!] Here is an example of Twitter in action with me posting a comment about having to put together a slideshow, and hearing immediately back from a student (pchristoperson) and colleague (knighthawk).

Source: Joanna Dunlap

Step 3. Model effective use. Don't assume learners know how to effectively use social media tools in a professional setting. Be sure to talk about and model effective use.

Step 4. Encourage learners' active and ongoing participation. The power of social working lies in part in active and ongoing participation. Instructors should be sure to encourage active and ongoing participation and participate themselves. If instructors stop participating, it's just a matter of time before most (if not all) learners stop.

Technologies used: social media tools

Figure 3.8. Patrick's Twitter Stream

Source: Patrick Lowenthal

Adopt or Adapt

Connecting with learners is especially important in online courses in order to overcome feelings of distance and isolation and provide additional means for communication and support. There are numerous social media tools, and more are likely to become available, so a variety of tools can be used for this purpose. The steps provided make it more likely that the tools chosen will be used well and provide the desired benefits.

Attribution

Submitted by Patrick R. Lowenthal, academic technology coordinator, University of Colorado–Denver, Denver, Colorado, USA

Contact: patrick.lowenthal@ucdenver.edu or www.patricklowenthal.com

Also involved: Joanna C. Dunlap, associate professor and faculty fellow for teaching, University of Colorado–Denver

Patrick R. Lowenthal is an academic technology coordinator at the University of Colorado–Denver (UCD), where he supports faculty who teach online. He also regularly teaches online in the master of arts in e-learning design and implementation program at UCD. Prior to coming to UCD, Patrick spent a number of years at Regis University as an assistant professor of instructional technology. Patrick is currently a doctoral student finishing his studies in instructional design and technology at UCD. His research interests focus on teaching and learning online, with a specific focus on social and teaching presence.

Comments, Please

The Big Idea

What

This idea shows how to use online review tools to facilitate peer comments.

Why

Using online review tools eliminates the need for multiple emails. It facilitates feedback from multiple people (learners, instructor, etc.) and keeps all feedback in one place.

Use It!

How

Linger uses free tools at acrobat.com, colaab.com, and voicethread.com to facilitate peer feedback on learner documents. These tools have different capabilities so it is worth looking at all of them to see which best meet your needs. For example, acrobat.com can also facilitate real-time discussions. Using these tools makes the review/comment process far less burdensome than it would be using email.

She uses tools like the one in Figure 3.9 in her business communications course to facilitate peer feedback on business letters. She also uses the tools to provide feedback on writing style and then she uses the tools to provide feedback on message organization.

Technologies used: commenting and review applications

Figure 3.9. Collaborative Peer Review Example

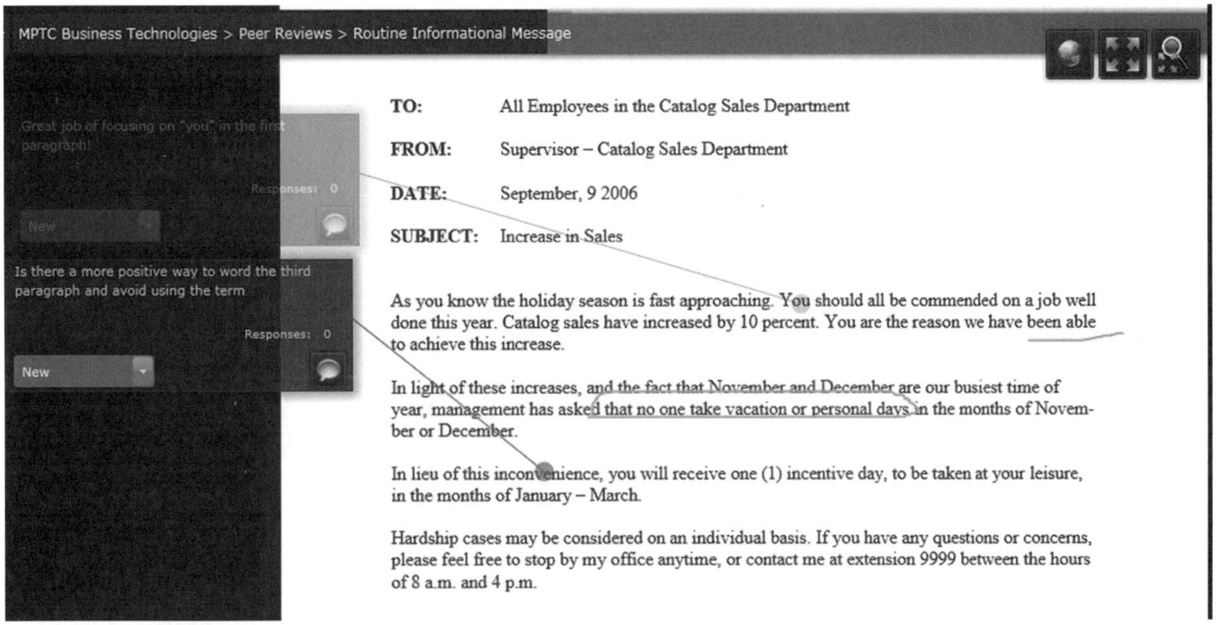

MPTC Business Technologies > Peer Reviews > Routine Informational Message

Great job of focusing on "you" in the first paragraph!

Responses: 0

New

Is there a more positive way to word the third paragraph and avoid using the term

Responses: 0

New

TO: All Employees in the Catalog Sales Department

FROM: Supervisor – Catalog Sales Department

DATE: September, 9 2006

SUBJECT: Increase in Sales

As you know the holiday season is fast approaching. You should all be commended on a job well done this year. Catalog sales have increased by 10 percent. You are the reason we have been able to achieve this increase.

In light of these increases, and the fact that November and December are our busiest time of year, management has asked that no one take vacation or personal days in the months of November or December.

In lieu of this inconvenience, you will receive one (1) incentive day, to be taken at your leisure, in the months of January – March.

Hardship cases may be considered on an individual basis. If you have any questions or concerns, please feel free to stop by my office anytime, or contact me at extension 9999 between the hours of 8 a.m. and 4 p.m.

Source: Nancy Linger, http://collab.com/

Adopt or Adapt

This idea is easily adaptable to a variety of content areas. The tools work well for commenting on the organization of a business letter, a design layout, or online learning course screens and could be used for other purposes such as to obtain opinions on a medical image such an a scan or x-ray.

Although the tools certainly lend themselves to use in all kinds of instructor-led courses, the tools could also work in self-paced online training courses to obtain comments on products built in these courses. For instance, a course on developing technical documentation could use these tools to have an expert comment on an assignment.

Attribution

Submitted by Nancy Linger, business technology instructor, Moraine Park Technical College, Beaver Dam, Wisconsin, USA

Contact: nlinger@morainepark.edu

Nancy Linger is a business technology instructor at Moraine Park Technical College. She holds a master's degree in office systems from the University of Wisconsin–Whitewater, a bachelor's degree in business education from the University of Wisconsin–Eau Claire, and a certificate in instructional development for online learning from Capella University.

Easy Collaborative Documents

The Big Idea

What

This idea shows how a web application can be used to support collaboration and learner feedback.

Why

Many online higher education courses encourage and use collaborative assignments. And collaborative writing is one of the most commonly used collaborative assignments in higher education courses. But sending word processing documents back and forth via email can cause potential problems such as loss of the documents or problems with version control. Having collaborative documents in a central location for participants to edit gets around these problems.

Use It!

How

Morris uses Google Docs (http://docs.google.com/) for collaborative writing assignments in her courses. This idea makes the collaborative process simpler and easier to accomplish, and the document is available to whoever is working on it at any time.

In addition, this tool can be used to provide feedback to learners. Figure 3.10 shows a portion of a learner's paper and the instructor's comments, suggestions, and edits. (All of these are input directly inside the paper.) The comments provide substantive feedback to the learner and save the instructor and the learner from having to download or email word processing documents back and forth.

Morris explains that it's easy for learners to start using Google Docs. An introductory video, Google Docs in Plain English, is available at www.youtube.com/watch?v=eRqUE6IHTEA.

Figure 3.10. Google Docs for Learner Feedback

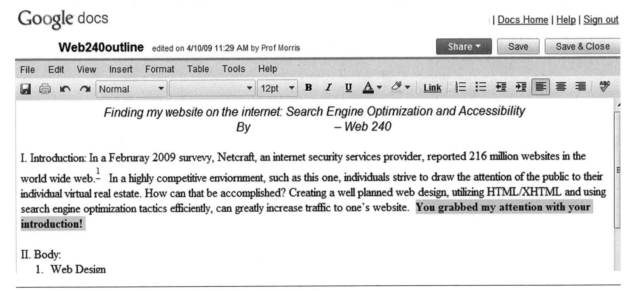

Source: Terry A. Morris

Morris also recommends these resources:

- Google Docs Web Tour: www.google.com/google-d-s/tour1.html

- Uploading Documents and Presentations to Google Docs: www .youtube.com/watch?v=_isaVcD8gXE

- How to Use Google Documents: How to Share Documents in Google Docs: www.youtube.com/watch?v=3MzcrQ4xUR0

Technologies used: online web application

Adopt or Adapt

This idea could be used in any course that utilizes collaborative writing or instructor feedback on writing and is applicable to almost any content area in both academic and corporate settings. In a corporate training course on writing performance appraisals, for example, an online collaborative writing tool could be used for feedback on a performance appraisal by the learner's supervisor or by a human resources representative. It could also be used as a peer review tool that allows peers to review written work in a (classroom or synchronous online) course setting.

In addition to Google Docs, other collaborative writing tools such as Writeboard (http://writeboard.com/), Zoho Writer (http://writer.zoho.com/), and Socialtext (www.socialtext.com/) can be utilized.

Attribution

Submitted by Terry A. Morris, associate professor, Harper College, Palatine, Illinois, USA

Contact: tmorris@harpercollege.edu or http://terrymorris.net

An associate professor at Harper College, Dr. Terry Morris has developed and taught online courses since 1999 in the subject areas of web development, computer fundamentals, and instructional technology. She has written several web development textbooks, including *Basics of Web Design* and the fifth edition of *Web Development & Design Foundations with XHTML*. Dr. Morris is a recipient of the Instructional Technology Council's 2008 Outstanding e-Learning Faculty Award for Excellence, the 2008 MERLOT Business Classics Award, and the 2006 Blackboard Greenhouse Exemplary Course Award (Online Course Category).

Virtual Job Interviews

The Big Idea

What

Mock interviews allow learners to practice job interviewing skills. But providing opportunities for mock interviews has been a challenge in online classes. Virtual environments such as Second Life (www.secondlife .com) provide an avenue for job interview interactions in a realistic online world. This virtual approach allows learners to experience an interview in a realistic manner.

Why

Mock interviews like the one portrayed in Figure 3.11 allow learners to put into practice the skills learned about interviewing. Just as in a real interview,

Figure 3.11. Virtual Interview in Second Life

Source: Susan Jennings

the learner experiences the realities of an interview in real time and does not know the questions in advance.

Use It!

How

Accounts with Second Life are free. Using it involves downloading the free application. Each person participating in the interview will need to use an avatar (which represents the person in the virtual world). The person can dress his or her avatar in appropriate business attire, which becomes part of the role play.

When entering the interview, learners introduce themselves and participate in the virtual interview with an interviewer avatar played by the faculty member or a businessperson with experience in interviewing.

Jennings provides some tips and guidelines for conducting this activity:

- Spend some time in Second Life in advance so you are familiar with its use, especially the voice function.

- Provide learners with Second Life training.

- Arrange for a private virtual location to hold the interviews, such as an office or conference room.

- Stress the importance of arriving at interviews on time. Provide an area for learners to wait in case they arrive early for the interview. Create an SL URL (Second Life URL) that will take learners directly to the waiting area.

- Meet with learners in a group setting before the interview date to allow learners a chance to practice their walking, sitting, and other body movements as well as their speech capabilities.

- Provide learners with information about where they can obtain free professional business attire.

- Invite a guest to interview the learners. If the guest does not have an avatar, help create one.

Technologies used: Second Life

Adopt or Adapt

This idea could be adapted for a variety of realistic interpersonal role plays such as interviewing techniques (journalism), performance reviews (management training), and therapeutic communications (psychology). Second Life and other virtual worlds are also valuable for a wide variety of interactive activities such as virtual field trips and virtual presentations.

Attribution

Submitted by Susan Evans Jennings, professor, Stephen F. Austin State University, Nacogdoches, Texas, USA

Contact: sjennings@sfasu.edu or www.sfasu.edu

Dr. Susan Evans Jennings has taught at SFASU since 2000. Prior to joining their faculty, she spent three years as an assistant professor at Valdosta State University in Georgia and eleven years as a high school business teacher at Parkers Chapel High School in El Dorado, Arkansas. She authored *Internet Office Projects* and co-authored the online textbook series *Administrative Office Professional*. Her research interests include communication technologies, including virtual worlds, social networking, and other Web 2.0 applications.

Who Are You? Alternative Online Meet-and-Greet Tactics

The Big Idea

What

This idea presents some unique tactics for meeting and greeting fellow online learners that are more engaging than the typical bio-sharing activities that are used in many online higher education courses.

Why

Typical bio-sharing activities at the start of an online higher education course ask learners to share a few facts about themselves (e.g., geographic location, position title, and purpose for taking the course), but are often uninspiring and leave learners with little more than a cursory impression of their peers. In addition, those types of activities can be a low-energy way to start an online course that does little to instill social presence or build trust and community among class members.

Use It!

How

Instead of eliciting creative responses that get at the core of an individual's personality, values, and purpose, typical bio-sharing activities encourage learners to share the most mundane facts. In online courses, when we need to do all we can to help people feel present and connected, a "just the facts" bio often fails to deliver the desired results.

Dunlap and Lowenthal suggest the following alternative meet-and-greet tactics:

- **Soundtrack of Your Life:** Learners create a playlist using an online digital jukebox tool like Tinysong (http://tinysong.com). In their playlist they include two songs that represent their past, two songs that represent their now, and two songs that represent their future.

- **Superhero Powers:** Using a tool like VoiceThread (www.voicethread .com), learners share their superhero monikers and powers, and explain how their powers help them in their professional and personal lives. (See Figure 3.12.)

- **Cartoon Network:** Using a tool like Xtranormal (www.xtranormal .com/), learners create an animated avatar to introduce themselves.
- **Virtual Photo Album:** Using a tool like Flickr (www.flickr.com/), learners put together a set of five photos that reflect who they are and what they care about.
- **A Few Words About Me:** Using a tool like Wordle (www.wordle.net/), learners create a word cloud that reflects who they are and what they care about. (See Figures 3.13 and 3.14.)
- **My Music Video:** Using a tool like Animoto (http://animoto.com/), learners put together a music video of their lives using photos and a music track of their choice.

Figure 3.12. VoiceThread Digital Storytelling, Text Response

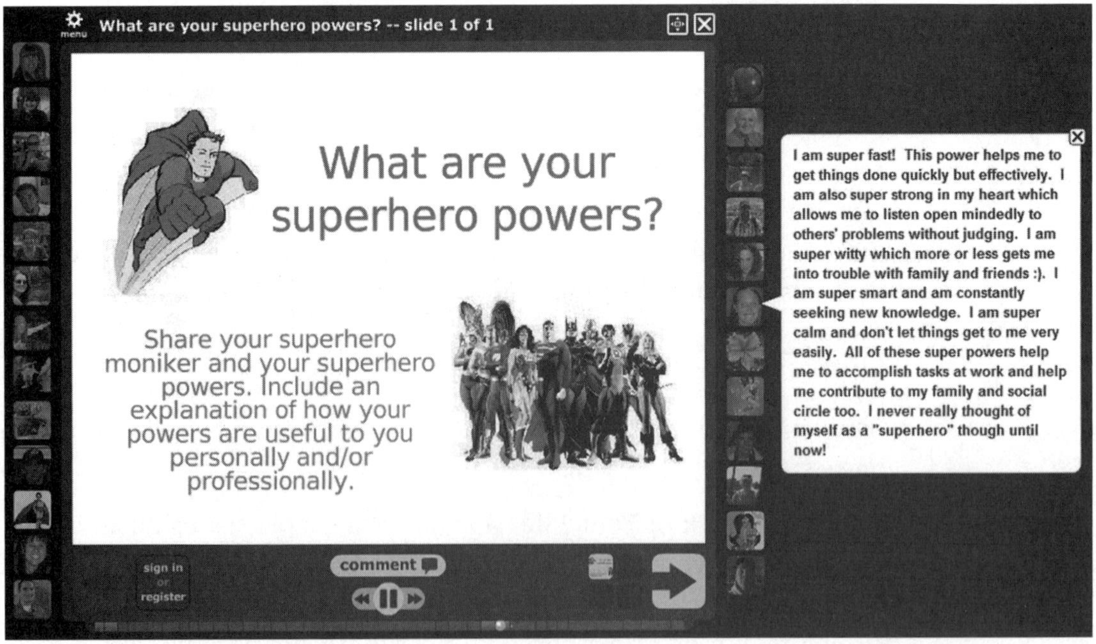

Source: Joanna Dunlap, http://voicethread.com/#q.b89809.i0.k0

Figure 3.13. Wordle Word Cloud, Example 1

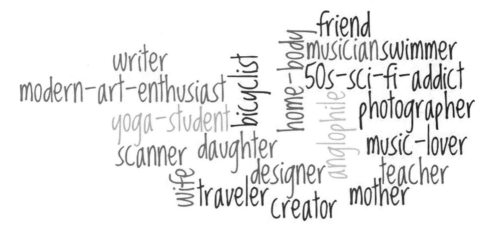

Source: Joanna Dunlap

Figure 3.14. Wordle Word Cloud, Example 2

Source: Joanna Dunlap

Technologies used: various web applications (tinysong, VoiceThread, Xtranormal, Flickr, Wordle, and Animoto)

Adopt or Adapt

Almost all online courses, regardless of discipline, use some sort of meet-and-greet activity at the start of the course. The tactics shared in this idea are not discipline or setting specific and therefore can easily be applied to any discipline or setting. These tactics could also be adapted for other purposes. For example, they could be used at the beginning of an extended (online or face-to-face) training program so that learners involved in the program can learn more about each other. They also could be used to introduce new board members or team members to each other.

Attribution

Submitted by Joanna C. Dunlap, associate professor and faculty fellow for teaching, University of Colorado–Denver, Denver, Colorado, USA

Contact: joni.dunlap@ucdenver.edu

Also involved: Patrick R. Lowenthal, academic technology coordinator, University of Colorado–Denver: CU Online/School of Education and Human Development

Joanna C. Dunlap is an associate professor of instructional design and technology at the University of Colorado–Denver. An award-winning educator, her teaching and research interests focus on the use of sociocultural approaches to enhance adult learners' development and experience in post-secondary settings. For over fifteen years, she has directed, designed, delivered, and facilitated distance and e-learning educational opportunities for a variety of audiences. Joni is also the university's assistant director for teaching effectiveness, working through the Center for Faculty Development to help online and on-campus faculty enhance their teaching practice.

Making Connections

The Big Idea

What

This idea shows how to use social networking groups to network with professionals in the field as part of course activities in a higher education course.

Why

Online networking with professionals in the field opens "the classroom" to the world and gives learners a chance to understand the issues of real-world practice from professionals' points of view.

Use It!

How

Linger suggests that instructors encourage learners, as part of course activities, to use the following methods for finding social networking groups aligned with career and professional goals:

- Identify professional organizations in the field and determine what online discussion groups they offer.

- Search LinkedIn Groups (Go to www.linkedin.com/. Then click Groups>Groups Directory) and Facebook Groups (Go to www .facebook.com/. Then search with keywords and then click on Groups to see related groups) for groups related to your field. LinkedIn is more professionally focused so it is usually a better place to start.

Learners should carefully read group descriptions to see whether the group is appropriate (you cannot always tell by the name alone). Look at how many people are enrolled in the group. Small numbers may mean the group isn't very active. (See Figures 3.15 and 3.16.)

Linger recommends that learners read postings without posting themselves for a while until they get a feel for how the group interacts and how they ask for and share information. She suggests that learners start

Figure 3.15. Finding Professional Groups on LinkedIn

Source: Nancy Linger, www.linkedin.com/

Figure 3.16. Responses from LinkedIn Group Members

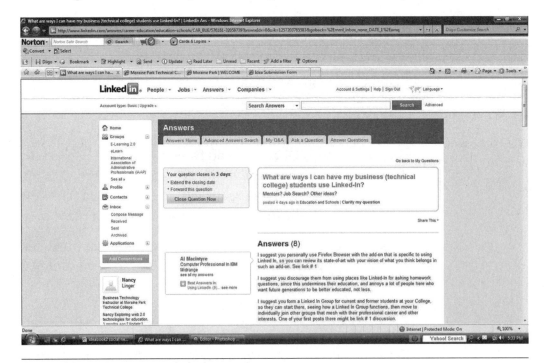

Source: Nancy Linger, www.linkedin.com/

to interact by asking a single question. It's usually best to not ask a *lot* of questions at once because they are less likely to be answered (professionals are busy!).

Instructors may need to help learners determine what types of questions are likely to get a good response and how to best ask for information. It will not be a good experience for learners if their first attempts are met with antagonism.

Linger shares the following professional development activity that shows how she has implemented this approach in one of her courses.

Professional Development Activity

Interview a minimum of three people employed in your career area. At least one of the people should be someone you don't personally know. Ask them what type of professional development they have been involved in over the course of their careers. Find out:

- Do they hold any certifications? How did they earn them?

- What professional organizations do they belong to? In what ways have these organizations been of benefit?

- What conferences do they think are most useful?

- What online resources do they regular use?

- What publications do they regularly read?

- What professional development opportunities do they recommend for people who are newer to the field?

For the person you don't know, consider Facebook Groups, LinkedIn Groups, or search out professional organizations in your career area to identify a discussion board you could use for this purpose.

Prepare a report summarizing the findings from this interview. Identify the person(s) you interviewed, their job titles, their organizations, and how you connected with them. Include a screen capture to document your questions and answers.

Technologies used: online social networking tools

Adopt or Adapt

This strategy can be used for gaining real-life perspectives on a given topic, soliciting opinions on a controversial topic, gaining international perspectives, and locating resources.

Attribution

Submitted by Nancy Linger, business technology instructor, Moraine Park Technical College, Beaver Dam, Wisconsin, USA

Contact: nlinger@morainepark.edu

Nancy Linger is a business technology instructor at Moraine Park Technical College. She holds a master's degree in office systems from the University of Wisconsin–Whitewater, a bachelor's degree in business education from the University of Wisconsin–Eau Claire, and a certificate in instructional development for online learning from Capella University.

Alternative Structures for Online Discussions

The Big Idea

What

This idea describes discussion protocols to ensure the continuing benefit of online discussions while minimizing the potential boredom that comes from misuse and overuse and maximizing learner responsibility and engagement.

Why

The same-old-same-old discussion forum format (i.e., instructor posts a question and each learner is required to post an original response and comment on posts from peers) can be detrimental to social presence and learner engagement. Online discussion protocols can prevent these problems and enhance engagement and learning.

Use It!

How

Online discussions are the bread and butter of higher education online courses. Besides providing opportunities for learner-content, learner-learner, and learner-instructor interaction—the foundation of social presence and learner engagement—online discussions allow learners to test their new knowledge, represent their conceptual understanding, and find their professional voices.

Using online discussion protocols has several benefits. They can:

* Encourage learner preparation in advance;

* Balance learner voices during discussion so everyone has a chance to contribute;

* Allow learners to test their understanding, and learn from others' testing;

- Provide additional structure that clarifies participation and assessment expectations; and

- Teach learners how to participate and contribute to discussions using online communication tools.

Dunlap and Lowenthal share the following online discussion protocols, modified from protocols described in Brookfield and Preskill (1999) and McDonald, Mohr, Dichter, and McDonald (2003).

For best results with these protocols, have learners work in discussion groups of four or five, with each group assigned to its own discussion forum. When using a protocol, it is helpful to debrief the activity with the whole group to reinforce what was learned from the discussion and explore any remaining questions. (*Note:* For all protocols, you can modify the words-per-post limit as well as the time frame. These structures are guidelines only, so modify as appropriate to your situation.)

The Final Post (for Asynchronous Discussion)

(Modified from McDonald, Mohr, Dichter, and McDonald, 2003)

Steps

1. Each learner identifies one of the most significant ideas from the reading, illustrated by a quote or excerpt. (Each learner should have a back-up quote/excerpt in case another learner has already posted the same quote/excerpt.)

2. Each learner starts a new thread by posting the quote/excerpt from the text that particularly struck her or him. The learner points out where the quote is in the text. In approximately 250 words, the learner describes why that quote/excerpt struck her or him. (Specify a deadline for the original posts.)

3. Each learner responds to that quote/excerpt and what the original learner wrote, using approximately 150 words. The purpose of the response is to expand on the original learner's thinking about the topic, to provide a different perspective on the topic, to clarify thinking about the topic, and to question the original learner's assumptions about the topic. (Specify a deadline for these posts.)

4. After each learner in the group has responded to the original post, the first learner has the "final word." In approximately 150 words, the original learner responds to what has been shared by the rest of the group, offering what she or he is now thinking about the topic, and her or his reaction to what the other learners have posted. (Specify a deadline for the "final word" post.)

5. This process continues until everyone has had the opportunity to have the "final word." This means that four or five discussions are happening simultaneously within a particular timeframe (e.g., one week), or that they are happening one at a time (each discussion over one or two days).

The Last Post (for Asynchronous Discussion)

(Modified from McDonald, Mohr, Dichter, and McDonald, 2003)

Steps

1. Each learner identifies one of the most significant ideas from the reading, illustrated by a quote or excerpt. (Each learner should have a backup quote/excerpt in case another learner has already posted the same quote/excerpt.)

2. Each learner starts a new thread by posting the quote/excerpt from the text that particularly struck her or him. The learner points out where the quote/excerpt is in the text, but does not explain why that quote/excerpt struck her or him.

3. The rest of the group discusses the quote/excerpt, why it is significant, what it means, and so on. Specify an amount of time for this discussion, such as two days.

4. After each learner in the group has participated in a discussion about the quote/excerpt, the first learner has the "last word." In no more than 250 words the original learner shares why she or he thought it was significant, what she or he is now thinking about the topic, and her or his reaction to what the other learners have posted.

5. This process continues until everyone has had the opportunity to have the "last word." This means that four or five discussions (depending on number of learners in a group) are happening simultaneously within a particular timeframe (e.g., one week), or that they are happening one at a time (each discussion over one or two days).

(continued)

Posting the Crux of the Matter (for Asynchronous Discussion)

(Modified from McDonald, Mohr, Dichter, and McDonald, 2003)

Steps

1. Set up four new threads: Sentences, Phrases, Words, and Insights. Designate a time frame for the discussion, such as two or three days.

2. First round: Each learner posts a sentence from the reading that she or he feels is particularly significant in the Sentences thread. Each new post must be unique; in other words, if a sentence has already been posted, it should not be posted again.

3. Second round: Each learner shares a phrase that she or he feels is particularly significant in the Phrases thread. Each new post must be unique; in other words, if a phrase has already been posted, it should not be posted again.

4. Third round: Each learner posts the word that she or he feels in particularly significant in the Words thread. Each new post must be unique; in other words, if a word has already been posted, it should not be posted again.

5. In the Insights thread, the small group discusses what they understand about the reading based on what everyone has posted, and any new insights about the reading.

Designated Readers (for Asynchronous Discussion)

(Modified from Brookfield and Preskill, 1999)

Steps

1. At some point in the course, each learner takes on the role of the designated reader.

2. During an online discussion, the designated reader does not contribute (except to ask for clarification of someone else's contribution).

3. At the end of the discussion, the designated reader is responsible for summarizing the online discussion. (*Note:* You can require a specific word count for summaries to help designated readers write concisely.)

Note: This protocol promotes active "listening" during online discussions because it requires the designated readers to read all contributions, look for themes and differing perspectives, ask clarifying questions, and summarize what has occurred during the discussion in a way that values everyone's contributions. Especially when written concisely, these summaries also serve to help the group feel a sense of closure, making it easier to move on to the next discussion.

Rotating Threads (for Asynchronous or Synchronous Discussion)

(Modified from Brookfield and Preskill, 1999)

Steps

1. Set up threaded discussion forums, with a different provocative issue to discuss in each forum.

2. In groups of four or five, have learners rotate to a new forum. In terms of timing, you could have each group spend one day in a forum, e.g., Forum A on Monday, Forum B on Tuesday, and so on.

3. Have each group record their ideas about the issue in the forum.

4. Once groups have rotated to each forum, give learners time to revisit all of the forums to see what other groups posted.

5. As a final activity, have learners summarize what they have learned about the issues.

Snowballing Threads (for Asynchronous or Synchronous Discussion)

(Modified from Brookfield and Preskill, 1999)

Steps

1. Discussion starts with small group discussions, with each small group having its own discussion forum.

(continued)

2. After a designated amount of time, each small group joins with another group in a new forum.

3. After a designated amount of time, each larger group joins with another group in a new forum, and so on, until the whole group comes together into the same forum.

Jigsaw Threads (for Asynchronous or Synchronous Discussion)

(Modified from Brookfield and Preskill, 1999)

Steps

1. Groups of four or five learners become experts on a particular issue/topic. Each group of experts has its own discussion forum to work in as they develop their expertise. Depending on the topic and level of desired depth of expertise, this could take one week.

2. Form new groups. Each new group includes an expert from one of the original groups. These new groups have their own discussion forums.

3. Experts lead new groups in an online discussion on their areas of expertise. Again, depending on the topic and desired depth, each expert could lead a discussion over one day to one week.

Chat Room of Voices (for Synchronous Discussion)

(Modified from Brookfield and Preskill, 1999)

Steps

1. Form learners into groups of four or five and set up a chat room for each group.

2. Post a question, a passage, etc., that focuses each chat.

3. After learners have a few minutes of quiet time to organize their thoughts (or you can ask learners to prepare in advance of joining the chat), each learner in the group then has three minutes of uninterrupted time to respond (this can be done

sequentially or in whatever order, as long as everyone writes for three minutes). *Modification:* Each learner must begin by paraphrasing the comments of the previous learner and must strive to show how his or her posting relates to the comments of the previous learner.

4. After everyone in the chat room has had three minutes, the discussion is opened up with the following ground rule: Learners are allowed to contribute to the chat only about other people's ideas, not expand on their own ideas (unless asked a direct question).

Chat Room Full of Quotes (for Synchronous Discussion)

(Modified from Brookfield and Preskill, 1999)

Steps

1. Set up a chat room for use with groups of ten to fifteen learners.

2. Prepare five or six sentences/passages/quotes from the text. Assign each learner a number based on the number of quotes you have (e.g., if you have six quotes, assign learners numbers from 1 to 6).

3. Share the quotes and explain that learners assigned number 1 will respond to quote number 1 and so on.

4. Give learners a few minutes to organize their thoughts about the quotes.

5. Call on each learner (randomly, by alphabetical order, or by order of entry into the chat room) to share the quote and comment on it.

6. Each learner has one or two minutes to respond in the chat room.

7. Once you have called on all learners to participate in the chat, you may want to have them write and post a 250-word summary describing the content of the chat session.

Note: Because learners are only reacting to five or six quotes, they are able to read others' views about the quote they posted on (or will post on).

Technologies used: asynchronous threaded discussion forum; synchronous text chat and voice discussions using online classroom applications such as Connect, Elluminate, Skype (including text-based chat, webcams, microphones)

Adopt or Adapt

These online discussion protocols not only support learner engagement in online courses at the secondary and post-secondary levels, but are great approaches to structuring webinars and online meetings. They could be easily adapted for traditional classroom training as well.

References

Brookfield, S. D., & Preskill, S. (1999). *Discussion as a way of teaching.* San Francisco: Jossey-Bass.

McDonald, J., Mohr, N., Dichter, A., & McDonald, E. (2003). *The power of protocols: An educator's guide to better practice.* New York: Teachers College Press.

Attribution

Submitted by Joanna C. Dunlap, associate professor and faculty fellow for teaching, University of Colorado–Denver, Denver, Colorado, USA

Contact: joni.dunlap@ucdenver.edu

Also involved: Patrick R. Lowenthal, academic technology coordinator, University of Colorado–Denver: CU Online/School of Education and Human Development

Joanna C. Dunlap is an associate professor of instructional design and technology at the University of Colorado–Denver. An award-winning educator, her teaching and research interests focus on the use of socio-cultural approaches to enhance adult learners' development and experience in post-secondary settings. For over fifteen years, she has directed, designed, delivered, and facilitated distance and e-learning educational opportunities for a variety of audiences. Joni is also the university's assistant director for teaching effectiveness, working through the Center for Faculty Development to help online and on-campus faculty enhance their teaching practice.

"Rad" Libs

The Big Idea

What

This idea shows a humorous "Mad Libs"–like activity for a higher education online course. It brings out commonality of experience among participants.

Why

It's easy to use the same-old activities in higher education online courses, such as sharing slides and asking learners to respond to poll questions. This activity is really different and can be extremely engaging.

Use It!

How

When dealing with the realities of limited time in online classroom courses, it's common to try to "cover" as much content as possible. But leaving out learner input and interaction usually isn't a good idea. Studies show that learners in online courses too often multitask (answer emails, etc.), and lack of interaction certainly makes this more likely. Plus, without input from the learners, the instructor is essentially doing a monologue and is unable to adapt what she or he is saying to the learners' needs.

Shank likes trying to come up with unique online course activities and developed this one for a course on typical online project management problems. She decided to create a "Mad Libs"–like activity. As she read out each line, learners typed an answer (to complete each fill-in blank) into the chat pod. At the end, Shank debriefed the commonalities in submitted answers. She brought up these commonalities again during the course as she discussed solutions to each common project management problem.

Shank found that learners were really interested in seeing what other learners typed in and that many were surprised to find that they had similar experiences. Shank suggests that, when building this activity, instructors carefully word stories so that learners clearly understand the types of answers they are supposed to submit (that's one reason why the directions provide an example). Make sure that you are, in fact, using experiences that many learners are likely to have in common, or adapt the activity so that you are debriefing both commonalities and differences. Examples are shown in Figures 3.17 and 3.18.

Technologies used: PowerPoint

Figure 3.17. "Rad" Libs Activity

Team Libs 1

Directions: As the numbers in the game are read by Patti, complete each blank by typing it into the Questions/Responses to Patti CHAT window. For example, type **1-storyboard.**

Don, the lead ID, committed to have the ___1___ (deliverable) completed by Wednesday so Toby, the SME, could ___2___ (something the SME needs to do) but guess what? Don didn't get it done. Don said he couldn't stick to the schedule because ___3___ (excuse or obfuscation).

www.learningpeaks.com

Source: Patti Shank

Figure 3.18. Show: Participant Answers

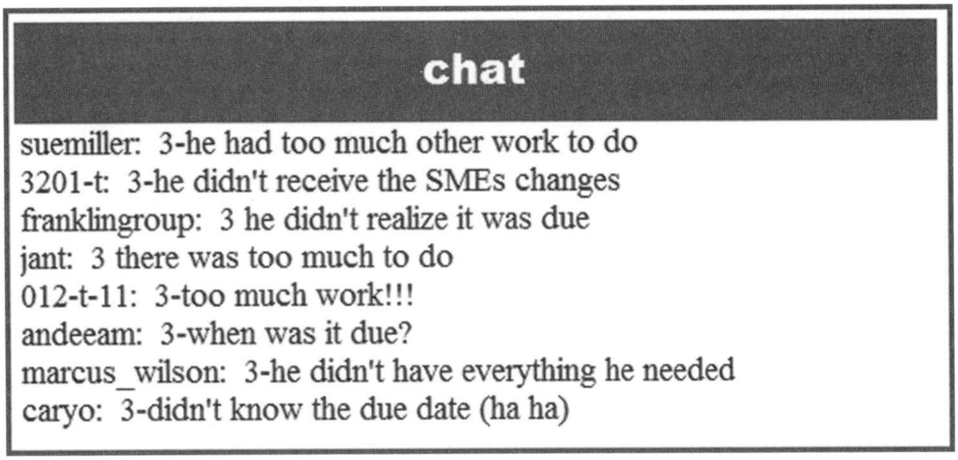

> **chat**
>
> suemiller: 3-he had too much other work to do
> 3201-t: 3-he didn't receive the SMEs changes
> franklingroup: 3 he didn't realize it was due
> jant: 3 there was too much to do
> 012-t-11: 3-too much work!!!
> andeeam: 3-when was it due?
> marcus_wilson: 3-he didn't have everything he needed
> caryo: 3-didn't know the due date (ha ha)

Source: Patti Shank

Adopt or Adapt

This idea could be adapted for a variety of purposes. "Rad Libs" is expected to be a funny activity (by anyone who has played "Mad Libs"), so adapting it for more serious use would require some rethinking. A serious story could be built as an introduction to or a recap of content.

Attribution

Submitted by Patti Shank, president, Learning Peaks LLC, Denver, Colorado, USA

Contact: patti@learningpeaks.com or www.learningpeaks.com

Patti Shank is the president of Learning Peaks LLC, an internationally recognized instructional design consulting firm that provides learning and performance consulting and training and performance support solutions. She is listed in *Who's Who in Instructional Technology* and is an often-requested speaker at training and instructional technology conferences. Patti is quoted frequently in training publications and is the co-author of *Making Sense of Online Learning*, editor of *The Online Learning Idea Book*, co-editor of *The e-Learning Handbook*, and co-author of *Essential Articulate Studio '09*.

Nonverbal Cues

The Big Idea
What

This idea suggests a unique and playful way to offer nonverbal cues in online discussions.

Why

It's easy to have communication disconnects when communicating using text (for instance, communication by email). For example, one person types a reply to an email very quickly before heading to a meeting, and the reader of that quickly typed reply thinks the sender is curt and tactless. If we can provide some image cues *along with* text, when appropriate, it may prevent miscommunications and improve the quality of textual interactions. (See Figure 3.19 for an example.)

Figure 3.19. Image Cue

Source: Leah Omilion

Use It!

How

Learning online involves a lot of text-driven communication. One problem with text-driven communication is that we lose the nonverbal cues we can get from someone's face and tone of voice.

Omilion, an online instructor who teaches business and organizational and group communication, found that text-driven communication sometimes didn't get things across as well as she hoped. She also realized that she sometimes missed cues that learners were confused or were having difficulties. Because she felt a strong obligation to ensure better flow of meaning in both directions, she decided on an unorthodox approach. Omilion began to use images that portrayed her thoughts (i.e., enjoyment, confusion, deep-in-thought) at times when responding to learners' posts in discussion forums.

Omilion also found that this was a great way to begin a discussion about the power of nonverbal communication in the context of her subject area. She doesn't announce ahead of time that some of her responses will come in graphic format. Her approach has had favorable reactions. So much so, that some responses to her postings and responses have begun to come in graphic format as well! Thus, not only does this approach add nonverbal messages, but it also improves enjoyment of the learning experience.

Initially, Omilion took some pictures of herself with a variety of expressions. The first images that she used included a cheerful expression, one that was quizzical, and another that showed her to be deep in thought. Because of the positive response, she began to take and use additional images.

When teaching in her subject areas, this approach also helps learners consider how expressions and gestures (such as crossed arms and lack of eye contact) impact how they are perceived. A benefit of this approach for online learners in any subject area is that learners begin to understand how easy it is to be misread in text (so they can consider how to improve their textual communications).

Technologies used: electronic images

Adopt or Adapt

Although Omilion uses this both to add nonverbal communications to a text-driven medium *and* to introduce the topic of nonverbal communication in the topics she teaches, this approach can be used in any content area just to add nonverbal messages. And imagine the other text-driven communications that this idea could be used in (email, memos, etc.).

Attribution

Submitted by Leah M. Omilion, doctoral candidate, Wayne State University, Detroit, Michigan, USA

Contact: Leah@wayne.edu

Leah M. Omilion is a doctoral candidate in the Department of Communication at Wayne State University. She teaches classes in group, health, and team communication. Her research focuses on leadership, organizational relationships, and social influence.

Online Classroom Clickers

The Big Idea

What

This idea describes ways to use the equivalent of student response systems, also known as "clickers," in online classrooms without actually having to use clickers.

Why

Polling can be a great way to check in with learners during a course and provide them with an anonymous way to voice their opinions. Here are some easy ways to do that!

Use It!

How

Higher education instructors are using student response systems more and more each year in a variety of ways in face-to-face classrooms. While threaded discussions are the most popular way to hold discussions in higher education online courses, they aren't anonymous, are often the only type of online discussion used, and are not effective at providing quick feedback the way that online polling does.

However, online polling applications offer online instructors ways to easily and effectively poll their learners on a variety of topics and then instantly display the results for other learners to see, thus acting a lot like "clickers." Some of these applications can even display the results in a course management system, as seen in Figures 3.20 and 3.21.

To get started, pick a polling tool to use. Poll Everywhere (www.pollevery where.com), micropoll (www.micropoll.com), and twtpoll (www.twtpoll .com) are a few options to check out. Most of these polling applications

Figure 3.20. Online Poll Created with Twtpoll

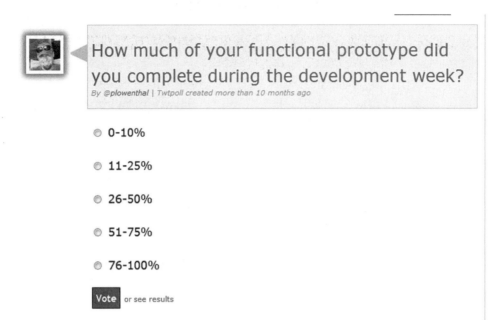

Source: Patrick Lowenthal

work the same. You first set up an account. Most offer some sort of free accounts. Once you set up your account, you can then create polls (often with the option for both yes/no, multiple-choice, or even short-answer questions). Once you create a poll, you can embed it into a web page or your course management system.

Technologies used: online polling tools, course management system

Figure 3.21. Online Poll Embedded in a Course Management System

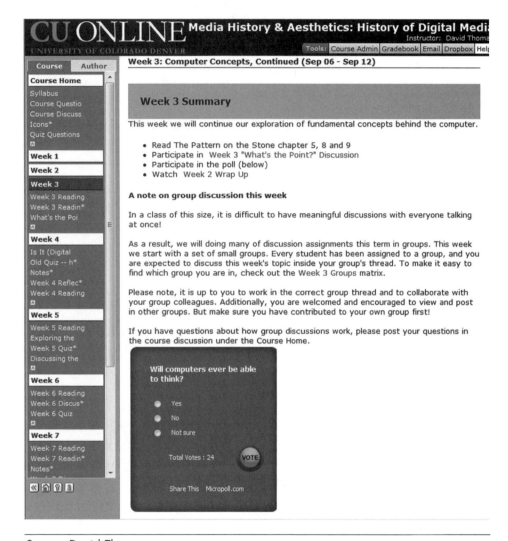

Source: David Thomas

Adopt or Adapt

Polls are good for a variety of purposes. Using them to gain learner opinions is the most obvious, but they can also be used as a self-check to see whether learners are on track with what is being taught. This idea discusses use in higher education courses, but they are also useful in corporate training. Online classroom systems often have polling capabilities built in, but you might also use polls in self-paced online courses as well. For example, it could be exceptionally interesting to embed opinion polls in self-paced courses so that learners could see how previous learners reacted to a specific question or questions.

Attribution

Submitted by Patrick R. Lowenthal, academic technology coordinator, University of Colorado–Denver, Denver, Colorado, USA

Contact: patrick.lowenthal@ucdenver.edu or www.patricklowenthal.com

Also involved: Joanna C. Dunlap, associate professor and faculty fellow for teaching, University of Colorado–Denver, and David Thomas, manager of academic technology, University of Colorado–Denver

Patrick R. Lowenthal is an academic technology coordinator at the University of Colorado–Denver (UCD), where he supports faculty who teach online. He also regularly teaches online in the master of arts in e-learning design and implementation program at UCD. Prior to coming to UCD, Patrick spent a number of years at Regis University as an assistant professor of instructional technology. Patrick is currently a doctoral student finishing his studies in instructional design and technology at UCD. His research interests focus on teaching and learning online, with a specific focus on social and teaching presence.

Online vs. On-Campus Competition

The Big Idea

What

This idea shows how to set up a friendly competition between learners in online and on-campus sections of the same course.

Why

This activity encourages interaction between learners in on-campus and online sections of the same course. This helps online teams feel more connected to the campus and improves engagement in the course for all involved. Chasteen uses this in his program's final (capstone) course and all the teams see each other at graduation, so it also helps them connect to each other prior to and during graduation.

Use It!

How

Chasteen says that learners in his business capstone courses tell him that their favorite part of the course is the simulation game. He felt that his online students missed some of the fun that occurred during the simulation in his on-campus section, so he modified the simulation so that online teams compete with on-campus teams.

After teams compete against classmates in their own online or on-campus sections, Chasteen has the top online teams and the top on-campus teams compete against each other. When the top teams compete against teams in other sections of the course, the competition becomes even more exciting because these teams feel that they are representing their entire section.

Here's a bit more about how the competition works. Each team's goal is to maximize stock price and total profits over eight rounds (eight "years") of running their companies. After each round (one "year"), each team can see other teams' results, including annual reports, balance sheets, and how much product the other teams sold during that round. Based on what they see and how well the other teams are doing, each team decides on its strategy for the next round.

Technologies used: simulation game, course communication tools

Adopt or Adapt

This approach could be used for competition on any project, deliverable, or game involving online and on-campus sections of the same course or different online or on-campus sections of the same course. It could also be adapted so that different groups going through the same training course or program compete against each other. For example, teams from two management development programs could compete to develop the best how-to documents for new supervisors.

Attribution

Submitted by Larry Chasteen, associate professor, Stephen F. Austin State University, Nacogdoches, Texas, USA

Contact: chasteenlh@sfasu.edu

Dr. Larry Chasteen is an associate professor of management at Stephen F. Austin University. He received a BSME and MSME from SMU and completed his Ph.D. in management at the University of Texas at Dallas with research in corporate entrepreneurship and innovation. He was a B-52 pilot during the Viet Nam War. His twenty-five-year civilian career was as a program manager in the defense industry for Texas Instruments and Raytheon in the areas of radar and smart weapons. He served as Fulbright professor in Germany in 2006 and as a science advisor at the U.S. State Department in 2008.

Polling for Engagement

The Big Idea

What

This idea shows how to use online polling technologies to engage learners and to solicit feedback on instructional elements or the learning environment.

Why

Polls are used to collect data from learners that instructors can use to improve courses. Instructors can collect feedback from learners about their understanding of and the effectiveness of learning strategies.

Use It!

How

Linger uses polls to collect information from learners and then shows learners aggregate responses. Her tool of choice is Poll Everywhere (www .polleverywhere.com/). Poll Everywhere uses the web to gather live responses in classes, presentations, conferences, and elsewhere. There are four ways to respond to a poll: sending a SMS (text) message, using a mobile web browser, sending a "tweet" (using Twitter), or using a web browser on a computer. As responses come in, the results are updated and charted and these results can be shown to learners. Figure 3.22 shows an example.

There are myriad applications that can be used for polling. Poll Anywhere is a standalone web application for this purpose, but some higher education course management systems may have built-in polling. Online classroom applications may have polling functionalities as well. Some social networking tools such as Facebook and LinkedIn allow users to set up polls. There are other online polling applications such as 99polls (www.99polls.com/), acepols (www.acepolls.com/), Pollcode (http://pollcode.com/), Polldaddy (http://polldaddy.com/), and twtpoll (http://twtpoll.com/).

Technologies used: polling application

Figure 3.22. Everywhere Poll Example

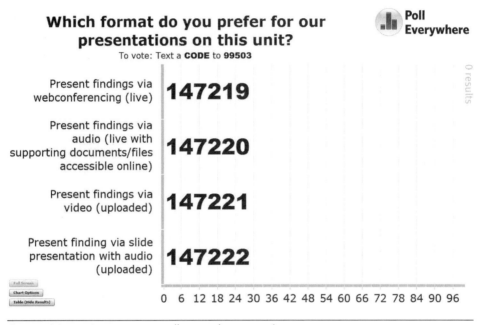

Source: Nancy Linger, www.polleverywhere.com/

Adopt or Adapt

Polling can be implemented in a wide variety of instructional situations and for a wide variety of purposes. For example, polls can be used in face-to-face courses, conference presentations, self-paced online courses, and synchronous online courses. They can be used to solicit feedback about the course, opinions about different topics, and to gauge understanding and need for support.

Attribution

Submitted by Nancy Linger, business technology instructor, Moraine Park Technical College, Beaver Dam, Wisconsin, USA

Contact: nlinger@morainepark.edu

Nancy Linger is a business technology instructor at Moraine Park Technical College. She holds a master's degree in office systems from the University of Wisconsin–Whitewater, a bachelor's degree in business education from the University of Wisconsin–Eau Claire, and a certificate in instructional development for online learning from Capella University.

Back in the Day, Facebook Style

The Big Idea

What

This idea shows how to use Facebook to hold engaging discussions about historical events.

Why

Role playing historical characters who are posting to a Facebook page makes history truly come alive in a fun and engaging way! Rather than writing a report on a historical figure or event, the information can be presented from multiple perspectives. This activity is more a conversation than a history "report," yet it imparts significant information in an appealing way. And because it's fun and involves multiple perspectives, it is likely to uncover insights that might not be uncovered in more traditional instructional activities.

Use It!

How

Learners and instructors role play historic figures through role-play profiles and posts to a Facebook page like the one in Figure 3.23. After researching the events and characters, learners can contribute role-played stories about the events from the perspective of their roles and receive comments from their role-played "friends."

This activity encourages learners to discuss, comment, and share information, links, and pictures in role. Quite a challenge—but fun!

Anderson's ideas for implementing the activity:

1. The instructor sets up a Facebook page for the activity or uses another medium to simulate this type of social interaction.

2. The instructor assigns roles and asks learners to prepare for the activity, including:

   a. Reading and explorative activities (online or elsewhere) to help learners understand the lives of the people they are role playing and the events of the time.

   b. Thinking through the following aspects of each role as it is likely to evolve on Facebook:

      i. What kind of personality does the role have and how will this be portrayed as they post?

      ii. What kinds of status updates will they add?

      iii. What personal information can they share that isn't well known?

      iv. What kinds of comments will they make to the status updates of others?

      v. What links will they share? What perspectives will they share on these links?

      vi. What pictures will they share? What will they say about them?

      vii. What issues of the day are they likely to agree with and disagree with? How is the person being played likely to handle these types of disagreements with others?

      viii. Are there some people they likely wouldn't accept as Facebook "friends"?

3. The instructor encourages continuing activity and handles any "problems" by deleting objectionable posts or emailing learners.

4. A final debriefing allows learners and the instructor to make sure that everyone benefitted from the activity.

Technologies used: Facebook

Figure 3.23. Facebook-Like Mockup

Source: David Anderson, http://multimedialearning.com/abraham-lincoln-and-facebook-for-learning/

Adopt or Adapt

This activity could be adapted using different kinds of content, for example, a role play of a city council disagreement over where to locate specific amenities in a town or a role play of different points of view regarding a government program.

What if you don't have access to Facebook or don't feel comfortable using Facebook for this purpose? The same activity could be accomplished using a wiki, blog, or collaborative writing tool (such as Google Docs) or even using a printed activity sheet that learners pass to other learners for handwritten comments.

Attribution

Submitted by David Anderson, community manager, Articulate, Phoenix, Arizona, USA

Contact: danderson@articulate.com and http://multimedialearning.com/

Also involved: Anderson saw a Lincoln Facebook parody posted by Jane Bozarth (http://bozarthzone.blogspot.com/) and Cammy Bean (http://cammybean.kineo.com/) and this idea came from it. A screenshot from the parody is available at www.indyweek.com/pdf/020409/LincolnFacebook.jpg.

David Anderson is a community manager at Articulate with over thirteen years of experience designing e-learning. He supports the e-learning community by helping users get the most from their tools, while finding creative ways to build more engaging courses. He also shares e-learning tips and tricks through his screencasts at http://screenr.com/user/elearning.

Side by Side

The Big Idea

What

This activity is used in online classroom instruction and offers a way for learners to brainstorm multiple things at the same time.

Why

In online classroom instruction, it's common to see mostly one-way delivery of content—from instructor to learners—and little contribution from learners. Structured group activities like this one provide the opportunity for learners to contribute to the discussion and engage with each other.

Use It!

How

Many online classroom applications have chat pods that can be used for textual discussion during the course. Some allow you to use multiple chat pods (Connect, for example). You can use two or more chat pods to have learners brainstorm multiple, related things at the same time. For example, you might ask learners to add benefits of using tables in Word in one chat pod and challenges of using tables in Word in another chat pod. Or you could ask learners to list the before, during, and after tasks of a complex process or the advantages and disadvantages of a course of action.

The process is as follows:

1. Prepare chat pods and give them names that correspond with the desired contents of the pod, such as "closed" and "open." (See Figure 3.24.)

2. Pose a question to the learners using a PowerPoint slide and prepare verbal instructions to give while displaying chat pods on-screen.

3. Invite learners to type their answers or insights into the available pods.

4. Wait for responses to appear in chat pods.

5. Discuss what learners have entered into the pods. Add or clarify as needed. If needed, prompt learners to elaborate verbally or in chat.

Chat pods are available in most online classroom applications, but very few allow for typing in separate chat pods at once. Connect has no limit on the number of pods you can have on-screen, so this is Hyder's choice of tools when using this activity.

Figure 3.24. Side-by-Side Chat Pods

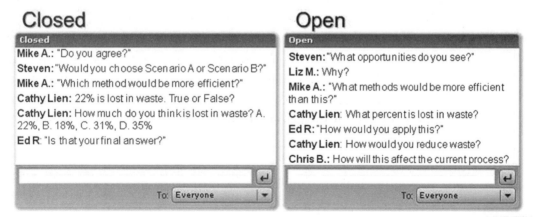

Source: Karen Hyder

Hyder's tips for this activity:

- Make sure that the activity contains self-explanatory, concise instructions. Learners should be able to read it and participate even if they didn't catch your verbal instructions.

- Be sure your directions are clear, concise, and worded well. Instructions that are too vague or too specific might not yield good responses. Think through what types of answers learners might give based on the question. Edit the wording to improve clarity and focus.

- Ask questions that generate interesting answers. For instance, by listing "possible causes" and "possible solutions," each learner has a chance to see others' perspectives.

- Be sure the answers you're looking for are reasonably short. "What are some potential problems?" might yield answers like "time," "money," and "expertise." If the question asks "How will you apply this in your own situation?" the responses might require quite a few sentences, which could take a lot of time to type.

Technologies used: virtual classroom chat pods

Adopt or Adapt

This strategy is useful for an online classroom course on almost any topic. (I know because I regularly use it myself!) If it is not possible to have multiple chat pods in the online classroom application that you use, use one chat pod, but focus on one aspect first, then switch to the other. The same idea could be implemented using the whiteboard tool, but this can become confusing if there are more than fifteen or twenty learners. Although it could be challenging to manage, the activity could also be accomplished using instant messaging, Twitter, or mobile texting. This activity can easily be used in a face-to-face classroom by asking learners to write on the board, a flip chart, or on sheets of paper.

This activity would work in an asynchronous setting as well and could be accomplished using a wiki, email, or dynamic web pages that include tables or forms that can be populated by viewers.

Attribution

Submitted by Karen Hyder, managing director, online event producer, and speaker coach, Kaleidoscope Training and Consulting, Palmyra, New York, USA

Contact: Karen@KarenHyder.com or www.karenhyder.com

Karen Hyder is a thought leader on how to best use synchronous online software tools to create learning environments. In her work with The eLearning Guild and in her consulting work, Karen has trained and coached thousands of individuals and helped them to adopt new styles of training and achieve new levels of competency. Karen started teaching technology topics for Logical Operations (now Element K) in 1991 and five years later became director of trainer development. In 1999, Karen transitioned from delivering train-the-trainer courses to connecting from her home in upstate New York to learners around the world.

Turn Up the Music

The Big Idea

What

The rise of Web 2.0 and social networking technologies, specifically those focused on digital music, provide new opportunities to integrate music into courses.

Why

Music has the potential to humanize, personalize, and energize a learning environment or experience, elicit positive feelings and associations for learners, and help learners with conceptual learning and knowledge construction.

Use It!

How

We rarely use music as an instructional strategy, but we really should consider using it because it has numerous benefits for learning. Internet jukeboxes like Songza (www.songza.com), 8tracks (www.8tracks.com), and Grooveshark (listen.grooveshark.com) provide exciting new ways to integrate music into the online classroom.

These new Web 2.0 applications let us incorporate music in our online courses in meaningful (and legal) ways. Lowenthal and Dunlap posit that music-driven instructional activities can increase social presence in online courses, tap into learner interest and increase learning motivation while leveraging each learner's background knowledge, and offer unique ways to encourage learners to interact with content. Activities such as having learners create soundtracks of their lives, create concept-specific soundtracks, and produce music videos are just a few ways to involve learners with music-driven instructional activities.

For example, Lowenthal and Dunlap frequently use a "soundtrack of your life" activity. With this activity, they ask learners to share a set of three

Figure 3.25. Music-Driven Activity, Example 1

INTE 6710 ~ Creative Designs for Instructional Materials
Virtual Paper Bag, Part 3

Music is a part of our lives, whether we hear it on the radio, stereo, Internet, in our mp3 player or listen to wind blowing through the trees. It is all music. Many of us can point to specific music that identifies who we are (as individuals, members of various communities, members of a family, and so on), or reveals a detail about ourselves that others rarely see.

For this assignment, please prepare a soundtrack that supports your previous two *Virtual Paper Bag* components: your collection of five photos, and your 250-350 word story. Include 3-6 songs (more if you want). Please provide a title for your soundtrack with a url/link to your soundtrack.

In terms of tools to use to create a shareable playlist, there are several out there. Two that I use are Grooveshark and blip.fm. Check them both out, they are both pretty easy to figure out and use. You can use any tool you wish (it doesn't have to be Grooveshark or blip.fm), as long as you can create an online playlists to share with the group. Once you create your playlist you can post that url for the group.

Here is a playlist I created in Finetune (a great tool that no longer exists in the same way as it once did). Note that you can access several other playlists I created via the "Finetune Playlists" drop-down menu:

Living in London 1978 ~

Source: Patrick Lowenthal

or more songs that represent the soundtracks of their lives or a set of six songs with two representing their past, two representing their present, and two representing their future. Sometimes they ask learners to share a brief explanation of why each song is included. Alternatively, the group asks questions to ferret out why each learner selected those particular songs.

Figure 3.26. Music-Driven Activity, Example 2

INTE 6710 ~ Creative Designs for Instructional Materials
Soundtrack of Our Lives

In the forum below, please discuss your views on any of the following questions regarding the playlists shared last week as Part 3 of the *Virtual Paper Bag* activity. [Note: You don't have to respond to all of them, just pick the one or ones that interest you.]

1. What commonalities do you see across playlists? What do you think the song selections say about the individual's life?

2. How did the songs/playlists make you feel? What information and emotions did they convey to you?

3. What is the purpose of this activity, and how is it related to the creative design of instructional materials? How is this activity related to this week's readings (Medina on Sensory Integration and Reynolds on Harmony)?

4. How should we try to use music for instructional purposes, if at all?

5. Bonus question: Each week I have been sharing an image with musical accompaniment in the Weekly Agendas. Why? What have you learned about me, if anything, based on my weekly sharing?

Source: Patrick Lowenthal

Finally, they ask questions that help the group consider shared interests, differences, and so on (e.g., how many folks like jazz, female songwriters, or sad songs). These activities help everyone get to know each other so they can better work together in an online course, and it provides a foundation for productive interactions and relationships. Some examples are shown in Figures 3.25 and 3.26.

Technologies used: various Internet Jukeboxes

Adopt or Adapt

While instructors in all subject areas can use music-driven activities to help improve social presence and build community, the usefulness of specific music-driven instructional activities will likely depend to some degree on the content area and/or setting. For instance, a literature course might focus on the lyrics of music, whereas a communication course might focus more on music as a communication medium.

Ideas for incorporating music-driven activities in synchronous online courses might include asking learners to select music to fit a specific scenario.

Attribution

Submitted by Patrick R. Lowenthal, academic technology coordinator, University of Colorado–Denver, Denver, Colorado, USA

Contact: patrick.lowenthal@ucdenver.edu or www.patricklowenthal.com

Also involved: Joanna C. Dunlap, associate professor and faculty fellow for teaching, University of Colorado–Denver

Patrick R. Lowenthal is an academic technology coordinator at the University of Colorado–Denver (UCD), where he supports faculty who teach online. He also regularly teaches online in the master of arts in e-learning design and implementation program at UCD. Prior to coming to UCD, Patrick spent a number of years at Regis University as an assistant professor of instructional technology. Patrick is currently a doctoral student finishing his studies in instructional design and technology at UCD. His research interests focus on teaching and learning online, with a specific focus on social and teaching presence.

YouTube YouTalk

The Big Idea

What

This idea describes using YouTube's commenting feature to support learner discussion of a YouTube video.

Why

This activity encourages learner discussion. The YouTube video hosting service is free and is web-based (so videos can be uploaded without having to go through IT/hosting services).

Use It!

How

The instructor can upload a video clip presenting a problem or idea (or still photos with titles or dialogue text balloons could work) to YouTube. Learners can then use the YouTube comments feature to provide answers or insights, as shown in Figure 3.27.

Technologies used: video, YouTube

Figure 3.27. YouTube Discussion

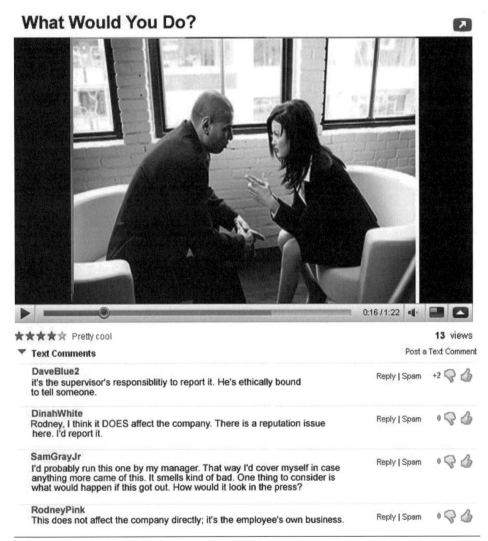

What Would You Do?

0:16 / 1:22

★★★★☆ Pretty cool   **13** views

▼ **Text Comments**   Post a Text Comment

DaveBlue2
it's the supervisor's responsiblitiy to report it. He's ethically bound   Reply | Spam   +2 👎 👍
to tell someone.

DinahWhite
Rodney, I think it DOES affect the company. There is a reputation issue   Reply | Spam   0 👎 👍
here. I'd report it.

SamGrayJr
I'd probably run this one by my manager. That way I'd cover myself in case   Reply | Spam   0 👎 👍
anything more came of this. It smells kind of bad. One thing to consider is
what would happen if this got out. How would it look in the press?

RodneyPink
This does not affect the company directly; it's the employee's own business.   Reply | Spam   0 👎 👍

Source: Jane Bozarth

Adopt or Adapt

This approach could be adapted to any video content in which learner feedback or interaction is desired. As an alternative, the instructor could record him- or herself asking questions, such as, "What can you do to expand your own circle of influence?" or "What would you do with an excellent employee who has suddenly shown a marked drop-off in performance?" For those who can't create video clips, it is an easy matter to assemble still photos and titles/text with the free Windows Movie Maker program (www.microsoft.com/windowsxp/using/moviemaker/) and then upload the result to YouTube.

Attribution

Submitted by Jane Bozarth, author of *Better Than Bullet Points* and *Social Media for Trainers*, State of North Carolina's Human Resource Development Group, Raleigh, North Carolina, USA

Contact: info@bozarthzone.com or http://bozarthzone.blogspot.com

Jane Bozarth has been a training practitioner since 1989. She holds an M.Ed. in training and development and a doctorate in adult education. She is the author of several books: Pfeiffer's *e-Learning Solutions on a Shoestring; Better Than Bullet Points; From Analysis to Evaluation;* and new in 2010, *Social Media for Trainers*. Following a ten-year stint as a member of *Training* magazine's "In Print" book review team, she began writing *Learning Solutions* magazine's popular "Nuts and Bolts" column. She has received numerous awards, including a Live and Online Award and a *Training* magazine Editor's Pick Award.

Wiki Review

The Big Idea

What

This idea shows a unique and engaging way to use wiki content as an interactive learner activity.

Why

Using wiki content with errors and omissions allows learners to work together to make the content accurate and sufficient. The process of editing helps learners clear up areas of confusion and make sense of the information. The end result, the edited content, can be used later and made available to others.

Use It!

How

To prepare for a post-course review, Biddle sets up a page on a wiki that contains information from her training course, but with a twist—it contains errors and omissions. Learners work together to edit the wiki to make it accurate. The entire group can work on all of the content together, or specific individuals or groups can edit specific topics.

Biddle shares an example of how she uses this idea in an online course she teaches on using charts and graphs. She creates a wiki page using a free wiki site (there are many available) and on the page provides incorrect content (Figure 3.28).

All of the "facts" on this page are actually incorrect; they are common misperceptions about charts. As the course progresses, she returns to look at each of the incorrect statements in turn and uses each to begin a discussion of what's wrong with the statement.

For each statement, she builds a sub-page that will subsequently hold additional information about that statement, such as why the statement is false, examples, how-tos, and common traps to avoid. Learners edit the

Figure 3.28. Completed Wiki Page

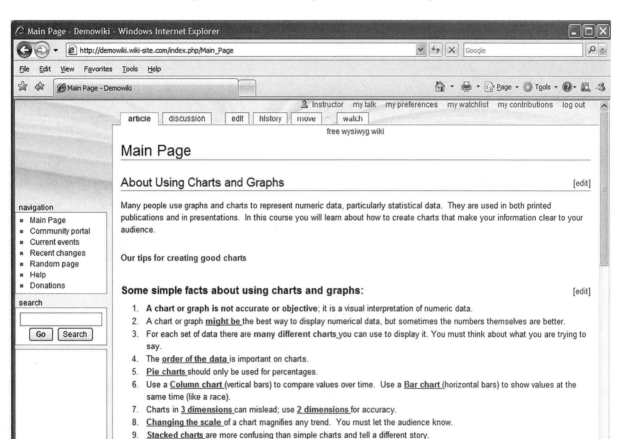

statements on the first page (to make them correct) and populate the subpages with needed information. Biddle is available for help during this activity and jumps in if incorrect information is added.

The resulting wiki (Figure 3.29) is a reference that learners can use after the class as a reminder and it often provides information unique to that class because of the specific examples learners add.

Technologies used: wiki

Figure 3.29. Wiki Page with Statements

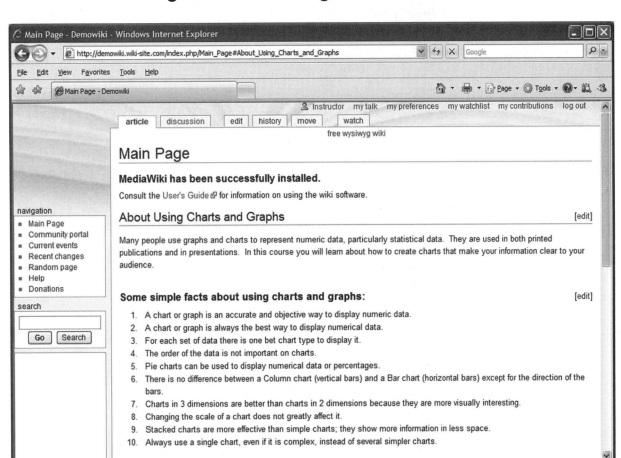

Adopt or Adapt

This idea can be easily adapted. It can be used as an end-of-day exercise to review learning, as an opening activity to determine what knowledge level the learners already have, or as a learning activity for a course on collaboration or social networking tools. It could also be used to examine different perspectives. For example, various pages could each be started with the same facts. Learners or groups of learners could then edit these pages to provide different perspectives. Following this activity, a discussion could be held to discuss how and why the perspectives are different. It could be used by different learners or groups of learners to respond to a story prompt.

Attribution

Submitted by Julie Biddle, owner/operator, You're Laughing, Toronto, Ontario, Canada

Contact: Julie@urlaughing.ca

Julie Biddle has been teaching folks about using technology for a very long time; the first computer course she taught was DOS version 2.21 (word processing before that). Today she combines technology with soft skills for a total learning experience. After more than twenty-five years, she still loves to make her students' jobs, and lives, easier.

Julie has developed and delivered many popular courses dealing with exciting topics like managing email, organizing files, and using database systems. The duller and dryer the topic, the more creative her sessions become. She finds the "fun" in fundamentals and laughter in learning.

Word Me

The Big Idea

What

This idea presents a word search activity used in online classroom instruction to review previously covered content.

Why

In online classroom instruction, it helps to include engaging activities that provide the opportunity for learners to review.

Use It!

How

A word search is a list of terms that are scrambled into a grid of letters. Learners locate and, using online classroom annotation tools, mark the found words on the screen. Software tools such as Discovery Education's Puzzlemaker (http://puzzlemaker.discoveryeducation.com/WordSearchSetupForm.asp) or the Free Online Puzzle Maker shown in Figure 3.30 (www.puzzle-maker.com) automatically create the grid based on a list of words the instructor provides. The number of words and size of grid are adjustable.

Hyder developed this activity because she was looking for a way to engage learners who returned early from break and to review content at the end of sessions. She also keeps extra word search puzzles handy to use just in case she needs to delay or fill time.

Hyder's Tips

- Use to encourage learners to review key terms, as a warm-up to engage participants, to fill time before the official start of a synchronous online course or when learners are returning from a break, OR to give learners an activity to do when you need to troubleshoot.

• Be sure to include instructions on the puzzle screen to eliminate the need to explain to each learner as he or she joins.

Technologies used: word search puzzle application, online classroom file sharing, and annotation tools

Figure 3.30. Word Search Puzzle and Online Classroom Annotation Tools

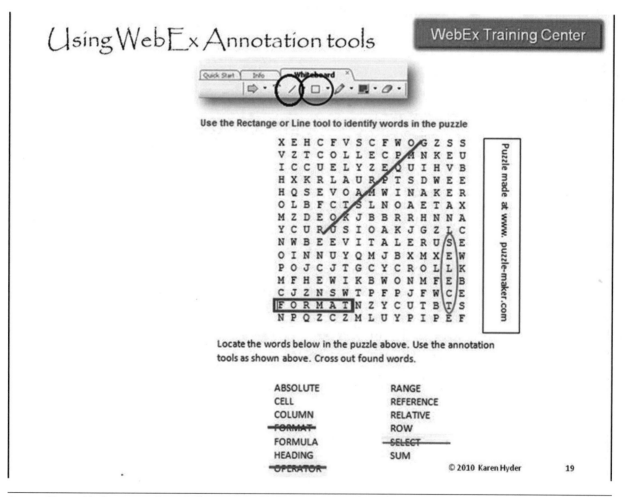

Adopt or Adapt

This strategy works for an online learning course on almost any topic. It could be done collaboratively, as described, or each learner could download the puzzle and do it offline and then compare it to the finished puzzle (shown by the instructor at the end of the activity).

Attribution

Submitted by Karen Hyder, managing director, online event producer, and speaker/coach, Kaleidoscope Training and Consulting, Palmyra, New York, USA

Contact: Karen@KarenHyder.com or www.karenhyder.com

Karen Hyder is a thought leader on how to best use synchronous online software tools to create learning environments. In her work with The eLearning Guild and in her consulting work, Karen has trained and coached thousands of individuals and helped them to adopt a new style of training and achieve a new level of competency. Karen started teaching technology topics for Logical Operations (now Element K) in 1991 and five years later became director of trainer development. In 1999, Karen transitioned from delivering train-the-trainer courses to connecting from her home in upstate New York to learners around the world.

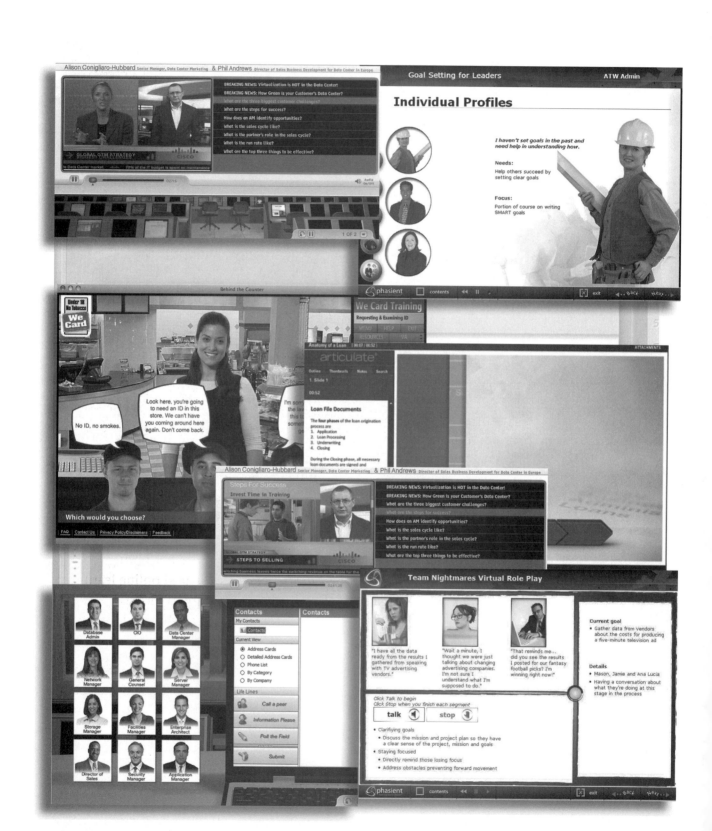

CHAPTER 4

Ideas for Self-Paced Learning

S elf-paced, online learning refers to learning "on demand," learning materials and communication methods that the learner can call upon when needed or when time is available. Self-paced makes lots of sense in many situations because adult learners are often busy and need to fit learning, whether workplace-oriented or higher education–oriented, into an already busy schedule.

Too many people assume self-paced online learning is likely to be boring, one-dimensional, lockstep, or unengaging. No reason it needs to be, except lack of imagination. And that goes for supposedly "boring" topics as well. As authoring tools become better and self-paced online learning becomes more mature and accepted, quality should increase. The examples in this chapter show that great quality and self-paced can go hand-in-hand.

This chapter illustrates numerous ideas for self-paced learning that should start your creative juices flowing. If you are looking for ideas for self-paced learning, also review Chapter 5, Ideas for Media and Authoring, as many of those ideas will also help you make self-paced learning more engaging. And don't forget to consider adding some of the strategies in Chapter 3, Ideas for Synchronous and Social Learning, as blending synchronous and social activities with self-paced learning can greatly improve learner energy and results.

Branched Scenarios with Three Cs and Placeholder Content

The Big Idea

What

Building branched scenarios allow learners to see the consequences of their choices but can be time-consuming to create. This idea shortens the time. Yes!

Why

Using a templated process for building branched scenarios makes designing and building them easier.

Use It!

How

Kuhlmann explains that branched scenarios, where the learner takes one path in the materials versus another based on his or her choices, can be used for different purposes, including testing understanding, allowing the learner to interact with a story, and sorting learners into a specific path based on some characteristic, such as interest or job level. Well-built branched scenarios can give the learning environment a realistic feel and be more engaging than linear content that provides the exact same feedback to all learners.

Kuhlmann created what he calls, the "3C" model to make designing branched scenarios easier. Each scenario consists of a **challenge** (what the learner has to do), **choices** (what options the learner selects from), and **consequences** (the result) of each choice.

Figure 4.1 represents the structure for a simple three-choice branch. Kuhlmann starts designing scenarios by determining what the challenge, choices, and consequences will be.

In the example in the figure, the learner receives a challenge. He or she selects one of three choices. The choice that the learner selects presents

Figure 4.1. Simple 3C Structure

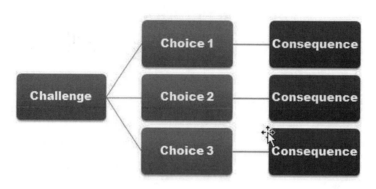

This is the starting branch. There's a challenge and three choices that produce consequences.

Source: Tom Kuhlmann

consequences—feedback or a separate path based on that choice. (In the simple example shown, there is no additional branching based on the choice selected.)

In the simple 3C example in Figure 4.1, the learner reaches the consequence and that's the end of the branching. For additional branching, you add another 3C structure at the end of any or all of the consequences. Figure 4.2 represents the structure for a more complex three-choice branch where another 3C branch is appended to one of the consequences.

There are a few ways to structure continuing branches. You could provide feedback and then present another challenge. Or instead of providing feedback, you could simply have the learner jump right into another challenge.

Figure 4.2. More Complex 3C Branched Scenario

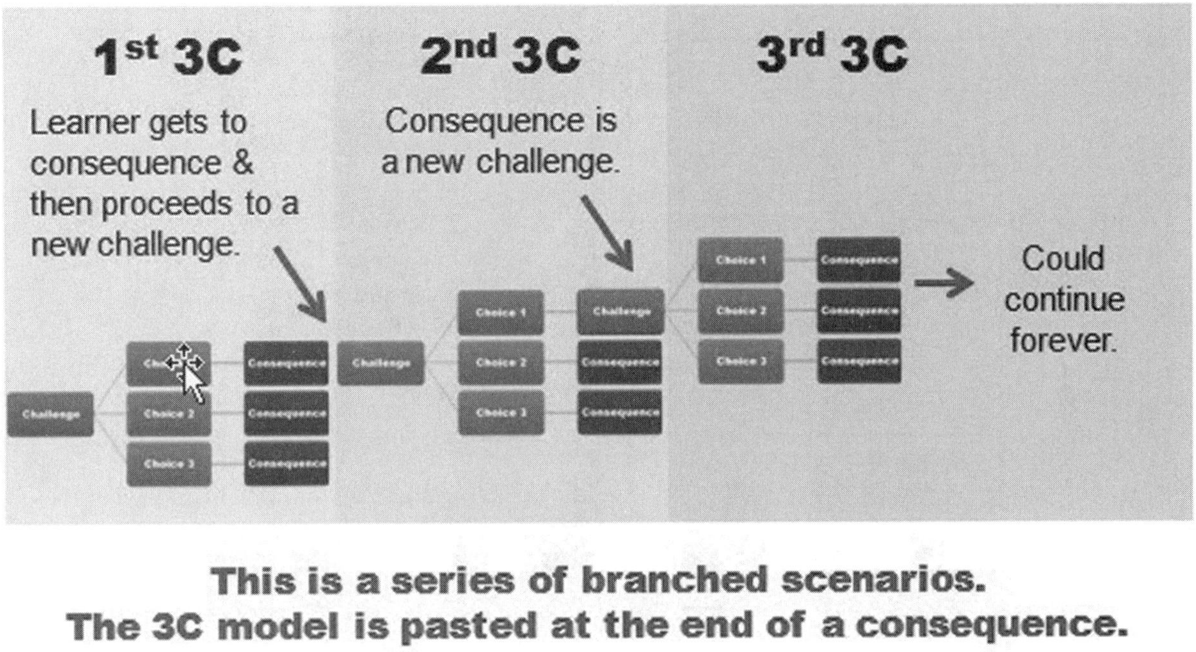

1st 3C
Learner gets to consequence & then proceeds to a new challenge.

2nd 3C
Consequence is a new challenge.

3rd 3C
Could continue forever.

This is a series of branched scenarios.
The 3C model is pasted at the end of a consequence.

Source: Tom Kuhlmann

The 3C process makes the branched scenario design process more clear, which can save time designing scenarios. To save even more time, prepare branched scenario templates that can be dropped into courses as needed. Kuhlmann builds branched scenarios in PowerPoint with placeholder content and images in PowerPoint slides for use in PowerPoint–based authoring programs (specifically Articulate Presenter). The branching navigation is built and tested (so that each choice goes to the appropriate PowerPoint slide for feedback or continued branching) so when it is needed in a course, he can drop in the branched scenario slides, as shown in the example in Figure 4.3. He then swaps out the content and images with the content and images needed in the course.

Technologies used: PowerPoint

Figure 4.3. Pre-Built Branched Scenarios with Placeholder Text and Final with Content and Images Swapped

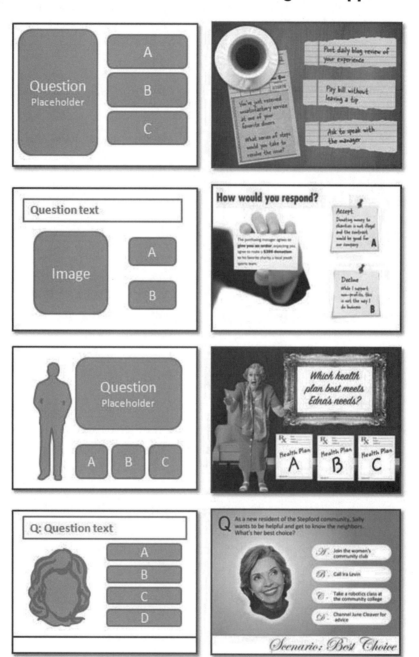

Source: Tom Kuhlmann

Adopt or Adapt

> This idea is super useful for streamlining development of branched learning scenarios. Although PowerPoint is used here to build the scenarios, these techniques should work in any authoring environment.

Attribution

Submitted by Tom Kuhlmann, vice president, community, Articulate, Seattle, Washington, USA

Contact: www.articulate.com/rapid-elearning/

> Tom Kuhlmann writes The Rapid e-Learning Blog, where he shares practical e-learning tips and tricks. He has close to twenty years of experience in the training industry, where he's worked on e-learning projects for both large and small organizations. Currently he manages Articulate's e-learning community.

Talking Head Video, CNN-Style

The Big Idea

What

This idea shows a fun and easy way to "spice up" videos of people talking (also known as "talking head" videos).

Why

Talking head videos are easy to create but boring to watch. If you have talking head videos to include in your e-learning content, they will be more engaging when broadcast and online news techniques are used.

Use It!

How

Cisco Systems came up with the idea to create CNN-style videos (Figure 4.4) because of a dilemma they had when trying to shoot videos

Figure 4.4. Split Screen–Two "Talkers" (Left) and User Selection (Right)

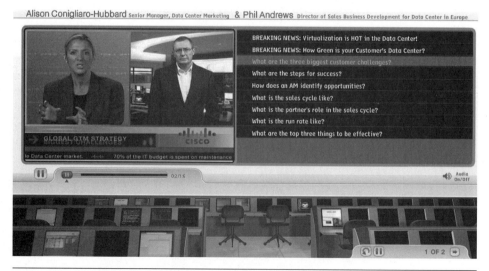

Source: Dawn Adams Miller, Cisco Systems

that included multiple experts: It was hard to get everyone to the same studio at the right time. For example, Alison was in San Jose, California, and Phil was in Bedfont, UK. Cisco has studios in both locations, but getting both people to the studio at the same time was a logistics problem.

They decided to shoot the video at both locations, at separate times, and then edit them together. They first developed a script with questions and answers. Adams Miller taped Alison in the San Jose studio. She then taped Phil in the UK studio a week later. They used green screen techniques so they could put the person filmed onto other backgrounds and into other interviews. They then added Flash graphics, a headline crawl at the bottom, and the ability to jump to specific points in the video.

From this experience, Adams Miller learned how to make these kinds of videos more engaging by using some techniques used by news organizations. (Figures 4.5 and 4.6 show examples.) Techniques she uses and recommends include:

- Show a "reporter" interview of an industry expert or corporate representative rather than just the expert.

- Use Flash or other graphics tools to add a headline crawl at the bottom of the screen.

- Show a combination of full screens and split screens.

- Use fades and transitions between segments.

- Add a menu to allow learners to jump to different portions (questions asked by the reporter) of the interview.

With heterogeneous audiences, it's tough to know what individual learners already know about a particular topic. By making the look and feel more engaging and covering a full range of questions while allowing them to select the questions they are interested in, you meet several needs: learner control, interesting presentations, and short content chunks.

Technologies used: Flash, video

Figure 4.5. Split Screen–One "Talker" Plus Important Points (Left) and User Selection (Right)

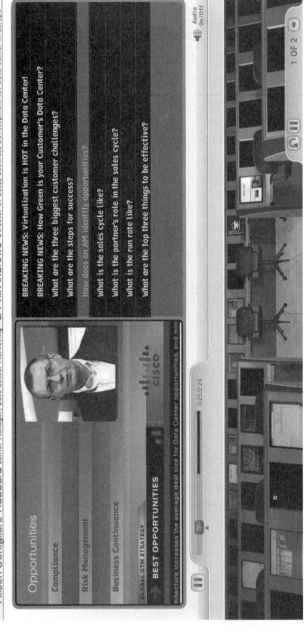

Alison Conigliaro-Hubbard Senior Manager, Data Center Marketing & Phil Andrews Director of Sales Business Development for Data Center in Europe

Opportunities

Compliance

Risk Management

Business Continuance

GLOBAL GTM STRATEGY

BEST OPPORTUNITIES

chitecture increases the average deal size for Data Center opportunities, and min

cisco

0:25/2:26

BREAKING NEWS: Virtualization is HOT in the Data Center!

BREAKING NEWS: How Green is your Customer's Data Center?

What are the three biggest customer challenges?

What are the steps for success?

How does an AM identify opportunities?

what is the sales cycle like?

what is the partner's role in the sales cycle?

what is the run rate like?

what are the top three things to be effective?

Audio On/Off

1 OF 2

Source: Dawn Adams Miller, Cisco Systems

Figure 4.6. Split Screen and User Selection (Right)

Alison Conigliaro-Hubbard Senior Manager, Data Center Marketing & Phil Andrews Director of Sales Business Development for Data Center in Europe

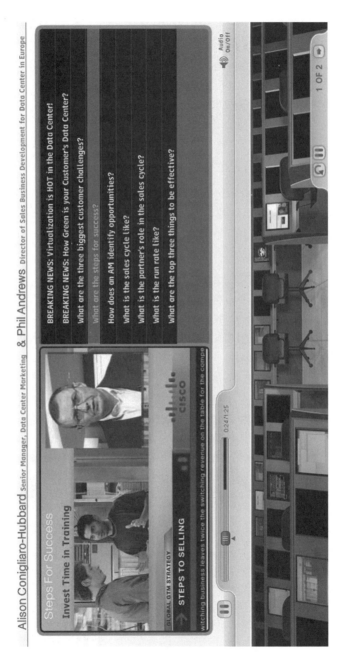

Source: Dawn Adams Miller, Cisco Systems

Adopt or Adapt

This approach is highly adaptable to all kinds of content. Even if you don't have the graphics and video editing capabilities to implement some of the techniques, adding a menu that allows learners to select from a variety of segments can be easily implemented in most of the simpler authoring programs.

Attribution

Submitted by Dawn Adams Miller, business engagement manager, enterprise initiatives, Learning Development Solutions Group, Cisco Systems, Charlotte, North Carolina, USA

Contact: dawadams@cisco.com

Dawn Adams Miller has been an instructional designer for more than twenty years. She has worked for herself, for major learning technology vendors, and for major corporations, including TIAA-CREF and Microsoft. Dawn specializes in technology-delivered instruction and has presented on this topic at major conferences around the world. At Cisco Systems for the past four years, Dawn has created sales-focused e-learning for new product releases and is currently focused on determining and executing on learning solutions for large global, enterprise-wide initiatives. Dawn has an M.S. in learning technology from Boise State University and is a lifelong learner in this area.

Bad Advice?

The Big Idea

What

This idea presents an activity that requires learners to differentiate good from bad advice.

Why

In the real world, learners often have to determine whether advice, documentation, or other resources are valid, correct, accurate, and so on. This activity provides a realistic and fun way to practice this skill.

Use It!

How

The screenshots in Figures 4.7 and 4.8 are from The We Card Program, Inc. The We Card training program covers FDA-suggested elements in a fun manner that allows learners to practice the skills they need to prevent selling tobacco products to underage buyers.

In this decision-making activity, the learner is presented with a realistic scenario (what to do when a customer won't or can't provide the requested identification). After hearing three store clerks provide three different potential responses to the customer (in this situation, advice is provided in audio format as well as in a text bubble), the learner has to judge which response is most appropriate.

The learner selects the most appropriate response and then receives feedback on his or her choice. This activity allows learners to practice key skills

Figure 4.7. Advice for This Situation

Source: The We Card Program, Inc.

in a realistic way. It is especially valuable because learners will likely have to make similar decisions while doing their jobs and will certainly have to deal with people who are not willing to show or who do not have proper identification. Skill training is needed to prepare for dealing with situations on the job.

Technologies used: Flash throughout: combination of ActionScript 2, timeline manipulation, web-format graphics, .wav narration, and native Flash elements (text, shapes); crucial narration synchronization/control by AS2

Figure 4.8. Correct Answer

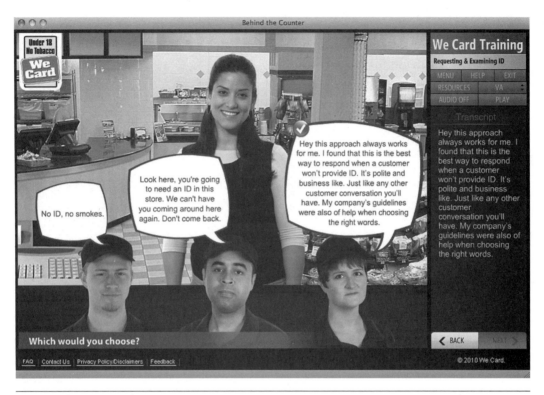

Source: The We Card Program, Inc.

in specific frames; scripted photo shoots of characters and elements; and professionally recorded narration by skilled voice actors

Adopt or Adapt

This idea is easily adaptable to other content for which a learner might have to determine whether advice, documentation, or other resources are accurate. Although this example uses realistic graphics and programming, a similar activity could be built with less fidelity but similar

impact using text scenarios with text or audio responses. It could be
built using question development tools such as Articulate Quizmaker
(www.articulate.com/products/quizmaker.php), Questionmark
Perception (www.questionmark.com/us/perception/index.aspx), or
Respondus (www.respondus.com/). There are free tools for building
questions that could be used as well.

Attribution

Submitted by The We Card Program, Inc., and Doug Reed, director of interactive technology,
OTM Partners, LLC, Arlington, Virginia, USA

Contact: dreed@otmpartners.com

Also involved: Lee Noel and Read deButts of OTM Partners, LLC; Doug Anderson, president, The
We Card Program, Inc.; and Patti Shank, president, Learning Peaks, LLC

OTM Partners are award-winning interactive training experts, delivering
content, reducing costs, and boosting results. They build consumer
awareness campaigns, product launches, sales force education, compliance
training, and legal presentation services.

Point It Out

The Big Idea

What

This idea shows how annotations that emphasize important information on the screen can make it easier for learners to understand complex visual information.

Why

In online courses that show and ask learners to discuss complex images, annotations help learners focus on what is currently being discussed. Without annotations, learners may look at the wrong part of an image (or the wrong image) and find it hard to follow how the narration relates to what they are looking at.

Use It!

How

Annotations are typically used to label or mark up text or images on the screen. The screenshot in Figure 4.9 is from a course designed by The We Card Program, Inc., to teach retail employees how to prevent underage access to tobacco products. The We Card Employee Training Course covers FDA-suggested elements in a fun manner that allows learners to practice the skills they need to prevent selling tobacco products to underage buyers.

The lesson describes the parts of an identification card an employee needs to check to determine whether a buyer is eligible to purchase tobacco products. Figure 4.9 shows the use of multiple annotations. First, the parts of the ID that need to be checked are annotated with a red box. Second, the reasons why a close inspection of the ID reveals that the buyers are ineligible to purchase tobacco products are also annotated with a red box. The annotations make it much easier to zero in on critical information.

Figure 4.9. Annotations on Driver's License

Source: The We Card Program, Inc.

Technologies used: Flash throughout: combination of ActionScript 2, timeline manipulation, web-format graphics, .wav narration, and native Flash elements (text, shapes); crucial narration synchronization/control by AS2 in specific frames; ultra-smooth scrolling and zooming (à la Ken Burns), combined with precise timing for annotations and narration, greatly enhance the basic Flash technology in this idea

Adopt or Adapt

Annotating complex images as the instructor discusses them makes sense because it helps learners focus on the right elements.

Attribution

Submitted by The We Card Program, Inc., and Doug Reed, director of interactive technology, OTM Partners, LLC, Arlington, Virginia, USA

Contact: dreed@otmpartners.com

Also involved: Lee Noel and Read deButts of OTM Partners LLC; Doug Anderson, president, The We Card Program; and Patti Shank, president; Learning Peaks; LLC

OTM Partners are award-winning interactive training experts, delivering content, reducing costs, and boosting results. They build consumer awareness campaigns, product launches, sales force education, compliance training, legal presentation services.

Simulate It

The Big Idea

What

This idea shows the need to simulate performance of tasks in task-oriented instruction.

Why

Instruction that teaches learners to perform specific tasks greatly benefits from simulations that mimic or simulate the tasks to be learned. Otherwise, learners learn about the task but don't have a chance to practice! And lack of practice usually means lack of know-how when they return to the job.

Use It!

How

Task simulations provide learners with an opportunity to think through the process and decisions as if they are doing the real task. For example, in a course teaching how to complete an I-9 form (U.S. Citizenship and Immigration Services Employment Eligibility Form), a simulation would typically include a simulated I-9 form and the ability to complete the form. Tasks would include choosing the appropriate forms of ID and completing the simulated I-9 form. The information could be validated so the learner could receive immediate feedback. For example, when typing in a zip code, validation could determine whether all characters are numeric. A sample form simulation is shown in Figure 4.10.

Another task-oriented simulation might include online interactions with other people. They may include audio or video files that permit the learner to hear what people are saying or see facial expressions. Typically, these types of simulations (see the sample in Figure 4.11) provide learners

Figure 4.10. Form Simulation

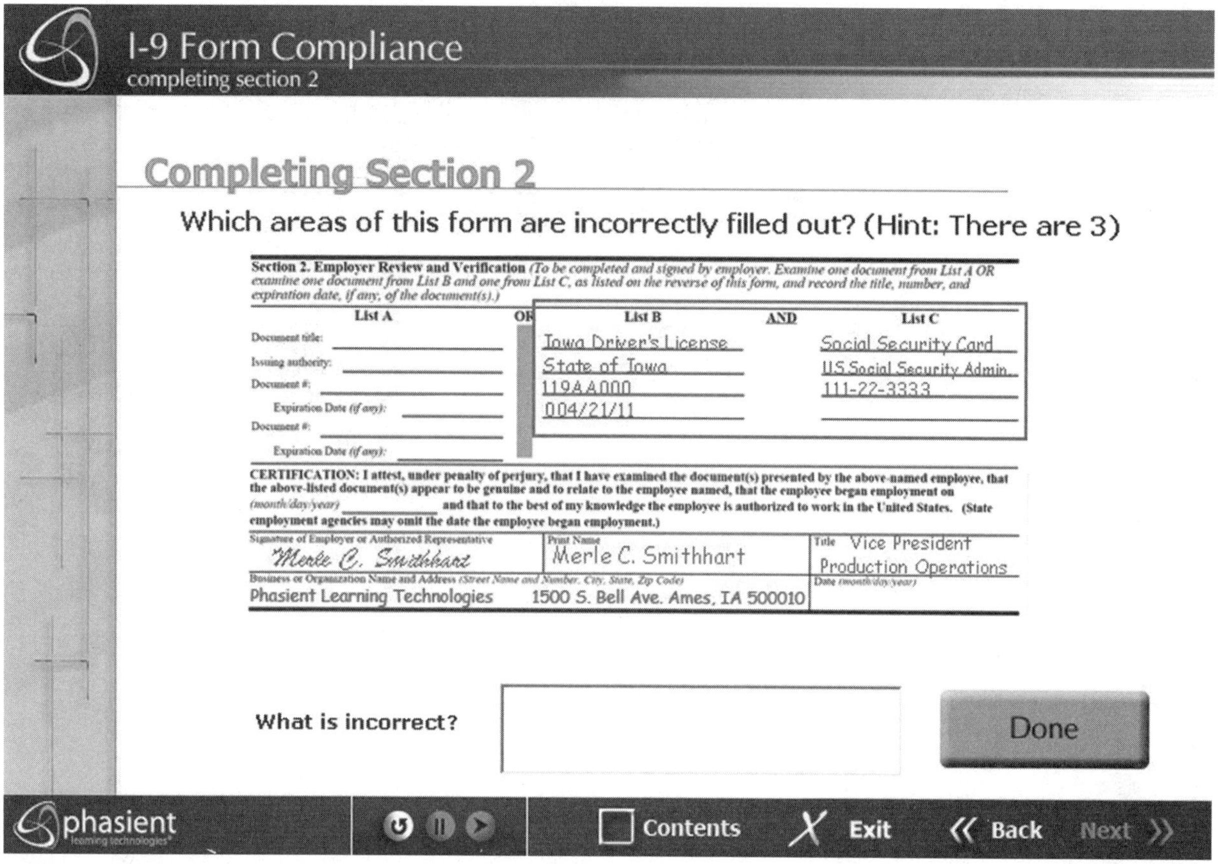

Source: Denise Link

with decisions to make, and the choices they make impact the feedback they are given or the path they take through the content.

By practicing the tasks in a realistic simulation, learners are better prepared to perform the tasks on the job. Providing this practice in a controlled environment allows designers to build instruction that adequately guides the learners through the tasks and allows them to practice in a safe environment.

Figure 4.11. Role-Play Simulation

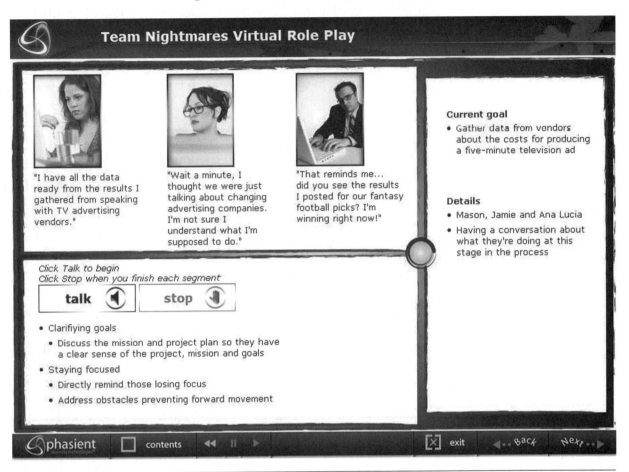

Source: Denise Link

Some ways to simulate tasks in an online course include:

- Software: Use software simulations software such as Camtasia (www
  .techsmith.com/camtasia.asp) or Captivate (www.adobe.com/
  products/captivate/) to capture elements of the task and choose which
  elements the learners will complete.

- Use Virtual Role Play to allow learners to interact with virtual customers (www.phasient.com/website/Pages/VirtualRolePlay.html).

- Soft skills: Develop branched scenarios or case studies that allow learners to interact with virtual co-workers or customers. Add audio and video files for realistic practice.

- Process: Capture elements of the process using a screencasting tool such as Captivate or Screenr (http://screenr.com/) and pair these with questions about next steps, decisions, and so on.

Link says it's critical to fully understand the complexities of the job tasks you want your learner to learn before attempting to simulate them. Once you understand the job tasks, create relevant and realistic scenarios that include typical decisions and feedback tailored to the choices the learner selects. For incorrect choices, feedback should state why the answer is incorrect or less correct than the correct answer.

When Link began using job task simulations in her online courses, a client reported that he had made the largest sale of his career to date as a direct result of the courses her team had created. He felt that the opportunity to practice gave him the skills he needed to succeed.

Technologies used: authoring software

Adopt or Adapt

Task simulations should be used when it is important that learners bring back real job task skills from instruction to the workplace, which means they should be used a lot in corporate training! But it may also be a good idea to include them in higher education courses, so that learners understand the real-world context of what they are learning. For example, physics courses would likely benefit from real-life scenarios and simulations that involve learners in the real-world contexts in which the topics under study are used.

Attribution

Submitted by Denise Link, vice president, Phasient Learning Technologies, Ames, Iowa, USA

Contact: denise@phasient.com or www.phasient.com

Denise Link is a founder and vice president of Phasient Learning Technologies. She has more than ten years of experience designing and developing online training and documentation as well as significant experience teaching secondary, university, and adult students. Denise holds a master of arts degree from Iowa State University (rhetoric, composition, and professional communication). At Phasient, Denise leads a team of instructional designers and graphic artists to create engaging e-learning courseware. Each course is customized for individual company needs to assure a successful learning experience.

Who's Who

The Big Idea

What

Teaching sales skills can be dreadfully boring, or—as in this idea—tons of fun (and especially impactful at the same time).

Why

Salespeople often don't think they have time for training. But good training helps them fulfill customer needs and thereby make more sales. In this idea, a game approach is used to teach salespeople how to recognize good contacts, as seen in the Contacts Game in Figure 4.12. Instead of just telling learners who to talk to and why (which is common in online sales training content), the game asks them to make work-related choices and obtain feedback. The game approach makes the process look easy, but learners find that they have something to learn. And because learners aren't spoon-fed the answers, they remember the primary points better.

Use It!

How

This activity helps salespeople target their sales by populating a contact list using a realistic gaming interface. The game starts with a brief animation describing why it's critical to expand sales contacts and why traditional methods for doing this don't work. After the introduction, learners drag and drop potential contacts into their contact lists. They receive feedback about their choices. To add to the drama and fun, the "game" provides help lines and two chances to complete each activity.

The help lines are similar to the ones used in the "Who Wants to Be a Millionaire" show: 50/50, Phone a Friend, and Ask the Audience. For example, when the learner selects the 50/50 help line, he or she sees a partial list of correct choices. When the learner selects Phone a Friend, a text bubble pops up and provides the "friend's" advice (for instance, "Not sure about that choice but I can tell you that the Application Manager is one of the people you will need to connect with").

Figure 4.12. Contacts Game

Source: Dawn Adams Miller, Cisco Systems

Learners can use all of the lifelines before making any moves or they can wait until they have made a preliminary attempt that isn't correct. If learners choose an incorrect contact twice, they see a list of the correct contacts. Each contact includes icons that represent characteristics about that contact. The eight icons represent pain points, things the contact might say indicating a need, and questions the contact might ask.

The game approach works for several reasons. First, learners come into the game thinking that they know the right answers, but the game shows them that they might not know everything they need to know. The shock of experiencing this stays with learners. In addition, the game mirrors how learners set up their client contacts. It calls on learners' experiences, the tasks are clearly related to work tasks, it helps them assess their typical approaches, it doesn't spoon feed the answers, and learners can try again without fear of looking stupid in front of others. Most learners feel this will be fun but a no-brainer, but almost all of them find that they learn more than they expect.

Technologies used: Flash

Adopt or Adapt

Populating a contact list with people you need to work with could be used in other contexts. For example, it could work when learners need to select the right people to contact for help with a problem. Or it could be adapted for making other types of choices. For example, a hiring course could have learners drag and drop candidate pictures or their resumes to the correct location (don't interview, find out additional information, interview).

Learners could also play the game with paper or electronic assets in a classroom or synchronous course.

One of the benefits of a game like this is that it can be adapted with different content without starting from scratch. It can be developed using simpler authoring tools as well.

Attribution

Submitted by Dawn Adams Miller, business engagement manager, enterprise initiatives, Learning Development Solutions Group, Cisco Systems, Charlotte, North Carolina, USA

Contact: dawadams@cisco.com

Also involved: Justin Lambakis, senior media developer, Sales Learning Group, Cisco Systems, San Jose, California, USA

Dawn Adams Miller has been an instructional designer for more than twenty years. She has worked for herself, for major learning technology vendors, and for major corporations, including TIAA-CREF and Microsoft. Dawn specializes in technology-delivered instruction and has presented on this topic at major conferences around the world. At Cisco Systems for the past four years, Dawn has created sales-focused e-learning for new product releases and is currently focused on determining and executing on learning solutions for large global, enterprise-wide initiatives. Dawn has an M.S. in learning technology from Boise State University and is a lifelong learner in this area.

Got a Clue?

The Big Idea

What

This activity prompts learners to look for clues. And looking for clues is often a very important part of decision making.

Why

When making decisions, people may have to look for subtle clues that point in the right direction. This activity lets learners practice in a realistic way.

Use It!

How

The screenshot in Figure 4.13 is from The We Card Employee Training Course used to teach retail and other employees how to prevent underage access to tobacco products. The We Card Employee Training Course covers FDA-suggested elements in a fun manner that allows learners to practice the skills needed to prevent them from selling tobacco products to underage buyers.

The lesson contains clues to help learners determine whether someone trying to purchase tobacco products is underage. In this activity, the learner sees the "customer" and is asked to click on clues to the customer's age.

Figure 4.13. Clue Activity, Example 1, Prompt

Source: The We Card Program, Inc.

In the screenshot in Figure 4.13 we see the prompt to the activity. The correct answer is her hair (it is gray).

In the screenshot in Figure 4.14 the learner is given another opportunity to find clues about the customer's age, but this time based on what the customer says instead of the customer's appearance.

Technologies used: Flash throughout: amalgamation of ActionScript 2, timeline manipulation, web-format graphics, .wav narration, and native

Figure 4.14. Clue Activity, Example 2, Feedback

Source: The We Card Program, Inc.

Flash elements (text, shapes). Crucial narration synchronization/control by AS2 in specific frames.

Adopt or Adapt

It would be beneficial in many instructional situations for learners to practice subtle skills like looking for clues. For example, a course on dealing with angry customers would benefit from exercises in "reading" facial expressions and voice inflections.

Attribution

Submitted by The We Card Program, Inc., and Doug Reed, director of interactive technology, OTM Partners, LLC, Arlington, Virginia, USA

Contact: dreed@otmpartners.com

Also involved: Lee Noel and Read deButts of OTM Partners, LLC; Doug Anderson, president, The We Card Program, Inc.; and Patti Shank, president, Learning Peaks, LLC

OTM Partners are award-winning interactive training experts, delivering content, reducing costs, and boosting results. They build consumer awareness campaigns, product launches, sales force education, compliance training, legal presentation services.

Reduce OnScreen Text

The Big Idea

What

This idea shows ways of reducing text in narrated self-paced courses.

Why

Self-paced online courses often have too much text. Too much text looks boring and can reduce understanding.

Use It!

How

In many self-paced online courses, screens (such as the one in Figure 4.15) have a lot of text and the narrator reads the text on the screen. Since the

Figure 4.15. Original Screen (Finished Output)

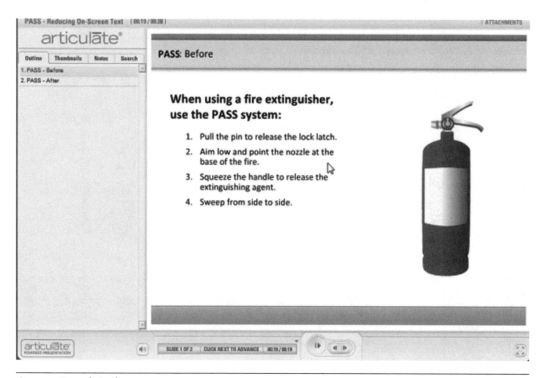

Source: David Anderson

narration adds context around what is on the screen, we can easily eliminate a great deal of the on-screen text. Eliminating redundant on-screen text prevents learners from reading the screen at the same time that the narrator is reading it aloud, which causes problems with understanding.

One technique for reducing text is to identify the main points and delete additional words from each bullet point, as shown in Figure 4.16, compared with Figure 4.15.

Figure 4.16. Reduced Bullet Text (PowerPoint)

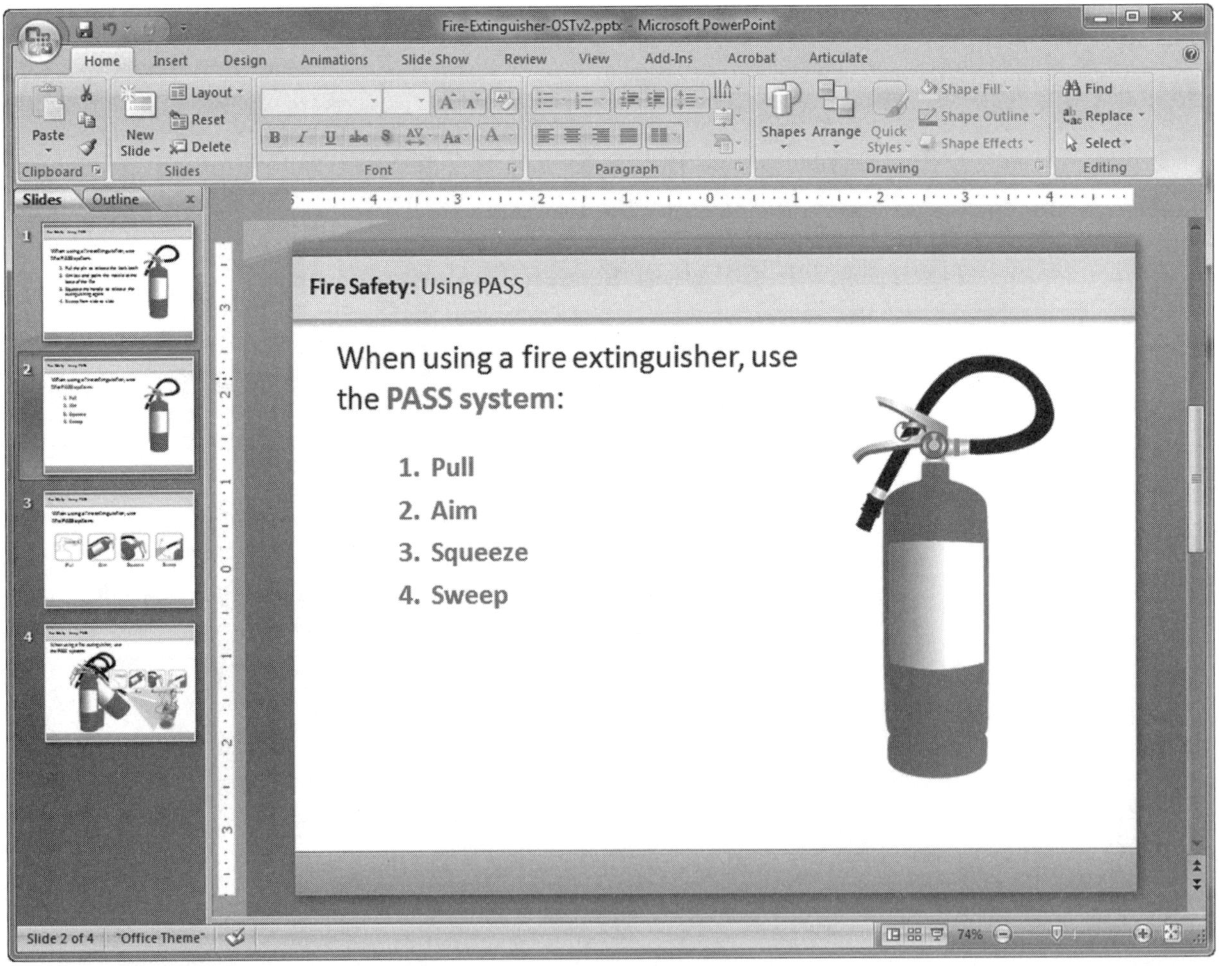

Source: David Anderson

Another way to eliminate on-screen text is by replacing on-screen text with graphics or animation, as in Figures 4.17 or 4.18.

Yet another way to reduce on-screen text is with progressive reveals, as in Figures 4.19 and 4.20. This technique involves showing only what is currently being discussed in narration on-screen. This

Figure 4.17. Images Instead of Text (Finished Output)

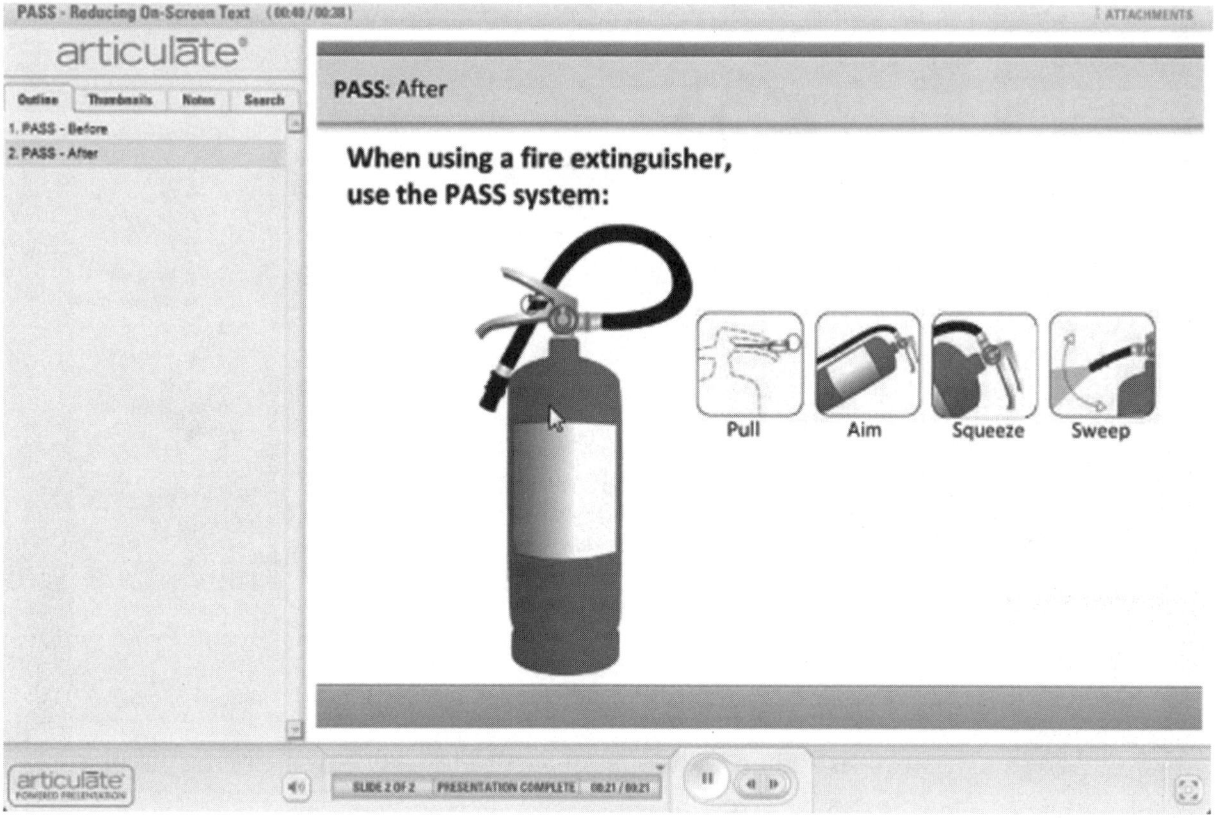

Source: David Anderson

Figure 4.18. Animations Instead of Text (PowerPoint)

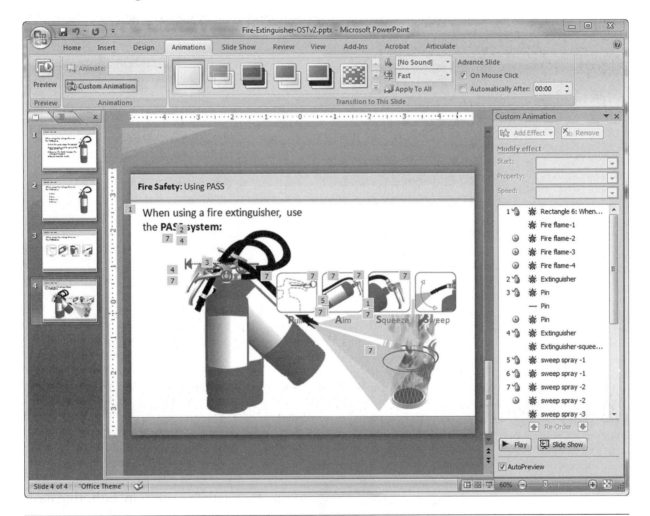

Source: David Anderson

involves adding additional images or text as items are being discussed (progressive reveal).

Some of these techniques involve using on-screen animation. For this idea, Anderson did the animations in PowerPoint and then brought those

Figure 4.19. Progressive Reveal, Initial State

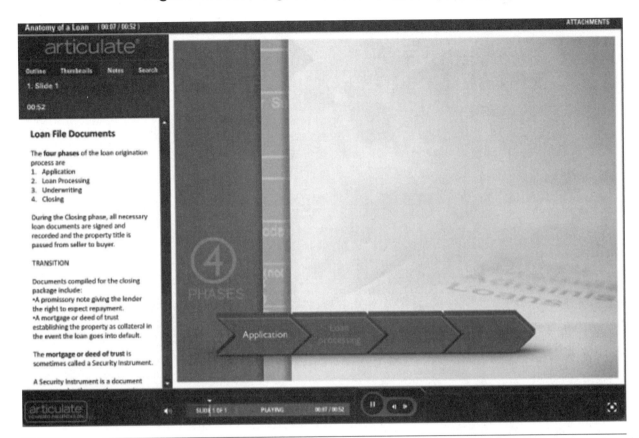

Source: David Anderson

and the non-animated slides into Articulate Presenter, an authoring tool. This is one of the easiest ways to do simple animations and it works well for authoring tools that use PowerPoint.

Technologies used: PowerPoint, Articulate Presenter

Figure 4.20. Progressive Reveal, Later State

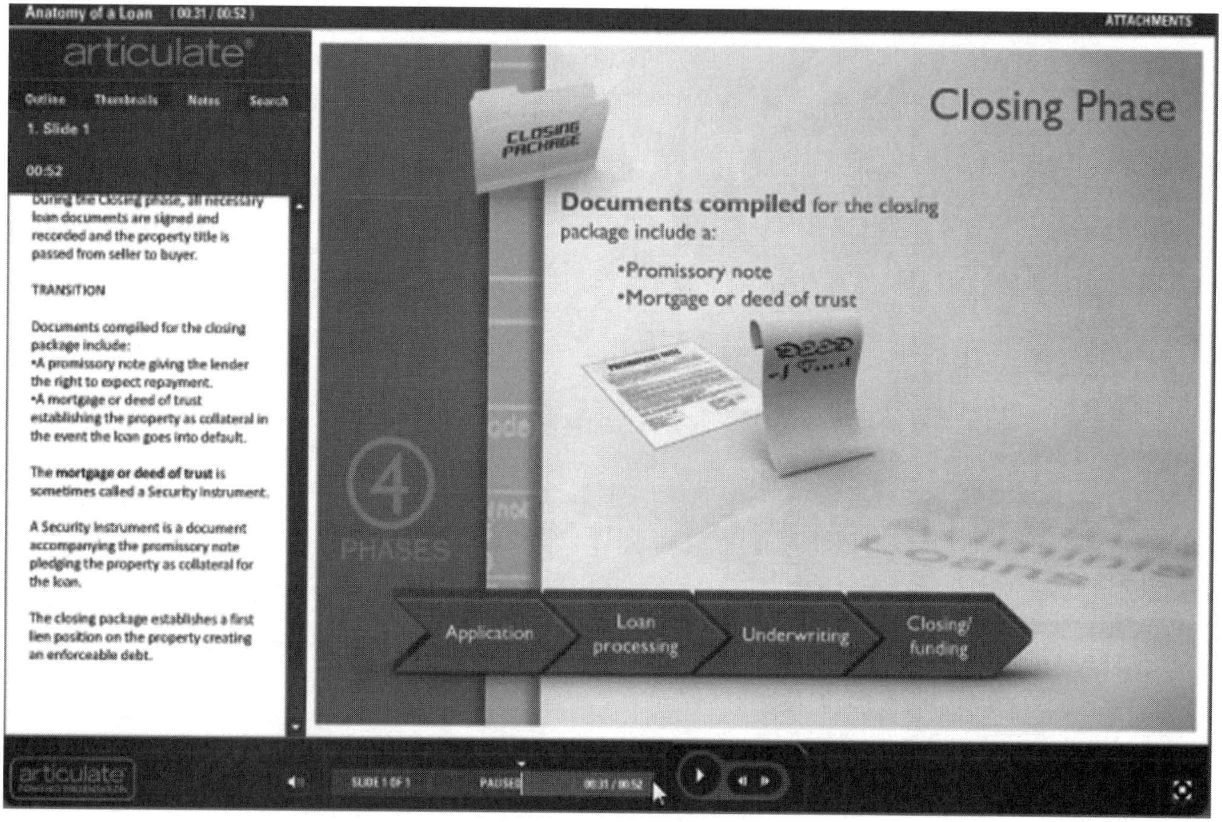

Source: David Anderson

Adopt or Adapt

These techniques can be used in self-paced online courses of all types to reduce on-screen text. This is most appropriate in narrated content. The ideas here can also be adapted for presentations.

Attribution

Submitted by David Anderson, community manager, Articulate, Phoenix, Arizona, USA

Contact: danderson@articulate.com and http://multimedialearning.com/

David Anderson is a community manager at Articulate with over thirteen years of experience designing e-learning. He supports the e-learning community by helping users get the most from their tools while finding creative ways to build more engaging courses. He also shares e-learning tips and tricks through his screencasts at http://screenr.com/user/elearning.

My Own Path

The Big Idea

What

This idea describes different ways to allow each learner to tailor his or her own path through learning content.

Why

Learning paths allow learners to view the content that best meets their needs. When learners can tailor their paths through the content based on their own needs, the online course can be far more relevant.

Use It!

How

There are many ways to allow learners to tailor learning content to learners' needs. One simple way is to include a "More Information" or "Additional Example" button that learners can click if they want more detail or another example.

A more elaborate way to allow learners to tailor their experience, based on their jobs, is to provide a button or link for learners to self-identify (their location, employment status, job title, or job level, for example) and use this information to present tailored information based on the selection. In the course screenshot in Figure 4.21, the learner identifies her employment status by clicking a button. Then the learner receives content relevant to her employment status and does not have to wade through information that does not apply.

A common issue for those developing self-paced online learning is the need to meet the needs of people with different levels of knowledge. Each person's experience can be customized by asking

Figure 4.21. Learner Selects Employee Status

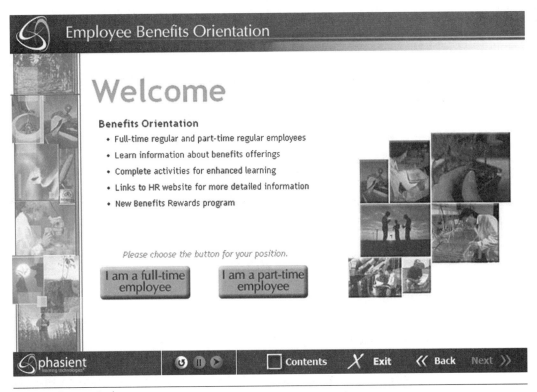

Source: Denise Link

a question and allowing those who answer correctly to move on to advanced information or the next topic, while providing additional (or remedial) information and exercises for those who answer the question incorrectly. Another way to identify learners with different needs is to ask them direct questions about their needs. In the course screenshot in Figure 4.22, the learner clicks the profile that best matches his or her own needs.

Based on the choice selected, the learner receives the content relevant to that choice, as in Figure 4.23.

Link provides the following suggestions for tailoring learning paths:

- Identify the basis for the tailoring paths before designing the course. Ideal bases for learning paths include:

  - Job role (for instance, some roles need only certain information or need more in-depth explanation of some information)

  - Location (if different locations have different needs)

  - Learner wants to know more or wants additional help (a "More Information" button, for example)

  - Learner displays mastery of subject (for example, answers a series of questions correctly) and is given the option to skip to advanced information

- Design the page or course so common information is presented first and information that differs based on the choice is presented afterward.

- Map out the potential paths on paper (or electronically, using a flow-chart, for example) before you try to develop them.

- Consider the tools available for development in light of the need for developing customized paths. Many of the commonly used author-ing tools (such as Captivate or Articulate Presenter) have functional-ities that make building different "branches" much simpler than in the past.

- Thoroughly test all paths. This kind of design requires a bit more advanced development, so it's common to encounter bugs that need to be worked out. Make sure that each path actually leads where you want it to go!

Learners often don't realize they are using tailored learning paths, and that's a good thing. If they are implemented well, each learner sees relevant information and thinks the course was well designed for his or her own needs!

Technologies used: authoring software or programming

Figure 4.22. Learner Selects Level of Information

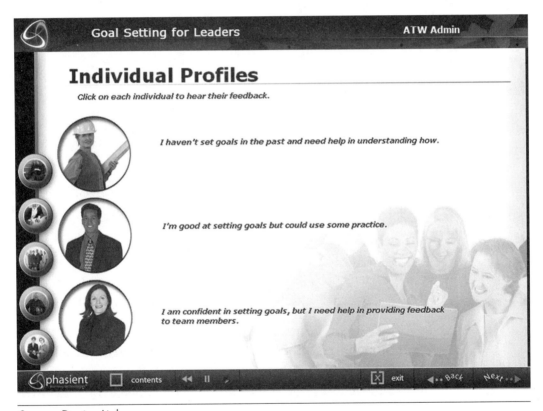

Source: Denise Link

Figure 4.23. Information Tailored for Selected Role

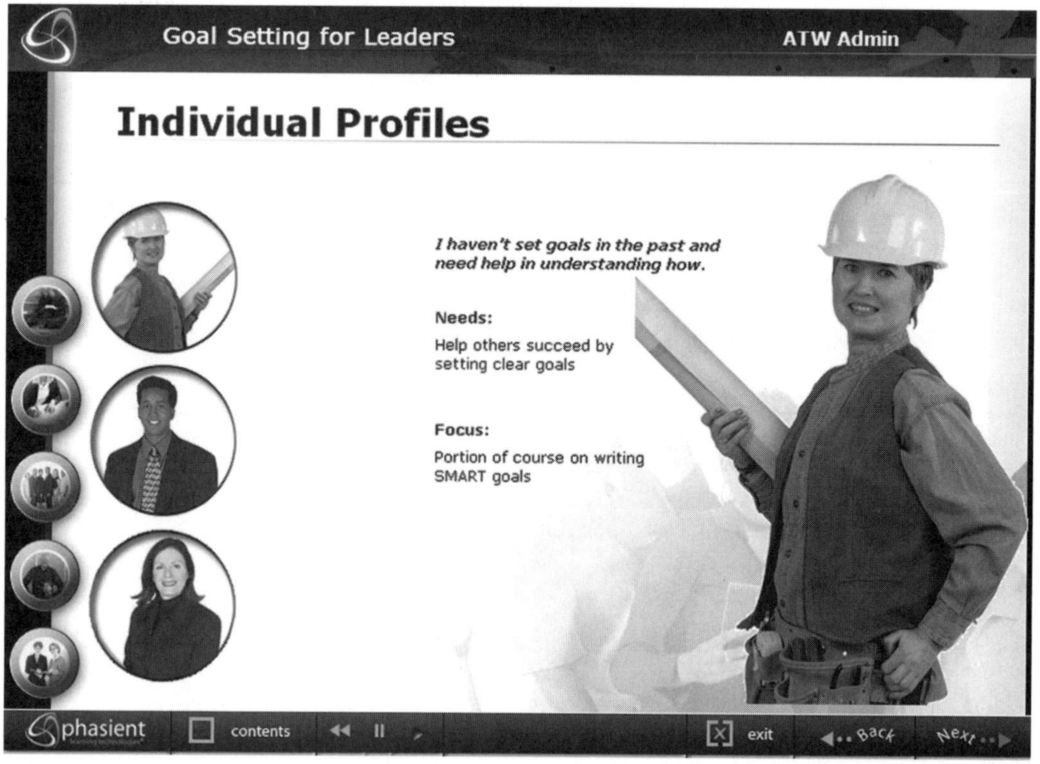

Source: Denise Link

Adopt or Adapt

This idea can be used for any content when learners have different needs. It can be adapted to work in higher education courses, too, by providing different readings or other content and allowing tweaks to assignments based on interests or needs of learners with different career plans or majors.

Attribution

Submitted by Denise Link, vice president, Phasient Learning Technologies, Ames, Iowa, USA

Contact: denise@phasient.com or www.phasient.com

Denise Link is a founder and vice president of Phasient Learning Technologies. She has more than ten years of experience designing and developing online training and documentation systems and has taught secondary, university, and adult students. Denise holds a master of arts degree from Iowa State University in English (rhetoric, composition, and professional communication). At Phasient, Denise leads a team of education-oriented instructional designers and graphic artists who create engaging e-learning courseware.

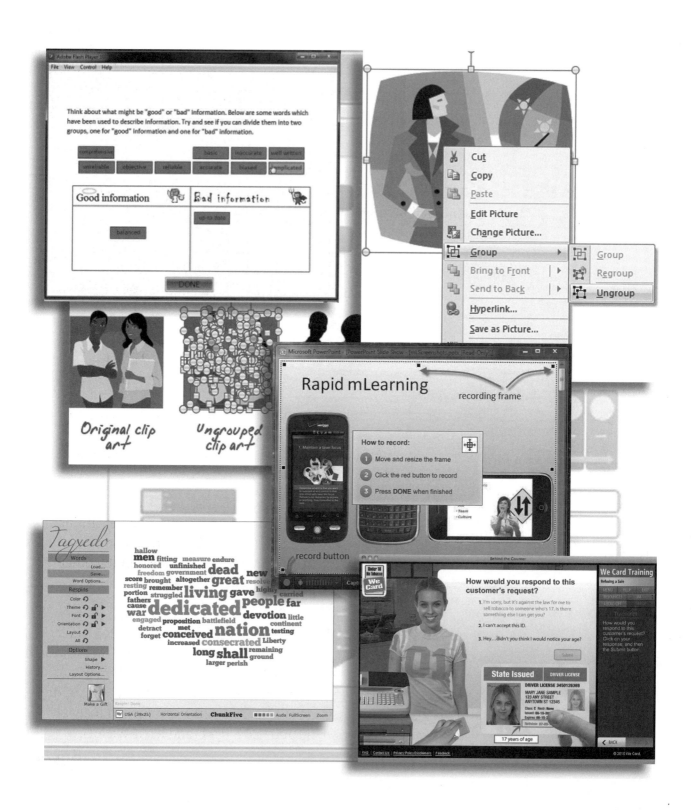

Ideas for Media and Authoring

This chapter shows how media, including images, audio, and video, are being used in creative ways to improve online learning. It also contains authoring ideas that can pump up the media and content you produce with media development tools. Although media *can* be used for the wrong reasons and these uses can detract from learning, media is often extremely important for learning. As the ideas in this chapter show, the right media can make ideas come alive.

Media and authoring are used to create many different types of learning materials, from self-paced to synchronous to tools that help people do their jobs. So you'll most certainly want to review the ideas in the other chapters to find synergies between a variety of instructional approaches and the use of media and authoring.

In case you haven't noticed, this is the largest chapter in the book. I think that's because media development and authoring have become far easier for the average instructional developer to do on his or her own. I think you'll see that, even if you aren't expert at building online instruction, you can do quite a lot, and these ideas are great places to start! I recommend that you spend time trying them out. I did and had a blast (and learned a lot).

Lose the Worn-Out Images, Up the Creativity

The Big Idea

What

This idea provides ways of getting away from the worn-out images that are too often used in self-paced online courses.

Why

Corporate online courses tend to use the same types of images over and over and they become predictable and boring. We tend to think that some learning needs to look dull. It doesn't.

Use It!

How

Anderson discusses replacing all-too-common images you see in corporate online courses, especially compliance courses, with images that are more playful. For example, he gives a "thumbs down" (Figure 5.1) to the

Figure 5.1. Say No to Thumbs Up

Source: Dave Anderson

all-too-typical thumbs-up graphic that tends to be overused in feedback in online compliance courses.

Anderson shows the images in Figure 5.2 and asks us to select the one that is more fun. The one on the right, of course! Better yet, dress up someone in your company learners will recognize and create a similar image (see also the Cheap Stock Photos idea later in this chapter).

Another idea to replace the worn-out thumbs up? An image of a fist bump. Anderson also recommends dressing up people in existing stock photos with sunglasses, leather jackets, hiking boots, and whatnot. (You can do this using image editing software.) Although these "playful" images may be inappropriate in some settings and for some content, the idea to rethink worn-out and often overused images is not inappropriate in any setting. Using these images over and over can become a visual sign to the learners that the content is going to be as engaging (not!) as the images.

Anderson suggests looking at the ad industry for creative inspiration for imagery and ways of presenting content. He suggests perusing AdCritic (http://creativity-online.com/adcritic) and Communication Arts (www .commarts.com/) for ideas. AdCritic hosts the best agency-created

Figure 5.2. Which Is More Fun?

Source: Dave Anderson

TV commercials. Communication Arts celebrates the best in visual communication.

"The ad industry realizes they have to make ads more engaging and unpredictable to connect with consumers. How much longer before e-learning does likewise?" muses Anderson.

Technologies used: images

Adopt or Adapt

Yes! This idea is adaptable in all kinds of learning content. Even though some learning content seems inherently dry and dull, that viewpoint is the problem, and there is a solution.

Attribution

Submitted by David Anderson, community manager, Articulate, Phoenix, Arizona, USA

Contact: danderson@articulate.com and http://multimedialearning.com/

David Anderson is a community manager at Articulate with over thirteen years of experience designing e-learning. He supports the e-learning community by helping users get the most from their tools while finding creative ways to build more engaging courses. He also shares e-learning tips and tricks through his screencasts at http://screenr.com/user/elearning.

Pecha Kucha for Learning

The Big Idea

What

Pecha Kucha (pronounced peh-cha ku-cha) is an alternative format for presentations that, when done well, stimulates creativity, enthusiasm, high energy, and engagement.

Why

Presentations are used in online courses to deliver content (by instructors) and to demonstrate new learning and comprehension (by learners). It can be challenging or even deadly boring to sit through bullet-pointed slide after bullet-pointed slide. And these kinds of bullet-point-driven presentations can be even more boring online.

Pecha Kucha (and similar formats like Ignite and Lightning Talks) offer a structured, timed approach that encourages instructors to be concise and get to the heart of the matter. This can enhance the quality of presentations, as well as the quality of the overall experience and the audience's engagement. Instructors and learners will find Pecha Kucha a refreshing change from what they are used to.

Use It!

How

The Pecha Kucha (Japanese for "chatter") format can easily be applied to all disciplines and contexts. The basic structure of a Pecha Kucha presentation is twenty slides/images, twenty seconds per slide/image (which is just under seven minutes for a presentation). Two architects in Tokyo developed it to structure presentations in an efficient informal way that is non-detrimental to the message.

Although often used for in-person settings, Pecha Kucha is an effective format for online presentations (e.g., stand-alone, kiosk, podcast, and synchronous live sessions) as well. Daniel Pink (contributing editor at *Wired* magazine) created a YouTube video on the topic of emotionally intelligent signage that is a good example of an online Pecha Kucha (see Figure 5.3).

Figure 5.3. Slide from Pink's Pecha Kucha Presentation

Source: Joanna Dunlap, www.youtube.com/watch?v=9NZOt6BkhUg)

Dunlap and Lowenthal provide the following guidelines for using Pecha Kucha for learning:

- **Select Images Thoughtfully.** The Pecha Kucha format requires a thoughtful selection of images that can speak for themselves with limited commentary. If an image is not worth looking at for twenty seconds, then maybe it is not the right image to contribute to the message of the presentation.

- **Use Silence Intentionally.** It is important to consider how silence can be used as part of the message. Your learners do not need constant noise to stay alert and engaged. Allowing for moments of silence provides the learners with space and time to process, reflect, and explore an intellectual and emotional connection with the image and overall message.

- **Tell Your Story.** Storytelling is a powerful instructional strategy that engages learners. Our typical presentation structure, which tends to be hierarchical, does not lend itself well to storytelling. Pecha Kucha does. With its reliance on strong visuals supported by the spoken word (as opposed to the other way around, as with typical presentations), the Pecha Kucha format provides a useful structure for telling important stories.

- **Don't Take Yourself Too Seriously.** While the Pecha Kucha format is quite structured in terms of number of images and time, it is intentionally informal. This means there is more room for presenter creativity. For example, there is room for audience participation and the use of props and music. Although this sort of creativity needs to be carefully planned given the constraint of time, knowing that the Pecha Kucha format invites creativity is very freeing.

- **Prepare and Practice.** Just because the Pecha Kucha format is intentionally informal, this does not mean that presenters do not have to prepare fully for their six minutes and forty seconds. To avoid uttering many "ummms" and "ands" and running out of time, it is necessary to prepare and practice. This becomes even more evident when recording a Pecha Kucha for online delivery.

If you have been looking for a way to spice up your lectures and presentations, consider Pecha Kucha. When used well, this format stimulates creativity, enthusiasm, high energy, and engagement. And if not used well, it is over in six minutes and forty seconds!

Technologies used: images, screencasting tools, PowerPoint

Adopt or Adapt

Pecha Kucha can be adapted for all kinds of content. Because of the format, the presenter must think about the message and the best way to get it across given the twenty slides/images, twenty seconds per slide/image format. This prompts a level of analysis and creativity that is often not given to "typical" presentations.

Attribution

Submitted by Joanna C. Dunlap, associate professor and faculty fellow for teaching, University of Colorado–Denver, Denver, Colorado, USA

Contact: joni.dunlap@ucdenver.edu
Also involved: Patrick R. Lowenthal, academic technology coordinator, University of Colorado–Denver: CU Online/School of Education and Human Development

Joanna C. Dunlap is an associate professor of instructional design and technology at the University of Colorado–Denver. An award-winning educator, her teaching and research interests focus on the use of sociocultural approaches to enhance adult learners' development and experience in post-secondary settings. For over fifteen years, she has directed, designed, delivered, and facilitated distance and e-learning educational opportunities for a variety of audiences. Joni is also the university's assistant director for teaching effectiveness, working through the Center for Faculty Development to help online and on-campus faculty enhance their teaching practice.

Find the Right PowerPoint Clip Art

The Big Idea

What

This idea presents two ways to find useful free PowerPoint clip art images for use in your presentations and PowerPoint–based online courses.

Why

It's not always easy to find the clip art you need, and these methods can widen your collection of free clip art.

Use It!

How

This idea is adapted from The Rapid e-Learning Blog (www.articulate.com/rapid-elearning).

When you search Microsoft Office Online for free clip art (http://office.microsoft.com/en-us/images/), you can find many additional images that you can download and use in your presentations and PowerPoint–based online courses. But there are many images there, so how can you find what you need?

When you select an image, you can see the image properties to the right. In the example in Figure 5.4, there are two things to focus on: keywords and styles. These two pieces of information are the key to finding additional clip art that can be useful.

Keywords identify what the clip art is about. If you click on one of the keywords, you'll find other images tagged with that keyword. Clicking on appropriate keywords on useful images will help you find additional useful images.

Figure 5.4. Clip Art Properties, Keywords, and Style

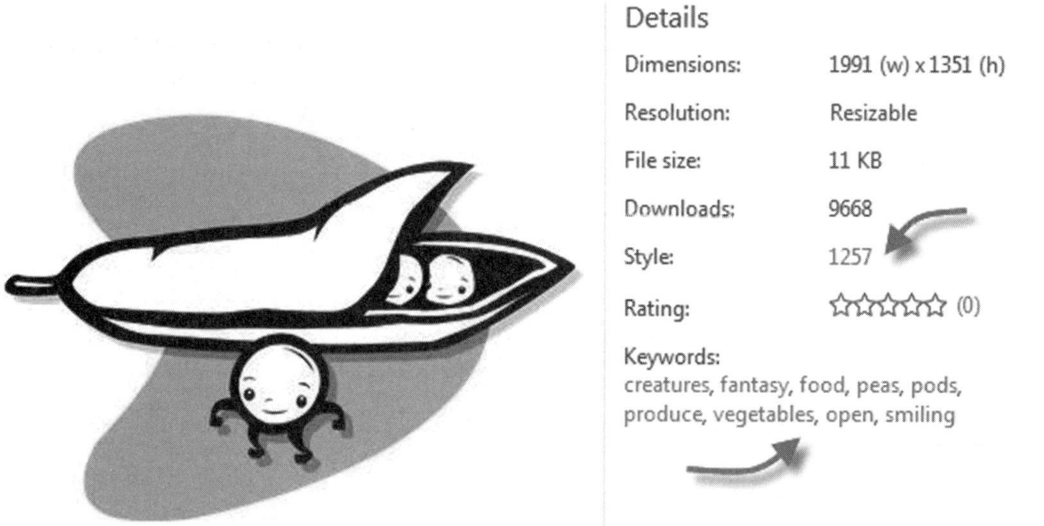

Details

Dimensions:	1991 (w) x 1351 (h)
Resolution:	Resizable
File size:	11 KB
Downloads:	9668
Style:	1257
Rating:	☆☆☆☆☆ (0)

Keywords:
creatures, fantasy, food, peas, pods, produce, vegetables, open, smiling

Source: Tom Kuhlmann

Style refers to images that share a common look. If you find a useful clip art image and want to find other images to use that look like they belong together, click on the style and you'll see the other images that are the same style (Figure 5.5). You can download them as a group to use in your presentations or online courses and can ungroup the grouped images (see the PowerPoint Clip Art Surgery idea that's the next idea in this chapter) so that you can delete parts you don't want, change colors of elements, or combine images to make new images. Keep in mind that not all images are part of a style group, nor can all images be ungrouped.

Kuhlmann suggests the following tips for saving clip art images with the same style so that they can be used later:

- Download all of the images to an open, empty PowerPoint presentation file.

- Spread the images out over a series of slides so that you can easily see them all.

- Save the file name with the style name (for example, style1257.ppt) so you know what style this collection of images is from.

- Play around with the images to make new images and save them in the file: break grouped elements apart to create custom elements, change element colors, etc.

Technologies used: PowerPoint

Figure 5.5. Microsoft Clip Art, Style 1257.ppt

Source: Tom Kuhlmann

Adopt or Adapt

PowerPoint has many clip art images, and these two methods will help you find additional ones to use. Although the idea describes using these in presentations and online courses, these images could also be saved as pictures (right-click>Save as Picture) and used in documents and on web pages.

Attribution

Submitted by Tom Kuhlmann, vice president, community, Articulate, Seattle, Washington, USA

Contact: /www.articulate.com/rapid-elearning/

Tom Kuhlmann writes The Rapid e-Learning Blog, where he shares practical e-learning tips and tricks. He has close to twenty years of experience in the training industry, where he's worked on e-learning projects for both large and small organizations. Currently he manages Articulate's e-learning community.

PowerPoint Clip Art Surgery

The Big Idea

What

This idea shows two ways to modify PowerPoint images in order to have additional free images to work with for your presentations and PowerPoint–based online courses.

Why

Many of us work with a tight budget and don't have access to graphic designers or illustrators or the ability to purchase the clip art images we need. The ability to modify existing PowerPoint graphics gives us access to additional free images that can better meet our needs.

Use It!

How

This idea is adapted from The Rapid e-Learning Blog (www.articulate.com/rapid-elearning).

PowerPoint clip art images are either bitmap images (such as .gif, .jpg, or .png) or vector images (such as .wmf). The .wmf images are made up of grouped objects. Grouped images can be ungrouped and edited. To ungroup a grouped image, right-click on the image and select Group> Ungroup. You typically have to do this twice—the first time to convert the image and the second time to ungroup it. (See Figure 5.6.)

Once you ungroup the image, you can click on the elements you don't want (such as the background) and delete them, as in Figure 5.7. Let's say you wanted a picture of someone presenting but didn't like all of the background elements that came with that image. So you would ungroup the elements, and then you would delete the background elements by clicking on individual elements and deleting them. Then

Figure 5.6. Ungrouping Grouped Clip Art

Source: Tom Kuhlmann

you would regroup the elements that remain by right-clicking the image and selecting Group>Regroup, as seen in Figure 5.8.

You can also *insert* elements to change an image. Let's say you want to add a flip chart to the image in Figure 5.6. You could insert a flip-chart image and then ungroup the flip-chart image and remove any elements you do not want and then regroup the remaining elements. Then you could arrange Image 1 (the woman) with Image 2 (the flip chart) to make the desired image (Figure 5.9). Finally, you would select both images and regroup them to make a single image.

Figure 5.7. Selecting and Deleting Ungrouped Background Element

Source: Tom Kuhlmann

The process is outlined below:

To Delete Elements

1. Right-click on the image and select Group>Ungroup. (*Note:* You will notice that some images cannot be ungrouped. That's because these are in bitmap format such as .gif, .jpg or .png.)

2. Select and then delete individual elements you don't want to keep.

3. Right-click on the final image and select Group>Regroup.

To Combine Two Images

1. For each image: ungroup the image (right-click on the image and select Group>Ungroup). Delete elements that you don't want to keep. When you are done deleting elements, regroup each image (right-click and select Group>Regroup).

2. Arrange both images together.

3. Select both images, right-click and select Group>Group to make into a single grouped image.

Figure 5.8. Regrouping Ungrouped Elements

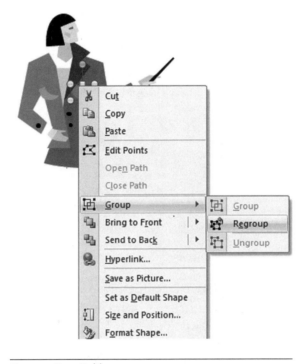

Source: Tom Kuhlmann

Don't forget that you can search Microsoft Office Online (http://office .microsoft.com/en-us/images/) to find thousands of additional clip art images.

Technologies used: PowerPoint

Figure 5.9. Grouping Two Elements

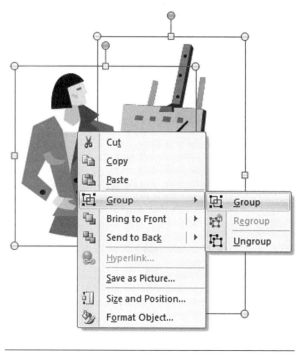

Source: Tom Kuhlmann

Adopt or Adapt

This process can be used to create additional images to use for your presentations and PowerPoint–based online courses.

Attribution

Submitted by Tom Kuhlmann, vice president, community, Articulate, Seattle, Washington, USA

Contact: /www.articulate.com/rapid-elearning/

Tom Kuhlmann writes The Rapid e-Learning Blog, where he shares practical e-learning tips and tricks. He has close to twenty years of experience in the training industry, where he's worked on e-learning projects for both large and small organizations. Currently he manages Articulate's e-learning community.

PowerPoint Graphics Library

The Big Idea

What

This idea shows how to create a stand-alone library of graphics inside a PowerPoint file to make it easier to collect and reuse PowerPoint graphics.

Why

You spend time creating and manipulating graphic files for your PowerPoint presentations and online courses that use PowerPoint slides. Then, when you want to use those graphics again, you have to remember what presentation they are in, open that PowerPoint file, cut and paste them into the new PowerPoint file . . . ugh. Want an easier way? A PowerPoint Library file makes it easier to reuse graphic elements and quickly make those elements available for other projects. This process can make rapid development even more rapid.

Use It!

How

Cook developed the following process to solve problems with finding and reusing graphic elements.

1. Open a new PowerPoint file for your Library items.

2. Save the file as ___Library.ppt (for example: DoctorandPatientGraphicsLibrary.ppt)

3. Add reusable graphics to the slides. You may want to organize slides by type of graphics, such as doctor slides, patient slides, medical items slides, medical background slides, and so on. Figure 5.10 shows an example.

4. When you want to reuse these graphics, open the appropriate graphics library and change the view of the Library file to Slide Sorter View.

5. Open the PowerPoint project file that you want to pull graphics into. Change the view of the project file to Slide Sorter View.

6. Arrange the two slide decks so they are side by side, as shown in Figure 5.11.

7. Drag and drop the slides that contain graphics you want to use from your Library file to your project file.

8. Give each Library file *slide* a title so that you can easily find the slides you need. You can quickly scan for desired slides in Outline View.

Figure 5.10. PowerPoint Graphics Library

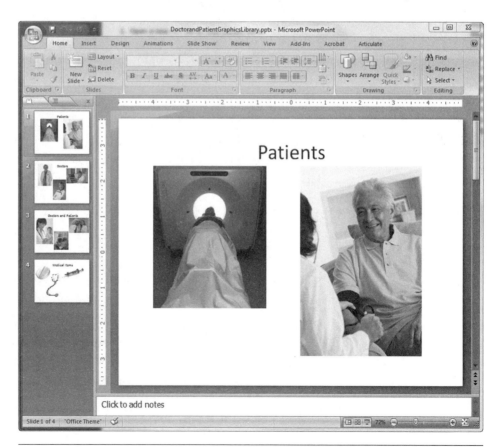

Source: Jenise Cook

Figure 5.11. Open Project File and Library File

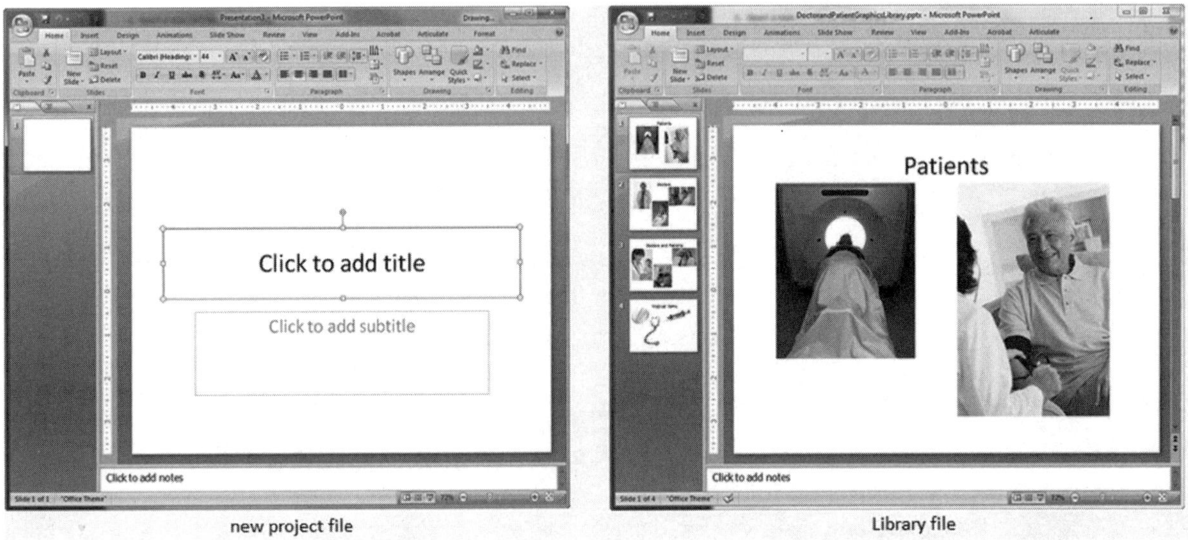

new project file   Library file

Source: Jenise Cook

Cook shares a few best practices:

- Whenever you are working on a new project, drag and drop slides with graphics you want to save and reuse later to the appropriate Library file.

- Save manipulated files (for example, cropped, grouped together, and alone) in a variety of ways that you might want to use in the future into the Library file.

- Save the graphics in your libraries as PowerPoint objects *and* as graphics files (save as picture). Cook keeps the original PowerPoint objects (shapes and SmartArt) on specific slides and puts the "Save as Picture" images (Figure 5.12) on different slides within the same library. Having both versions helps her go back and change the original images if needed. graphical elements.

Technologies used: PowerPoint, graphics files

Figure 5.12. Save Graphic as Picture

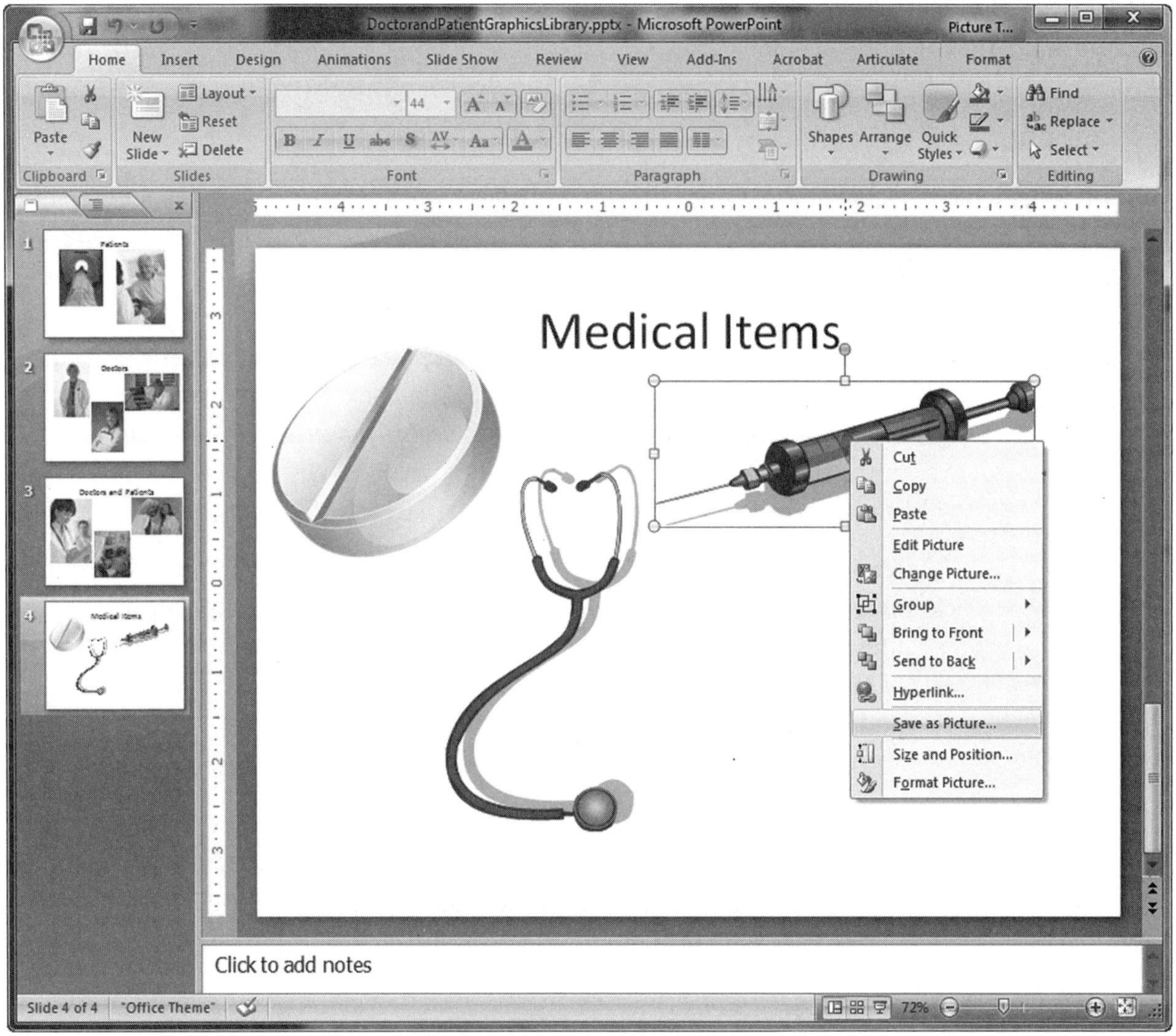

Source: Jenise Cook

Adopt or Adapt

This idea will help you collect graphics for reuse in PowerPoint presentations and online courses that use PowerPoint slides (such as Adobe Presenter projects, Captivate projects, and Articulate Presenter projects).

Libraries can be created for graphics that go with various topics or graphics of various types. For example, you might create a library of K through 12, university classroom scenarios, or medical office scenes.

Attribution

Submitted by Jenise Cook, Ridge View Media, Prescott, Arizona, USA

Contact: info@ridgeviewmedia.com or www.ridgeviewmedia.com

Jenise Cook designs and develops workplace learning solutions as a virtual consultant of Ridge View Media. She has over fifteen years of experience as an instructional designer and technical writer. She has designed and developed e-learning solutions since 2004, with experience in financial services, health care, consumer goods, manufacturing, and academia.

Jenise graduated from California State University, Northridge, with both master of arts and bachelor of arts degrees in Spanish language and literature, is certified in teaching English to speakers of other languages (TESOL), and holds memberships in the American Society for Training and Development (ASTD), and the eLearning Guild.

Show to Tell

The Big Idea

What

This idea provides some new ways to use graphics and images in PowerPoint for delivering content in online courses.

Why

Many of the more typical displays of information in PowerPoint are pretty boring. Bullet points work okay—in very small quantities. But PowerPoint is a *visual* medium and these capabilities should *really* be taken full advantage of!

Use It!

How

PowerPoint is often used by online instructors to provide course content. Milstid thinks it's very important to make use of PowerPoint's visual communication capabilities, so she analyzes her content to assess whether the content she wants to convey on a slide can be conveyed in the form of a graphic, as opposed to bullet points. "I try to think creatively about images that can convey what I am discussing on each slide," she explains. "And I don't always use obvious and literal photographs or images."

"With later versions of PowerPoint," says Milstid, "I have increased opportunities to create courses that are visually stimulating. To accomplish this, I use two specific approaches: First, I look for ways to incorporate visual elements, such as utilizing PowerPoint's SmartArt capabilities." SmartArt is one of the newer PowerPoint features that can help you turn textual information into interesting visual information. It is specifically used to represent steps in a process, flow of information, and the relationships between pieces of information in a visual way. Milstid analyzes her content and then looks at the SmartArt formats that are available to see whether she can use them to convey that information. See Figures 5.13, 5.14, and 5.15 for some examples.

Figure 5.13. SmartArt Options in PowerPoint 2007

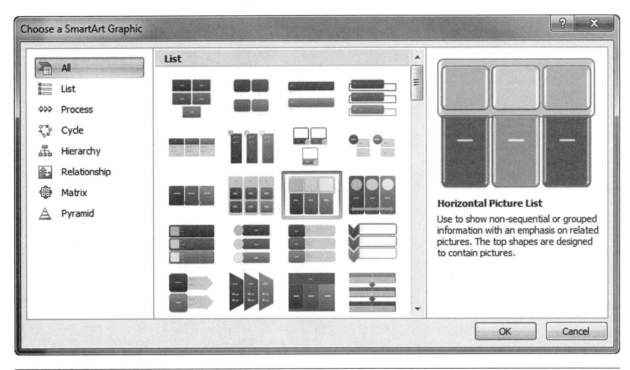

Source: Lauren M. Milstid

Figure 5.14. SmartArt Example 1

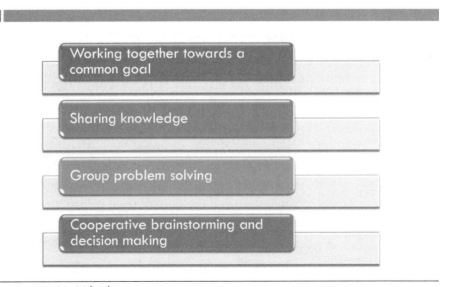

Source: Lauren M. Milstid

Figure 5.15. SmartArt Example 2

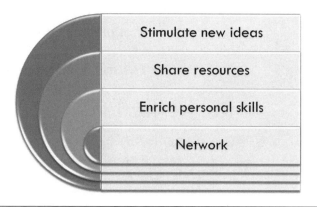

Why Collaborate?

Stimulate new ideas

Share resources

Enrich personal skills

Network

Source: Lauren M. Milstid

Another approach Milstid uses to incorporate effective graphics is to think of images that subtly represent the topic she is presenting so that learners are curious about what she is discussing. For example, when discussing dementia and an inability to encode information, she may use a photograph of jumbled letters, word fragments, and numbers intermingled together, as opposed to a person with a confused facial expression. On a slide about life reflections, she might use an image of a landscape. A sample is shown in Figure 5.16.

Milstid says that these approaches are more visually engaging and get away from bullet points and stereotypical imagery. The trick is to think like a graphic designer; learn graphic design best practices by reviewing books, websites, and marketing collateral; and then apply the design approaches to instruction.

To find images, Milstid uses three sources:

- Microsoft Office (http://office.microsoft.com/en-us/images/): The selection is limited but free, and is a great starting point for locating media.

- iStockphoto (www.istockphoto.com/index.php): Available media types consist of photos, illustrations, Flash animations, video, and audio. The selection is wide but images need to be purchased. Lower resolution images are inexpensive. iStockphoto offers one free photograph each week, in any size, and Milstid downloads the photo each week and saves it for later use.

- stock.xchng (www.sxc.hu/index.html): Free image gallery that is built by a community of photographers who offer their work for free.

Figure 5.16. Sample Imagery

Life Reflection

- Discuss life journey.
- Take pride in accomplishments.
- Reconnect with joyful memories.
- Reflect on lessons learned from hard times.
- Reflect on lessons learned from human relationships.

Source: Lauren M. Milstid

Milstid shares the following guidelines that she uses when selecting SmartArt and non-literal images.

Guidelines for SmartArt

- SmartArt works best with less text, such as keywords, lists, concise points, etc. If the slide needs to have a substantial amount of text, avoid using SmartArt because the text can quickly become illegible as it shrinks in size in order to fit into the selected SmartArt graphic.

- Pick SmartArt types that visually represent the type of content to be displayed. For example, use one of the process SmartArt graphics when discussing how events progress over time or one of the pyramid SmartArt graphics when wanting to describe concepts in a bottom-up or top-down manner.

- If the text doesn't fit well into the chosen SmartArt graphic, try selecting a different SmartArt graphic that allows more room for the text.

Guidelines for Non-Literal Images

- Pick out a keyword from each slide.

- Think of many different ways to interpret that word. For example, on her life reflection slide, using the keywords, "reflection," and "life review," instead of being literal and using a photograph of a person contemplating or smiling, Milstid considered how reflecting on one's life is much larger than a single emotion or facial expression and chose a visual depiction of sky, clouds, grass, and trees.

Technologies used: PowerPoint and digital graphics

Adopt or Adapt

These approaches can be adapted in any setting when using imagery, not just with PowerPoint. The key is to think about how your content can be conveyed using visual representations and evocative images.

Attribution

Submitted by Lauren M. Milstid, course developer, St. Petersburg, Florida, USA

Contact: MilstidL@yahoo.com or www.linkedin.com/in/laurenmilstid

Lauren M. Milstid completed her master of science degree in instructional technology in May 2009 at Chestnut Hill College in Philadelphia, Pennsylvania. She wrote her thesis on learning through games and also worked as a graduate assistant, serving as a project manager for various instructional design projects. She is currently a course developer for a health and human services training organization in St. Petersburg, Florida, and is involved in all phases of the instructional design process. Her responsibilities include script writing, voice-overs, sound editing, graphics production, interaction design and development, and client and SME management.

First-Person Point of View

The Big Idea

What

This idea presents a visual technique that calls upon an engaging and realistic first-person point of view that puts the learner squarely "inside" the training.

Why

Using this visual technique provides a realistic visual metaphor for the entire course and helps learners feel like they are actually there, dealing with the challenges of real work.

Use It!

How

The screenshots in Figures 5.17 and 5.18 are from The We Card Employee Training Course, provided by The We Card Program, Inc. The course covers FDA-suggested training elements in a fun manner that allows learners to practice the skills needed to prevent selling tobacco products to underage buyers.

The entire course is visual, with the learner behind the counter of a retail store. All the content and skills to be practiced are within a setting that is likely to be similar to the setting in which learners will be working and which feels like "real work." Many self-paced online training programs feel like they are about other people, but this visual technique (and the design of the content and activities around being "on the job") feels like it is about the learner doing the activities he or she will be doing on the job. Since the learner is practicing realistic skills in an environment that is very similar to a real work environment, the training is likely to feel very relevant and is more likely to result in skills transfer to the job.

Figure 5.17. First-Person Point of View, Example 1

Source: The We Card Program, Inc.

Figure 5.18. First-Person Point of View, Example 2

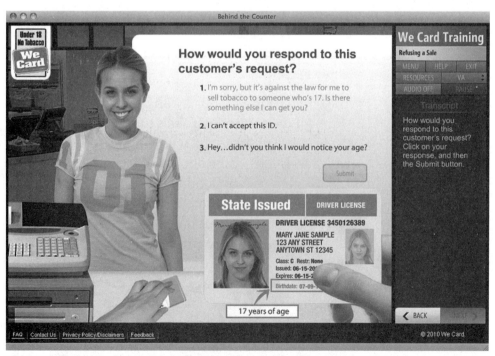

Source: The We Card Program, Inc.

Both screenshots show this first-person point of view. Notice that in the second figure, we even see "your" hand!

Technologies used: Flash throughout: combination of ActionScript 2, timeline manipulation, web-format graphics, .wav narration, and native Flash elements (text, shapes); crucial narration synchronization/control by AS2 in specific frames; Flash technology adapted to deliver a web-based variant of long-established cinematic first-person scene building techniques

Adopt or Adapt

This visual technique would be useful for many different types of training content. For example, it would work well for training customer service reps how to judge customer body language and wherever "seeing" the world from a learner's/worker's point of view would be effective.

Attribution

Submitted by The We Card Program, Inc., and Doug Reed, director of interactive technology, OTM Partners, LLC, Arlington, Virginia, USA

Contact: dreed@otmpartners.com

Also involved: Lee Noel and Read deButts of OTM Partners, LLC; Doug Anderson, president, The We Card Program, Inc.; and Patti Shank, president, Learning Peaks, LLC

OTM Partners are award-winning interactive training experts, delivering content, reducing costs, and boosting results. They build consumer awareness campaigns, product launches, sales force education, compliance training, and legal presentation services.

Create a Television in PowerPoint

The Big Idea

What

This idea shows how to use PowerPoint graphics tools to create a television image to display video content.

Why

This is a really fun way to present video content in online courses! And it is also a great activity to learn more about the graphic design and illustration capabilities of PowerPoint.

Use It!

How

This idea is adapted from The Rapid e-Learning Blog (www.articulate.com/ rapid-elearning) and was inspired by Ryan Putnam (http://vectips.com/).

PowerPoint image creation and editing tools can be used to create a television (Figure 5.19) that can be used to show video content. The techniques here require fairly advanced knowledge of the image creation and editing tools in PowerPoint, so if you don't yet have that knowledge, Kuhlmann suggests starting with his PowerPoint graphic creation exercise (www.articulate.com/rapid-elearning/ see-how-easily-you-can-create-graphics-in-powerpoint/).

1. Create the television set body using PowerPoint shapes, lines, and fills. Create three rectangle shapes (Figure 5.20). A rectangle with no border and a gradient fill is the main body of the set. Another rectangle (no fill and a gradient border that is the same as the main body box) makes the outer edge of the main body. For the screen, duplicate the border box but make the border thicker and flip it upside down so the lighter gray is on the bottom.

Figure 5.19. Television Graphic to Show Video Content

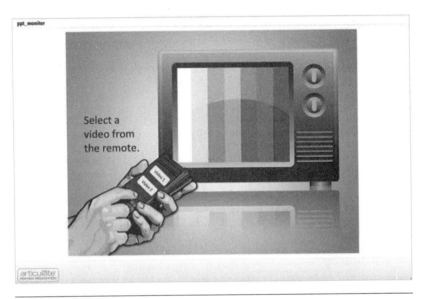

Source: Tom Kuhlmann

Figure 5.20. Create Television Body

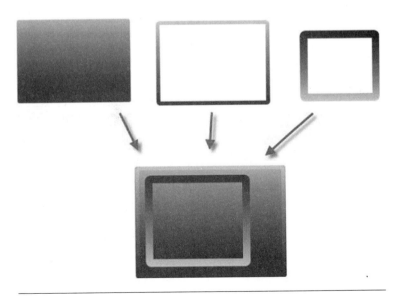

Source: Tom Kuhlmann

2. Create color bars and shimmer. The color bars are a grouped set of colored rectangles with a 60 percent transparent shape to give it a gel look. Create the color bars by building a series of rectangle shapes and filling with the colors (Figure 5.21). Then group all the rectangles (right-click>Group>Group) and then move behind the television image. The shimmer is a bit trickier. Take a rectangle and convert it to a freeform and then edit the points to give it a curve. Fill it with white and 60 percent transparent.

3. Add the television set details. The television set details are just basic shapes with simple gradient fills (Figure 5.22).

Figure 5.21. Create Television Bars and "Shimmer"

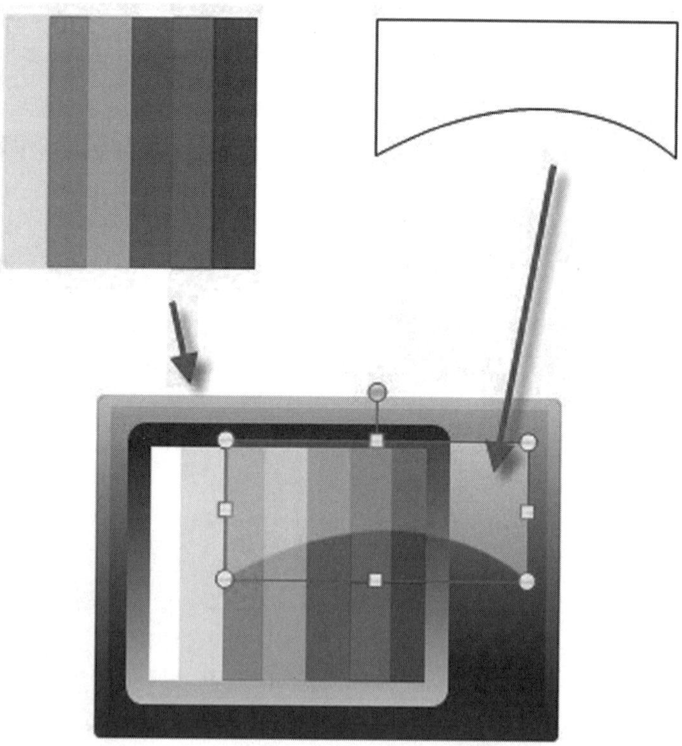

Source: Tom Kuhlmann

Figure 5.22. Create Rest of Television Set

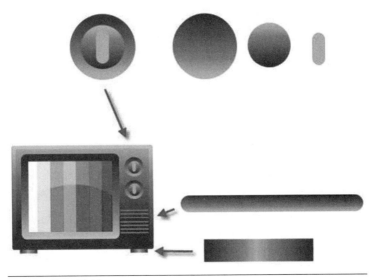

Source: Tom Kuhlmann

- *Knobs:* Create a circle and use the same gradient fill as the set. Duplicate the circle, flip it, and scale it down. Create a rounded rectangle with a lighter gray. Use the alignment tool to align them. Group the knobs and add to the set.

- *Grills:* Create a rounded rectangle and fill with a gradient. Duplicate them and use the alignment tool to distribute them equally.

- *Feet:* Create a rectangle and add a gradient with a lighter center and darker edges.

Now group all of the TV elements and save as an .emf or .png file and then bring it back in as a picture. This way it's a single object and easier to work with. To have more room to show video, you may want to create a big screen television without dials and grills.

How do learners get the video to "turn on"? In this example, when learners click on one of the transparent rectangles over the video titles, which are hyperlinked, they are taken to the slide where that video content plays inside the "television."

Technologies used: PowerPoint

Adopt or Adapt

This idea adds realism and fun to showing video content by viewing it through a television.

Attribution

Submitted by Tom Kuhlmann, vice president, community, Articulate, Seattle, Washington, USA

Contact: www.articulate.com/rapid-elearning/

Tom Kuhlmann writes The Rapid e-Learning Blog, where he shares practical e-learning tips and tricks. He has close to twenty years of experience in the training industry, where he's worked on e-learning projects for both large and small organizations. Currently he manages Articulate's e-learning community.

Easy Video

The Big Idea

What

This idea provides a simple way of producing web video that includes your photos, videos, and music, using an easy-to-use web application.

Why

Younger learners, especially, are more engaged with multimedia than text and pictures. But many instructors, designers, trainers, and subject-matter experts who create online learning content don't know how to create multimedia and don't have budgets for multimedia developers. Easy-to-use tools for this purpose allow them to create multimedia easily.

Use It!

How

Morris uses Animoto (http://animoto.com) to create video sequences for her online courses. She explains that you can preview and select a style of video from a list, upload photos and videos, add text and music, and edit your video (Figure 5.23). Videos can easily be created to introduce a topic, review a topic (think multimedia flash cards!), and produce learner assignments or presentations.

Completed Animoto videos (Figure 5.24) can be posted to Facebook, embedded in web pages, sent to YouTube, or sent via link by email. If off-line access is needed, there is an option to download and burn a DVD.

Technologies used: online web application

Figure 5.23. Animoto Development Environment

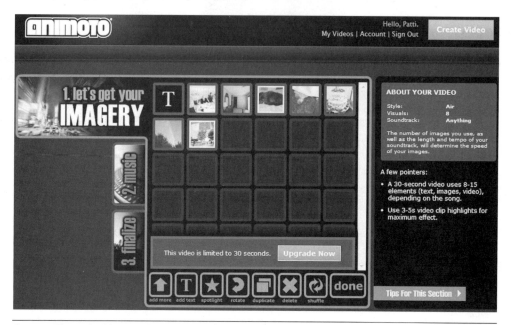

Figure 5.24. Example of Finished Output, Uploaded to YouTube

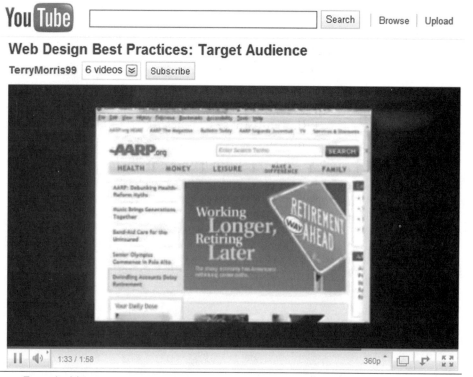

Adopt or Adapt

This idea can be used for a wide range of content and situations, in both academic and corporate settings. For example, paintings could be shown in an art history course, or web navigation tips could be provided in a web design course. Tips for being a successful online learner could show photos of learners completing the steps shown at the beginning of the video.

Educators can register for a free account with Animoto at http://animoto .com/education. Case studies are available at http://animoto.com/ education/casestudies.

Attribution

Submitted by Terry A. Morris, associate professor, Harper College, Palatine, Illinois, USA

Contact: tmorris@harpercollege.edu or http://terrymorris.net

An associate professor at Harper College, Dr. Terry A. Morris has developed and taught online courses since 1999 in the subject areas of web development, computer fundamentals, and instructional technology. She has written several web development textbooks, including *Basics of Web Design* and the fifth edition of *Web Development & Design Foundations with XHTML*. Dr. Morris is a recipient of the Instructional Technology Council's 2008 Outstanding e-Learning Faculty Award for Excellence, the 2008 MERLOT Business Classics Award, and the 2006 Blackboard Greenhouse Exemplary Course Award (Online Course Category).

VoiceThread Virtuosity

The Big Idea

What

This idea explores using VoiceThread (www.voicethread.com), an easy-to-use and readily available web application, to create narrated multimedia slideshows. And those who access your VoiceThread presentation can annotate and respond to the content using a simple voice-capture/video-capture function.

Why

The multi-voice feature of VoiceThread makes it a great tool for lectures, presentations, digital storytelling, status reports, peer reviews, and instructor feedback.

Figure 5.25. VoiceThread Course Introductions, Voice Response

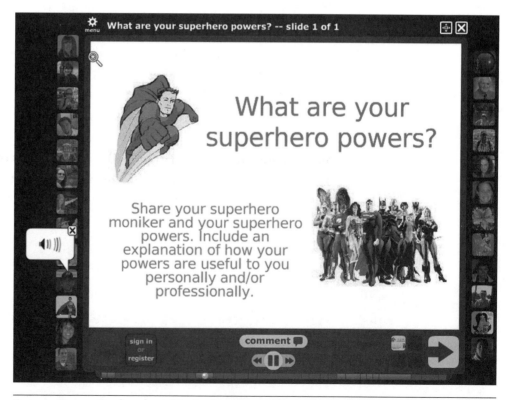

Source: Joanna Dunlap, http://voicethread.com/#q.b38310.i0.k0

Use It!

How

Dunlap and Lowenthal suggest using VoiceThread for:

- **Instructor lectures and mini-lectures:** VoiceThread's functionality allows instructors to quickly and easily create narrated presentation slideshows. Online instructors often struggle with finding easy and inexpensive ways to narrate their presentations—leading many to simply post an un-narrated presentation online. An additional benefit for online instructors is that the slideshows they create reside on the VoiceThread server, limiting the hassle of uploading presentations. Each VoiceThread presentation has a unique URL. VoiceThread presentations may also be embedded in web pages.

- **Learner presentations:** In some online higher education courses, learners need to deliver presentations to demonstrate conceptual understanding, share reflections on an experience (such as an internship), or report out on project status. Online narrated presentations can be technically challenging to create and make available to others. With VoiceThread, learners can easily add narration to a presentation and, because the narrated presentation is stored on the VoiceThread server, learners do not have to worry about uploading the presentation.

- **Central meeting place with advanced commenting features:** Online instructors can use VoiceThread to create a space for learners to present material and share ideas. For example, an instructor could upload a set of slides to VoiceThread, showing various classroom settings and activities. Then the instructor can ask learners to view the images on each slide, and share their perspectives on what they see that reflects effective teaching and what they see that does not. This activity could also be accomplished using a threaded discussion within a higher education course management system, but VoiceThread allows for a more personal (and possibly more complete) response to the prompt because learners can actually talk, as opposed to relying on typing.

- **Personal feedback:** VoiceThread lets instructors of online courses easily give audio feedback on learners' work. VoiceThread can similarly

Figure 5.26. VoiceThread Course Introductions, Text Response

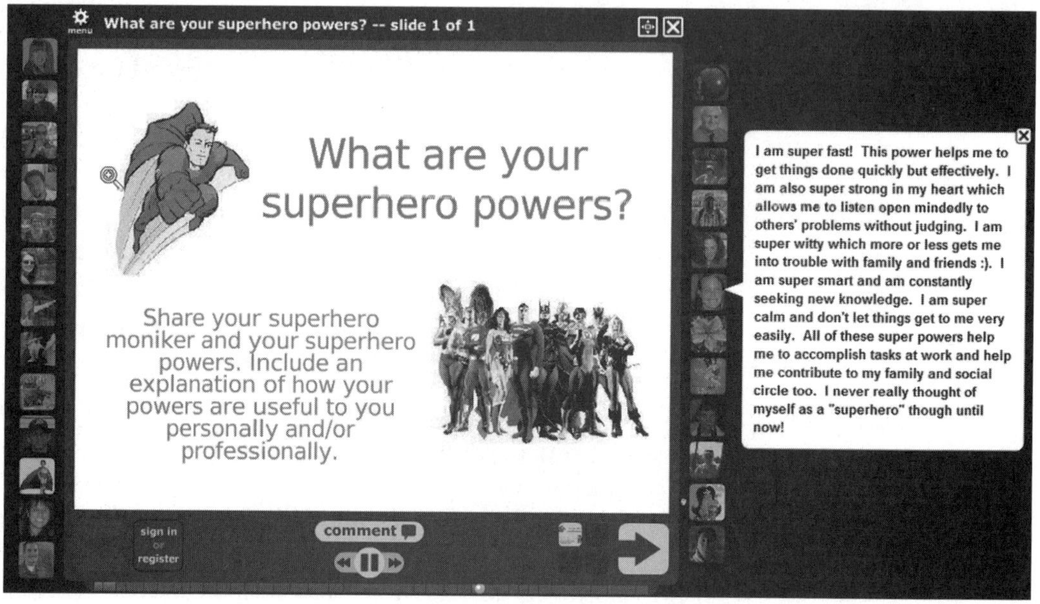

Source: Joanna Dunlap, http://voicethread.com/#q.b38310.i0.k0

be used to provide feedback among peer review groups, making it easy for peers to comment on each other's work.

VoiceThread supports the achievement of universal instructional goals related to social presence, content delivery, demonstration of new learning and comprehension, and learner assessment. The following are just a few of the ways that Dunlap and Lowenthal use VoiceThread in their online courses:

- Social presence: bios, discussion, collaboration activities (see Figures 5.25 and 5.26)

- Content delivery: mini lectures, digital stories, presentations (see Figure 5.27)

Figure 5.27. VoiceThread Digital Storytelling, Text Response

Source: Joanna Dunlap, http://voicethread.com/?#u75498

- Demonstration of new learning and comprehension: student-delivered mini lectures, digital stories, presentations

- Student assessment: peer review, instructor review of learners' work

To create a free account, go to www.voicethread.com. Pick a presentation/ lecture that you might give, upload the associated PowerPoint slideshow to VoiceThread, and use VoiceThread to narrate it. Then invite others to post comments.

Technologies used: VoiceThread web application

Adopt or Adapt

VoiceThread can be used in online higher education courses to support social presence, content delivery, demonstration of new learning and comprehension, and assessment needs. It can also be used to deliver online training content, submit comments on digital media, and share knowledge among members of a team.

Attribution

Submitted by Joanna C. Dunlap, associate professor and faculty fellow for teaching, University of Colorado–Denver, Denver, Colorado, USA

Contact: joni.dunlap@ucdenver.edu

Also involved: Patrick R. Lowenthal, academic technology coordinator, University of Colorado–Denver: CU Online/School of Education and Human Development

Joanna C. Dunlap is an associate professor of instructional design and technology at the University of Colorado–Denver. An award-winning educator, her teaching and research interests focus on the use of sociocultural approaches to enhance adult learners' development and experience in post-secondary settings. For over fifteen years, she has directed, designed, delivered, and facilitated distance and e-learning educational opportunities for a variety of audiences. Joni is also the university's assistant director for teaching effectiveness, working through the Center for Faculty Development to help online and on-campus faculty enhance their teaching practices.

Cheap Stock Photos

The Big Idea

What

This idea shows how to make your own stock photos using a digital camera.

Why

Downloading needed photos from stock photo sites can be expensive. So consider making your own!

Use It!

How

This idea is adapted from The Rapid e-Learning Blog (www.articulate.com/rapid-elearning).

Using a stock image site to find just the right photos can be time-consuming and expensive. Kuhlman suggests creating your own stock images. This approach requires practice, but taking good photos is a cost-effective approach and, with adequate practice, a very viable alternative to expensive stock photos.

Here are Kuhlmann's top tips for producing good stock photos of your own.

- **Flood the area with light.** Many photos appear grainy because there's not enough light. Most photos would benefit greatly from additional light. You can control shadows by bouncing the light off the walls or the ceiling instead of shining it directly on the subject. Or try moving the light source back a little.

- **Keep the image in focus.** One problem with many digital cameras is that the shot looks in focus on a tiny LCD screen, but less so on your computer screen because the camera wasn't held still. To take better pictures, use a tripod or at least rest the camera on a solid surface.

- **Use higher settings for better image quality.** You can't make a bad image good. For the best quality possible from the get go, use a higher resolution setting (see Figure 5.28). You can always reduce the file size later, but you won't be able to make a low-quality image better.

- **Remember the "rule of thirds."** The best pictures will have the subject intersect two perpendicular lines (Figure 5.29). Kuhlman says that his digital camera even has a grid feature to make this easier and he suggests finding out whether yours does, too. He recommends reading this explanation of the law of thirds: http://photoinf.com/General/ KODAK/guidelines_for_better_photographic_composition_rule_of_ thirds.html.

- **Don't take just one shot.** Take as many pictures as you possibly can. It's not film. There are no development costs. The more options you have, the better your choices will be. This is especially valuable when combined with some of the new image-editing applications that can combine similar shots from multiple images to create the "perfect shot."

Figure 5.28. Low Versus Higher Resolution Photo

It is easier editing a high resolution image.

Source: Tom Kuhlmann

Figure 5.29. Using the Law of Thirds

Source: Tom Kuhlmann

- **Create visual interest.** Make photos more interesting by shooting from multiple angles and distances. Take a wide-angle shot. Get another that's closer and tighter. And then do a close-up, or even an extreme close-up. Get down low. Get up high. Tilt the camera a little. You don't want all of your photos to look the same or be from the same angle. Also, try to keep the people from looking at the camera. You want things to look natural.

- **Use "real" people to make the images authentic.** People like to see people they know or at least real people (not actors) in courses. Take advantage of this! But be careful here. There's nothing worse than having John Doe (or your state's governor) in your ethics course and then finding out two weeks later that he was fired for lying, or worse.

- **Obtain signed releases.** You'll need signed releases to make sure all of your bases are covered. Kuhlman suggests this resource for learning more about releases: http://asmp.org/tutorials/property-and-model-releases.html.

- **Share your photos.** Consider putting your photos on a photo-sharing site such as Flickr (www.flickr.com/) and using a Creative Commons license so others can use them, too.

Technologies used: digital camera

Adopt or Adapt

This idea can be useful for any online instruction that uses photos. Shooting your own stock photos can save you a lot of time and money. With a little practice, there's no reason why you can't learn to do a good job.

Attribution

Submitted by Tom Kuhlmann, vice president, community, Articulate, Seattle, Washington, USA

Contact: /www.articulate.com/rapid-elearning/

Tom Kuhlmann writes The Rapid e-Learning Blog, where he shares practical e-learning tips and tricks. He has close to twenty years of experience in the training industry, where he's worked on e-learning projects for both large and small organizations. Currently he manages Articulate's e-learning community.

Silhouette Characters

The Big Idea

What

This idea presents two ways to make silhouette characters for use in online courses and some interesting ways to use them.

Why

Stock photos aren't cheap and are sometimes difficult to come by, so we tend to use the same ones over and over again. One day a group of stock photos represents managers and the next day they're representing customer service agents. The photos tend to be reused too much!

Use It!

How

Silhouette characters can provide you with new image options and make your online courses look a little different. Here are two methods that Kuhlmann shares for producing silhouette characters.

Method 1: Convert PowerPoint grouped images to a silhouette image (see Figure 5.30). (See the PowerPoint Clip Art Surgery idea earlier in this chapter for more information about ungrouping clip art.)

Process

1. Find a grouped clip art image that you want to use.

2. Right-click on the image and select Group>Ungroup. (*Note:* You will notice that some images cannot be ungrouped. You may need to repeat the command.)

3. Select the character (and anything else you want to be silhouetted) and fill with black (Format>Shape Fill>Choose color, as in (Figure 5.31). Kuhlmann suggests using colors in addition to black fills. And you can make use of some of the graphic effects in PowerPoint to add variety.

4. Right-click on the image and select Group>Regroup.

Figure 5.30. Silhouette from PowerPoint Clip Art

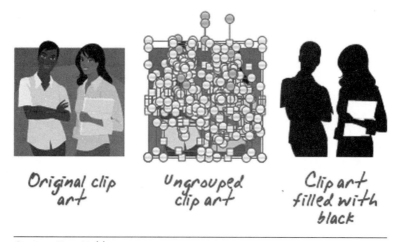

Source: Tom Kuhlmann

Figure 5.31. Colors and Effects on Silhouettes

Source: Tom Kuhlmann

Figure 5.32. Silhouette from a Photo

Original image *Remove background* *Fill image with black*

Source: Tom Kuhlmann

Method 2: Convert photos to a silhouette image. This method involves separating the character from the background in a photo and then re-coloring the character with a solid color. This is a great trick because you can shoot your own photos and not worry about lighting and getting the best image. As long as it is clear and has the right pose, you're fine. Once it's filled no one can tell what the original looked like. (See Figure 5.32.)

Process

1. Find the photo that you want to use.

2. Open the photo in an image-editing application (such as Photoshop (www.adobe.com/products/photoshop/photoshop/ whatisphotoshop/), Photoshop Elements (www.adobe.com/ products/photoshopel/), Artweaver (www.artweaver.de/products-en/artweaver-plus/features/), or a free tool such as paint.net (www .getpaint.net/).

3. Remove the background. (*Note:* You may need to use the program's help topics to find out how to do this, but most image editors make this possible.) A tutorial on creating transparent backgrounds in Artweaver is at http://screenr.com/T5S. PowerPoint

2007 and 2010 also offers a very simple background removal feature (Picture Tools>Recolor>Set Transparent Color).

4. Fill the character's shape with a solid color and save the image.

Silhouettes can help focus the learner's attention. For example, in the top of Figure 5.33 you see a group of people in an office. The learner clicks on

Figure 5.33. Silhouettes Narrow Focus

Silhouette used to isolate person or idea.

Source: Tom Kuhlmann

an employee to learn more. When that happens, to focus attention on just that one employee, the learner goes to another slide, where the others in the picture have become silhouettes.

Technologies used: PowerPoint, digital photos, image-editing program

Adopt or Adapt

Using silhouettes is an easy solution to having enough images to use in your online courses and creating something that is also visually compelling. Look at how silhouettes are used in advertising and print media to get some ideas that you can adapt in your courses.

Attribution

Submitted by Tom Kuhlmann, vice president, community, Articulate, Seattle, Washington, USA

Contact: /www.articulate.com/rapid-elearning/

Tom Kuhlmann writes The Rapid e-Learning Blog, where he shares practical e-learning tips and tricks. He has close to twenty years of experience in the training industry, where he's worked on e-learning projects for both large and small organizations. Currently he manages Articulate's e-learning community.

Create Polaroid-Like Images

The Big Idea

What

This idea shows how to create Polaroid-like images with digital photos using the Poladroid application.

Why

This is a really fun way to present images in online courses!

Use It!

How

This idea is adapted from The Rapid e-Learning Blog (www.articulate.com/rapid-elearning).

The free Poladroid application (www.poladroid.net/index.php?do=faq) lets instructors create Polaroid-like images for use in online courses. The application is really easy to use.

To create Polaroid-like images:

1. Download the application and install it (simple and fast).

2. Drag a digital photo onto the camera (Figure 5.34).

3. The image "develops" before your eyes (Figure 5.35). When the image is ready for use, a notification sounds and the image is marked with a red icon.

4. The final image file (Figure 5.36) is a .jpg file. It is located either in the original image folder or in a folder you select.

Kuhlmann recommends adding a curled edge drop shadow (Figure 5.37) to these images for additional realism and suggests reviewing David Anderson's screencast to learn how to do this (http://screenr.com/pV8).

Figure 5.34. Drag Digital Photo onto the Camera

Source: Poladroid application

Figure 5.35. Picture "Develops"

Source: Poladroid application

Figure 5.36. Final Image

Source: Poladroid Application and Patti Shank's cat, Redd

Figure 5.37. Image with Curled-Edge Shadow and Transparent Tape Effects

Source: Tom Kuhlmann

Kuhlmann also recommends adding a transparent tape effect to these images and recommends Stephanie Harnett's screencast to learn how to do this (http://screenr.com/aGh).

Technologies used: Poladroid application

Adopt or Adapt

These images can be put to use many ways in online courses. A great example is to create a screen that mimics a desktop or personnel folder. Then add the Poladroid images to them to add a little personality. You can use the images as hyperlinks to additional content. Or they can be used to tell a story using photos.

Attribution

Submitted by Tom Kuhlmann, vice president, community, Articulate, Seattle, Washington, USA

Contact: /www.articulate.com/rapid-elearning/

Tom Kuhlmann writes The Rapid e-Learning Blog, where he shares practical e-learning tips and tricks. He has close to twenty years of experience in the training industry, where he's worked on e-learning projects for both large and small organizations. Currently he manages Articulate's e-learning community.

Word Clouds

The Big Idea

What

This idea shows how a web application can create word clouds, a visual representation that shows the prominence of words in source text.

Why

A visual representation of the words in a passage of text is useful as a preview of the concepts about to be presented or as a review in an online course. They are visually engaging as well!

Use It!

How

Word clouds show words that appear more frequently in the source text larger and in different colors from words that appear less often. Wordle (www.wordle.net/) allows you to select fonts, layouts, and color schemes to get the effect you are looking for. You can share your Wordle images in any of the following ways: print out on paper or as a PDF file, do a screen capture and save as an image file, or save to the Wordle public gallery and share the URL with others.

A Wordle can be used in a variety of ways, such as to visually introduce topics and to provide a visual representation of the concepts discussed in an online (text-based) discussion. Famous speeches and news articles can also be made into engaging word clouds.

Morris creates visual word clouds of text using Wordle for her online courses. She has used Wordle word clouds for the following purposes:

- Introduce a topic or concept by visually representing the text in an assigned reading

- Assign learners to generate a Wordle with the text in their written work

- Wrap up discussion question responses by visually representing the text in learner written responses. The image in Figure 5.38 shows a Wordle that was created based on learner responses to the question, "What do you hope to learn from this course?"

Technologies used: online web application

Figure 5.38. Wordle Word Cloud with Learner Responses

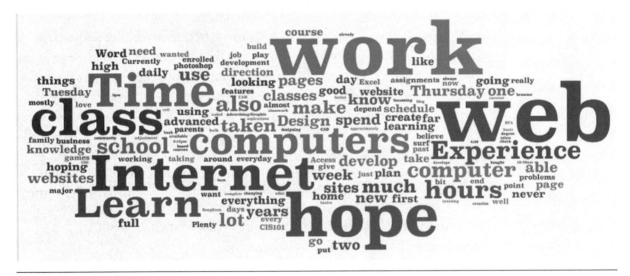

Source: Terry A. Morris

Figure 5.39. Tagxedo Word Cloud for Gettysburg Address

Source: Terry A. Morris

Adopt or Adapt

This idea can be used in almost any content area and in both higher education and corporate settings. It could also be used to create a visual representation of the topic for presentations. In addition to Wordle, some of the other word cloud creators include TagCrowd (http://tagcrowd. com/) and Tagxedo (www.tagxedo.com/). Tagxedo (Figure 5.39) lets you constrain your word cloud into specific shapes—cool!

Attribution

Submitted by Terry A. Morris, associate professor, Harper College, Palatine, Illinois, USA

Contact: tmorris@harpercollege.edu or http://terrymorris.net

An associate professor at Harper College, Dr. Terry A. Morris has developed and taught online courses since 1999 in the subject areas of web development, computer fundamentals, and instructional technology. She has written several web development textbooks, including *Basics of Web Design* and the fifth edition of *Web Development & Design Foundations with XHTML*. Dr. Morris is a recipient of the Instructional Technology Council's 2008 Outstanding e-Learning Faculty Award for Excellence, the 2008 MERLOT Business Classics Award, and the 2006 Blackboard Greenhouse Exemplary Course Award (Online Course Category).

EZ Forms

The Big Idea

What

Online forms are a great way to collect data from learners, but until recently, only technologically savvy instructors had the skill-set to create, use, and maintain forms in their online courses. Now instructors can easily create online forms using Google Docs.

Why

Forms, whether they are created using Google Docs (http://docs.google .com/) or another application, let instructors obtain data from learners to help them improve their courses, collect and publish resource lists, and create templates for projects.

Use It!

How

Instructors can easily create forms using the "form" tool in Google Docs for their online courses, embed forms into their course management systems, collect the data submitted by learners, and finally (if they choose), publish the results for anyone to see.

Forms can accomplish a number of things that are extraordinarily useful when teaching online (or face-to-face) courses. They provide an easy way to collect data about how the course is going (Figure 5.40). While end-of-course evaluations are helpful when it comes to improving a course for the following semester, they do little good for fixing problems in the here and now. Instructors can use forms (whether anonymous or not) throughout their course (as frequently as once a week or at certain key intervals—for instance once a month—throughout the semester) to see how things are going and to make any changes before the course is over.

Forms are useful for collecting and publishing resources from learners. For instance, instructors can ask learners to submit a list of annotated online

Figure 5.40. Google Docs Form for Course Feedback

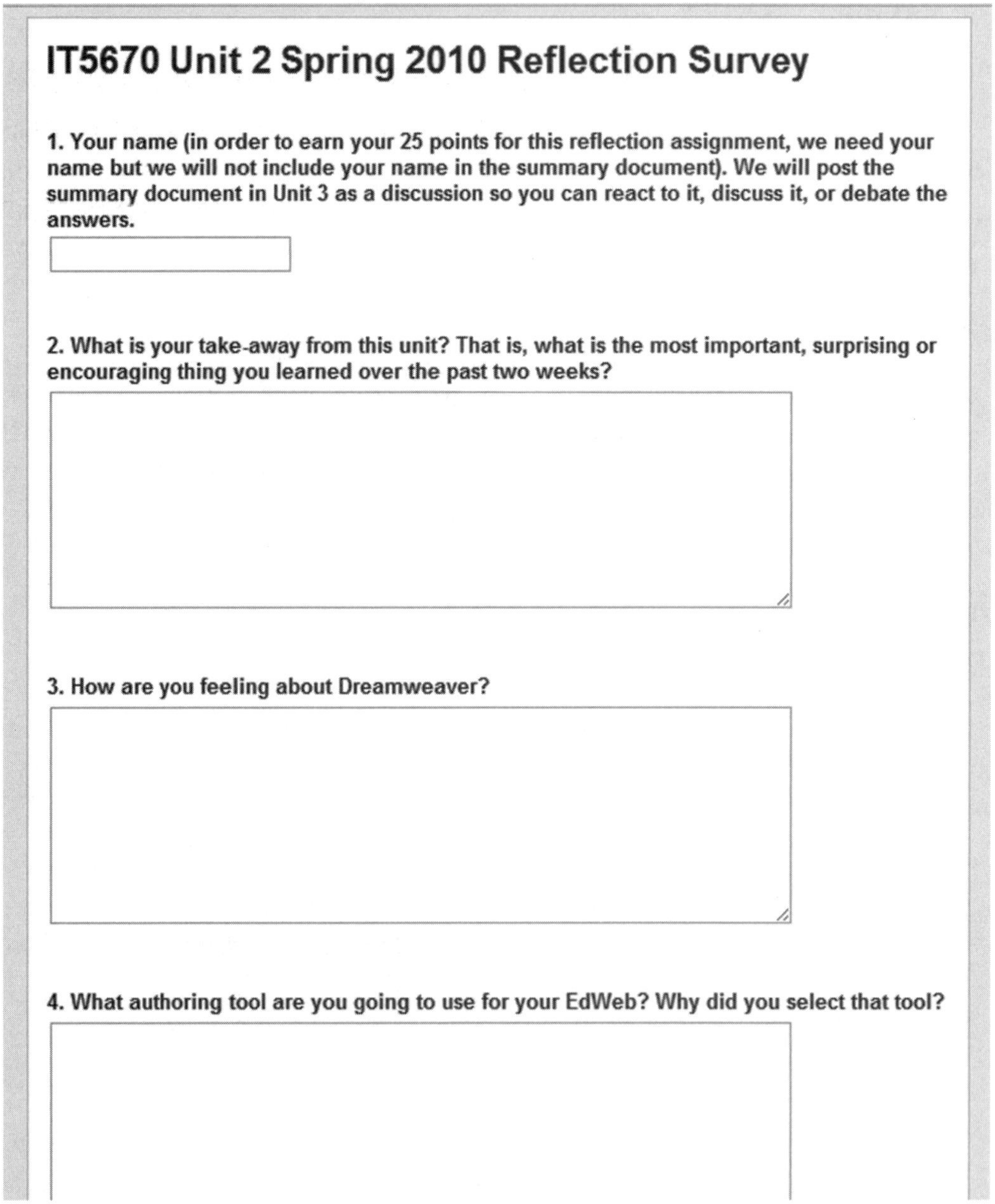

IT5670 Unit 2 Spring 2010 Reflection Survey

1. Your name (in order to earn your 25 points for this reflection assignment, we need your name but we will not include your name in the summary document). We will post the summary document in Unit 3 as a discussion so you can react to it, discuss it, or debate the answers.

2. What is your take-away from this unit? That is, what is the most important, surprising or encouraging thing you learned over the past two weeks?

3. How are you feeling about Dreamweaver?

4. What authoring tool are you going to use for your EdWeb? Why did you select that tool?

Source: Patrick Lowenthal

resources (sometimes called a webliography) that instructors can publish and make available online, as shown in Figure 5.41.

Figure 5.41. Google Docs Form for Annotated Resource List

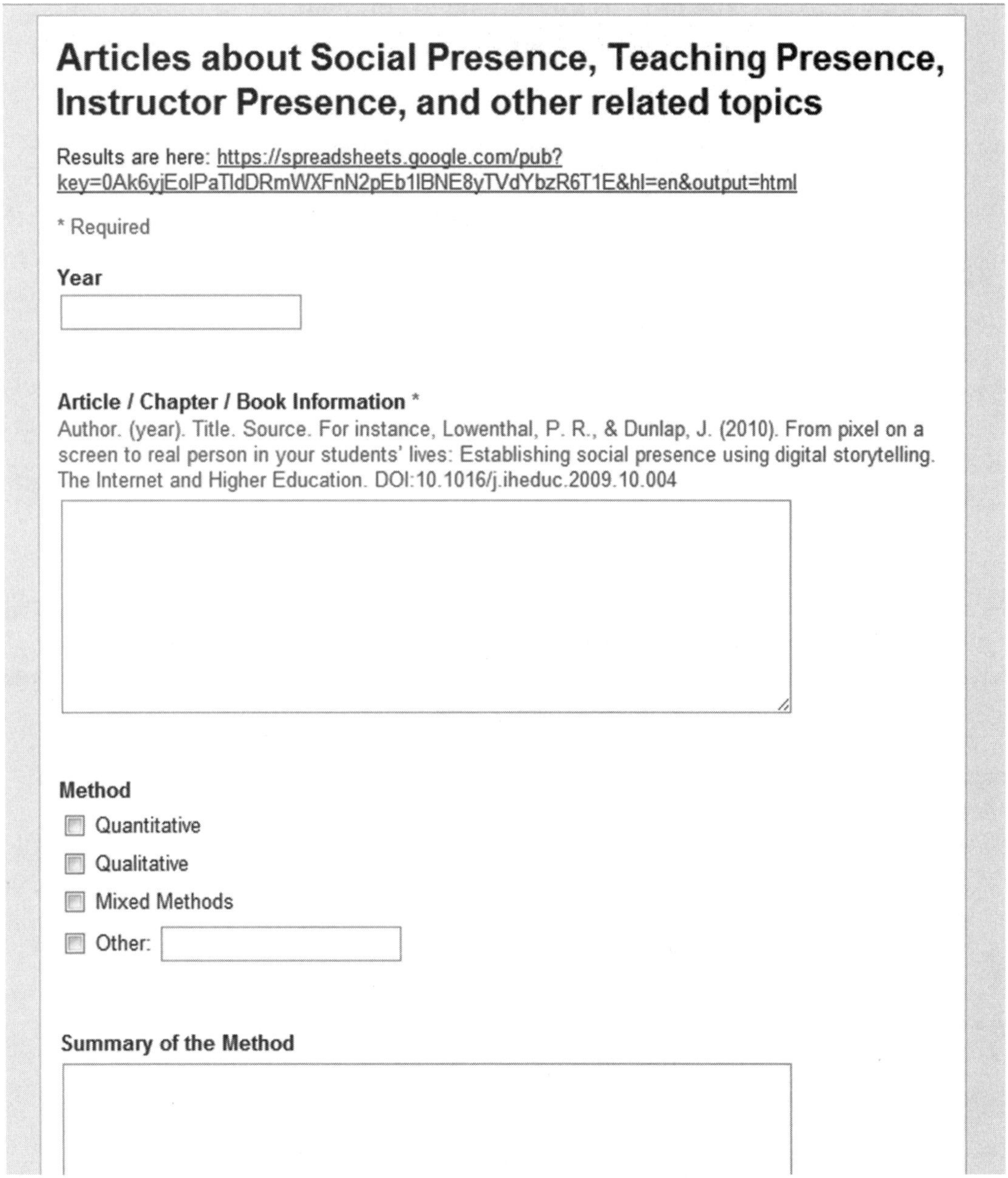

Articles about Social Presence, Teaching Presence, Instructor Presence, and other related topics

Results are here: https://spreadsheets.google.com/pub?
key=0Ak6yjEolPaTldDRmWXFnN2pEb1lBNE8yTVdYbzR6T1E&hl=en&output=html

* Required

Year

Article / Chapter / Book Information *
Author. (year). Title. Source. For instance, Lowenthal, P. R., & Dunlap, J. (2010). From pixel on a screen to real person in your students' lives: Establishing social presence using digital storytelling. The Internet and Higher Education. DOI:10.1016/j.iheduc.2009.10.004

Method
- ☐ Quantitative
- ☐ Qualitative
- ☐ Mixed Methods
- ☐ Other:

Summary of the Method

Source: Patrick Lowenthal

Instructors can also use forms as templates that learners can use to complete a project. For example, an instructor may want learners to describe the projects they intend to complete, so an online template would be valuable for assuring that all projects are described according to the same guidelines.

While most higher education course management systems (e.g., Blackboard) offer some type of survey tool, instructors are limited in how they use it and the results are contained in the system and, therefore, typically no longer available to learners after the course is over. And very few of them make it possible to deliver anonymous surveys.

To start, all you need is a Google account and access to Google Docs (Figure 5.42). From there, find the tool and create the form (Figure 5.43).

With a few clicks of the mouse you can have a form that can then be embedded into your course management system.

Figure 5.42. The Form Tool in Google Docs

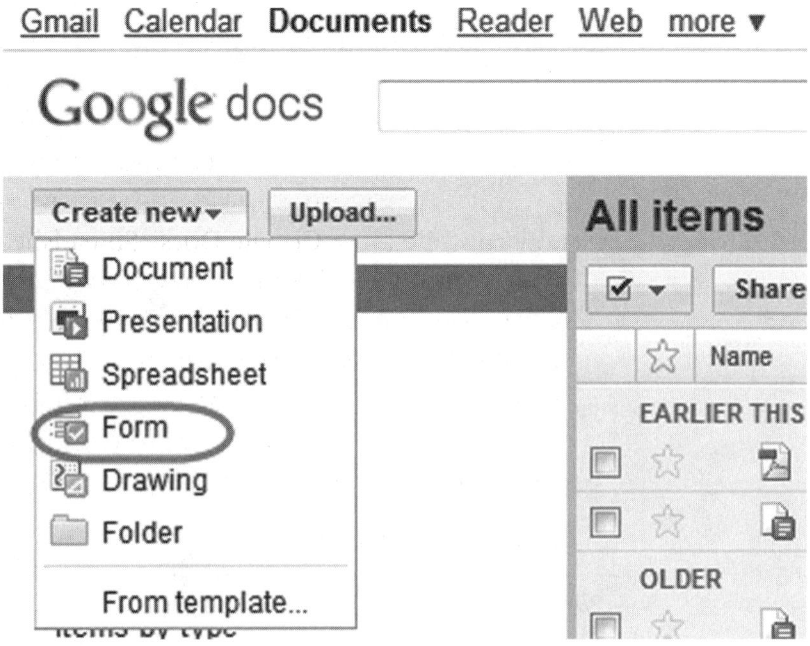

Source: Google Docs

Figure 5.43. Google Docs Form Creator

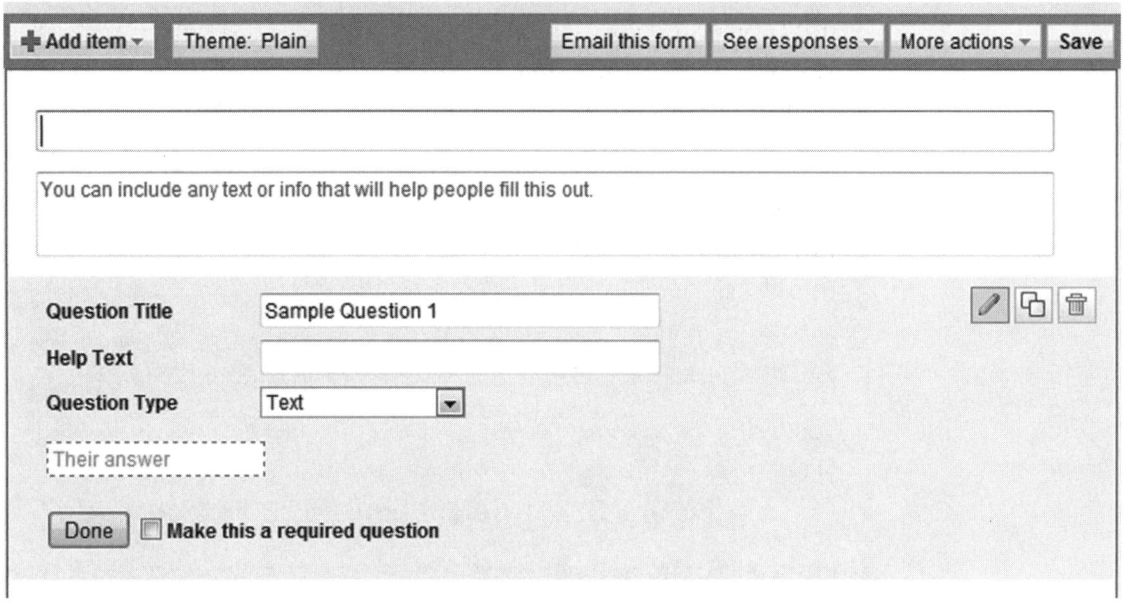

Source: Google Docs

To embed the form, simply click "More Actions" when editing the form and then "Embed." You will then be provided with some embed code (in the form of an iframe) that can be copy/pasted into your course management system. When it comes time to view and share the results (if you wish), you can simply publish them, as shown in Figure 5.44 (now compiled in a Google Docs "Spreadsheet") by clicking on the "Share" button and "Publish as web page"(Figure 5.45) or, if you want to aggregate the results and comment on them, you can do a File > Download As > Excel sheet, which then can be copied and pasted into a word processing program, as in Figure 5.46 (such as Google Docs or Word) and distributed as you see fit (e.g., by email or in the course management system, as seen in Figure 5.47).

Technologies used: Google Docs

Figure 5.44. Select Publish to Share Results

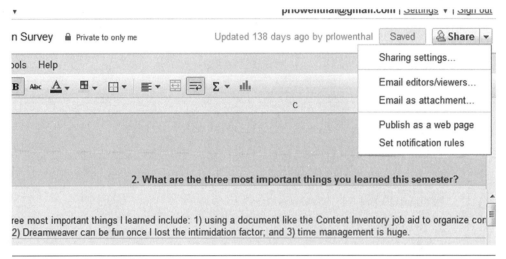

Source: Patrick Lowenthal

Figure 5.45. Select Embed to Embed Code

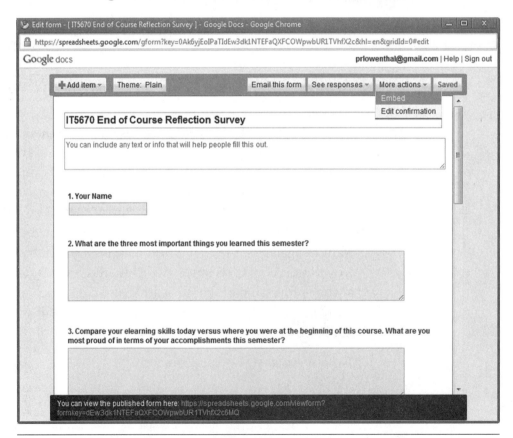

Source: Patrick Lowenthal

Figure 5.46. Embed Code to Paste into a Blog or Website

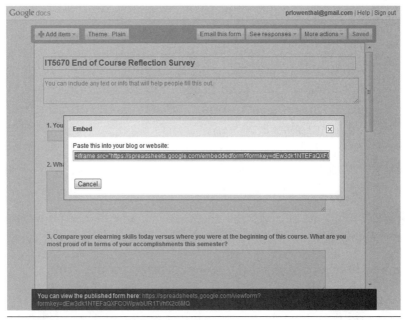

Source: Patrick Lowenthal

Figure 5.47. Google Docs Form Embedded in Course Management System

Source: Patrick Lowenthal

Adopt or Adapt

The ability to collect data to improve courses, collect and publish resource lists, and create templates for projects can be useful in any kind of online or classroom-based higher education course. You could also use forms for synchronous and self-paced corporate training for the same purposes.

Attribution

Submitted by Patrick R. Lowenthal, academic technology coordinator, University of Colorado–Denver, Denver, Colorado, USA

Contact: patrick.lowenthal@ucdenver.edu or www.patricklowenthal.com

Also involved: Joanna C. Dunlap, associate professor and faculty fellow for teaching, University of Colorado–Denver and Jacquie Dobrovolny, adjunct professor, University of Colorado–Denver, and owner of Triple Play: All Bases Covered

Patrick R. Lowenthal is an academic technology coordinator at the University of Colorado–Denver (UCD), where he supports faculty who teach online. He also regularly teaches online in the master of arts in e-learning design and implementation program at UCD. Prior to coming to UCD, Patrick spent a number of years at Regis University as an assistant professor of instructional technology. Patrick is currently a doctoral student finishing his studies in instructional design and technology at UCD. His research interests focus on teaching and learning online, with a specific focus on social and teaching presence.

Recording Better Audio

The Big Idea

What

This idea provides some techniques to use for producing better audio files for your online courses.

Why

If the audio quality in your narrated PowerPoint slides and online course is not very good, it detracts from the course and makes it seem less professional.

Use It!

How

This idea is adapted from The Rapid e-Learning Blog (www.articulate.com/rapid-elearning).

Some people use professional voice talent to produce the narration for their online courses, but this may not be an option if resources are tight. Here are Kuhlmann's tips for producing good audio files.

1. Purchase a good microphone. A good microphone is going to give you better audio quality than a poor microphone. This isn't to say that you can't make do with an inexpensive microphone. For the most part, they work fine, especially if you follow some of the other tips. But the truth is that when you compare the acceptable low-quality audio with similar narration recorded with a better microphone, there is a noticeable difference.

The good news is that you don't have to spend a lot to get a decent microphone for recording narration. Kuhlmann says he's had success with a Plantronics headset with microphone such as the Plantronics DSP400 and a Samsung Go Microphone Compact USB microphone. He says he's heard good things about the Blue Microphones Snowball USB microphone as well. Kuhlman prefers a desktop microphone because it gives him better control over the audio quality.

He also prefers a unidirectional microphone over an omnidirectional microphone. A unidirectional microphone records sound from one direction so only picks up the sound coming from the narrator. An omnidirectional microphone is likely to pick up more ambient noise.

2. Place your microphone in the right position. If you place the microphone too close to the narrator's mouth, you get a distorted clipping sound, and if it is too far from the source, you pick up more ambient noise. The best distance for the microphone is 6 to 12 inches from the narrator's mouth. Do a few test recordings to see what sounds best.

3. Maintain a consistent environment. The more you control the recording environment, the better quality audio you will record. One key is to develop a consistent routine for recording. By maintaining a consistent environment, you're better able to match the audio quality when you do retakes. Here are Kuhlmann's tips for developing a consistent environment:

- Use the same room and maintain the same settings on your computer and the same microphone setup.

- If you're using a desktop microphone, use a microphone stand and measure the recording distance so that the next time you record you have the same setup and use the same distance.

- Use a microphone screen to help prevent the popping p's that plague so many amateur recording sessions.

4. Get rid of ambient noise. There's very rarely a time when there is complete silence. But you do want to get rid of whatever noise you have control over. Here are Kuhlmann's tips for getting rid of ambient noise:

- Unplug office machines. Turn off fans and air conditioners.

- Place your microphone away from your computer. Your computer fan actually makes a lot of noise. And keep your microphone cord away from your computer's power cord.

- Let the people around you know you are recording and need quiet. Put signs on the door. Do whatever you have to do to keep the area as quiet as possible.

5. Dampen the sound. Recording studios have walls that absorb the sound waves. You can do something similar by using cubicle walls, which are designed to absorb sound. Even better, drag a cubicle into a room and close the door. You can also cover walls with blankets. Kuhlman suggests looking into a Porta-Booth, a portable sound booth. See www.harlanhogan.com/portaboothArticle.shtml for more information.

6. Record silence before and after speaking. By recording some silence, you won't cut off the narration accidently at the beginning or end of your narration clips. And having a recording of the ambient noise makes it possible to sample just the ambient noise and use a noise removal process in an audio editing program to filter it out later.

7. Don't slouch or ad-lib while recording. You'll feel more energized and be able to breathe better if you stand up while recording. If you do sit, don't slouch. Sit up straight and keep your chin up.

Stick to the script and don't ad-lib. Odds are that you'll have to do multiple takes, even with a script. If you ad-lib, you'll rarely have the same break points for editing. Sticking with the script lets you follow along with the audio and find a common edit point on re-takes.

Kuhlmann recommends free applications that can be used to create and edit better audio:

- Audacity (http://audacity.sourceforge.net/) for audio recording and editing

- Myna (www.aviary.com/tools/audio-editor) for online audio editing without needing to download an application

- Levelator (www.conversationsnetwork.org/levelator) to adjust the audio levels in your narration

Kuhlman recommends, in addition to recording narration, that you consider recording your own sound effects. For example, need some ambient office noise? Just set up a microphone in a busy area and record the audio. Or try the cafeteria.

Technologies used: microphone, audio creation and editing tools

Adopt or Adapt

Good audio is necessary if you are going to use audio, so use these tips and get better audio!

Attribution

Submitted by Tom Kuhlmann, vice president, community, Articulate, Seattle, Washington, USA

Contact: /www.articulate.com/rapid-elearning/

Tom Kuhlmann writes The Rapid e-Learning Blog, where he shares practical e-learning tips and tricks. He has close to twenty years of experience in the training industry, where he's worked on e-learning projects for both large and small organizations. Currently he manages Articulate's e-learning community.

Easy Mobile Learning Content: PowerPoint to MP4

The Big Idea

What

Many instructors want to create mobile learning content but don't want to invest in building custom applications or expensive mobile platform solutions. This idea shows how to use PowerPoint and free or almost free screen-recording tools to quickly develop engaging content for smart phones using MP4 video.

Why

Mobile learning is beginning to take off. Many learners have phones with advanced capabilities and the ability to play MP4 videos, so it makes sense to use these capabilities for instruction.

Use It!

How

Here's a simple way to start creating narrated, animated MP4 mobile learning content for smart phones with a few simple tools.

Sceenr (http://screenr.com/) and Jing (www.techsmith.com/jing/) are two of the many web tools that let instructors record anything that appears on a computer screen and immediately turn that into an MP4 "movie."

These two tools let instructors capture what is on a screen and immediately share the content online in Flash format or download it as an MP4 file. With Screenr, the MP4 file download is free; with Jing a Pro account is required.

Here are the steps to create a short MP4 video of animated, narrated PowerPoint content with Screenr. (The approach for Jing and other tools is very similar.)

Figure 5.48. Aspect Ratios for PowerPoint, iPhone, and BlackBerry Curve

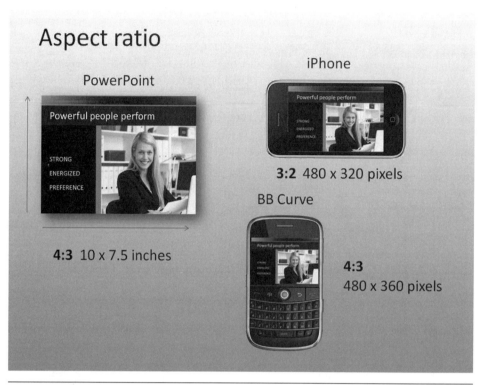

Source: Paul Clothier

1. Develop your content in PowerPoint, making sure that you have the same aspect ratio as the smart phone screen that will be viewing it (see Figure 5.48). Ensure that your font sizes and diagrams with be easily read on the mobile screen.

2. Add custom animations, if desired.

3. Choose Slide Show>Set Up Slide Show and change the show type to Browsed by an individual (window). (See Figure 5.49.)

4. Run the slideshow (Slide Show>From Beginning) and adjust the window to a suitable size to be screen-recorded (about twice the size of your mobile screen).

Figure 5.49. Set Up Slide Show to Play in Window

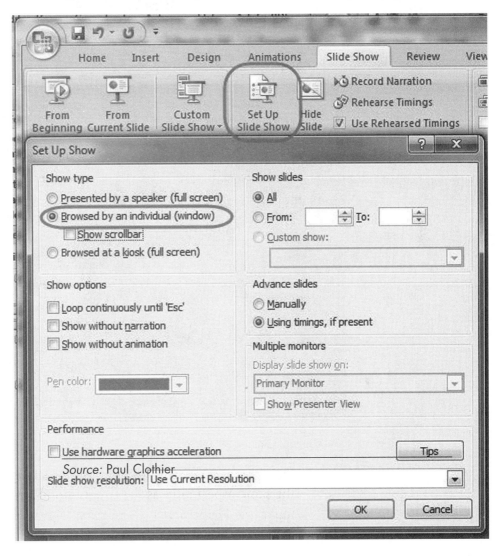

5. Go to Screenr and click **Record your screencast now!** Screenr will place a frame on your desktop. Resize the frame to record just inside the PowerPoint slide show, as in Figure 5.50.

6. Click the red button to start recording. Start the slide show. Record narration to go with each slide and animation.

7. Click the DONE button when you are finished (maximum five minutes).

Figure 5.50. Drag Frame Around What You Want to Record

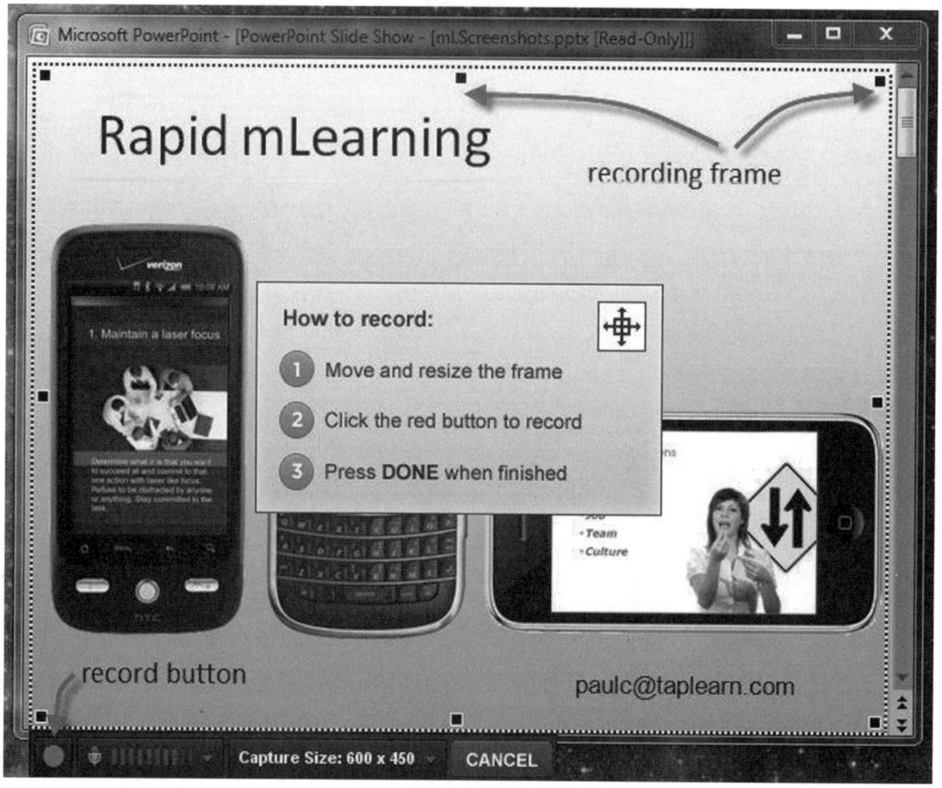

Source: Paul Clothier

8. When the preview appears on the Screenr website, click on the Don't tweet this screencast. I will tweet it through Twitter manually checkbox.

9. Type in a description and then click the Post it button.

10. When it finishes publishing, first click on the Download the MP4 file link on the right under More Actions. If you don't want the Flash file to remain on Screenr, click the Delete this screencast link on the right under More Actions.

11. You can distribute the MP4 file as you wish (email, a file manager app, a web application, etc.).

Screenr has a limit of five minutes of recording, but for mobile use this should be adequate for most projects. If you need to produce a longer MP4, use a screen recording tool like Camtasia that can publish to MP4.

Technologies used: PowerPoint, screen recording application

Adopt or Adapt

This idea can be adopted for any content you might show on PowerPoint slides! If you have pre-existing Flash content, you can also use this technique to record it and convert to MP4.

Attribution

Submitted by Paul Chothier, principal, TapLearn, Sausalito, California, USA

Contact: paulc@taplearn.com or www.taplearn.com

Paul Clothier is a learning specialist, e-learning and mobile learning developer, speaker, and writer who has been in the technology training and learning field for over twenty-five years. A published author, his articles on e-learning and mobile learning have been featured in numerous learning and training magazines. He has a special interest in mobile learning and instructional design for small screens.. Paul is the principal of TapLearn, a mobile learning consultancy.

Rollover Slidelets for Nonrectangular Rollover Areas in Captivate 5

The Big Idea

What

This idea shows how to use a rollover slidelet in Captivate 5 when you want to create a rollover for a nonrectangular shape.

Why

Rollover slidelets allow for nonrectangular rollover areas. By using a rollover slidelet rather than a rollover image or a rollover caption, you can display much more than an image or caption.

Use It!

How

In Captivate, a rollover slidelet is a specific area on a slide that responds to a mouse rolling over it by displaying a slidelet, a slide within a slide, which has much of the functionality of a regular slide. For example, you can create a rollover map slidelet that shows facts about each portion of the map when a mouse moves over it, complete with captions, image, video, and more.

One cool feature of rollover slidelets is the ability to make the rollover area any shape you wish. This is especially useful when you have a photo, diagram, or other image that has interlocking areas (the dark portion of Figure 5.51), any or all of which could serve as a rollover area. Examples might include adjoining countries on a map or the organs of the human body. Let's look at a simple example in the following image.

If you would like users to roll over each of the colors, it would be difficult to use rectangular areas, even if you only wish to show a caption or an image when rolling over an area. For example, rolling over the dark area in the middle of the image on the next page requires a rollover area the same shape as the dark area, not a rectangular one. If you use a rectangle,

Figure 5.51. Image with Interlocking Areas

Source: Joseph Ganci

such as is required by a rollover caption or rollover image, and the cursor is where you see it in Figure 5.52 during playback, it would trigger the caption or image.

Figure 5.52. Rollover of Intersection Area

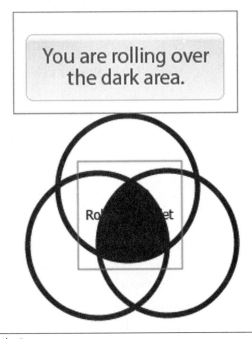

Source: Joseph Ganci

Figure 5.53. Insert Desired Rollover Contents

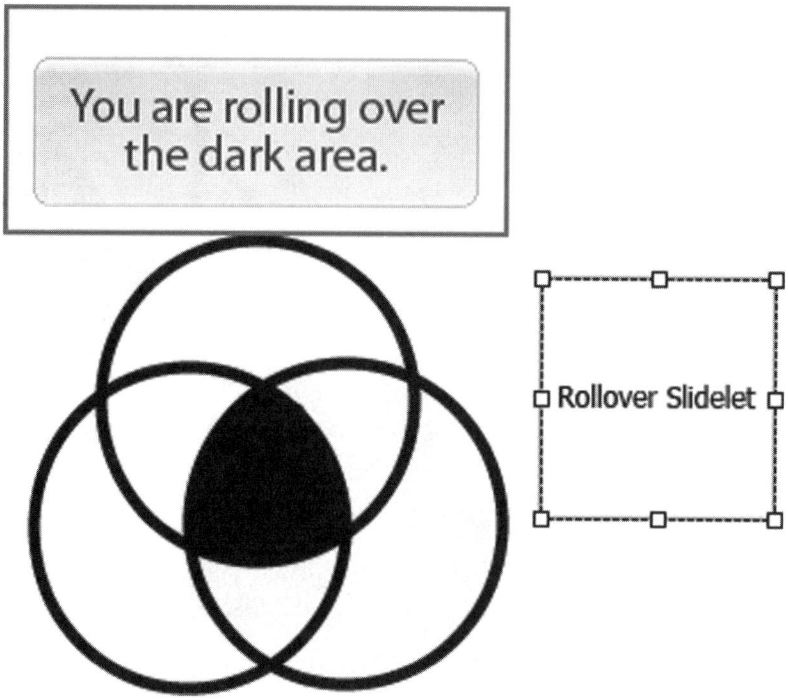

Source: Joseph Ganci

Here's how to make this work.

1. Insert an image. Insert → Image. (See Figure 5.53.)

2. Choose Insert → Standard Object → Rollover Slidelet.

3. Resize the slidelet as desired and add the text or image into the slidelet that you wish to see when the user rolls over the area. Place it in the desired position on the stage. Move the rollover area to where you can work with it, away from the image.

4. Right-click the rollover slidelet and choose Redraw Shape. Alternatively, click once on the rollover slidelet and choose Edit → Redraw Shape or press Ctrl-Alt-W.

5. Your rollover slidelet will disappear and your cursor will change into a crosshair.

6. Click on the image where you wish to start the rollover slide-let area. Then move the mouse and you will see a line drawn from the click point to where the cursor is at the moment. Click again and the line will become the first segment of your rollover area.

7. Continue to click to create new segments. When you have finished drawing the rollover area, double-click the mouse and the area will be closed.

8. While you still see a rectangle with handles around it, notice the internal blue lines that represent the true rollover area. When played back, the slidelet will be activated only when the cursor falls within the blue-lined area.

Technologies used: Captivate 5

Adopt or Adapt

This idea is useful for providing additional information about non-rectangular areas of a slide. For example, an instructor may want to provide an image with additional details, a diagram, or a video that appears when the mouse rolls over specific muscles or certain parts of a product.

Attribution

Submitted by Joseph Ganci, president, Dazzler Technologies Corp., Asburn, Virginia, USA

Contact: jganci@dazzletech.com or www. dazzletech.com

Since 1983, Joseph Ganci has been involved in every aspect of multimedia and learning development. Joe holds a degree in computer science and has written and continues to write many books and articles about e-learning. He is widely considered a guru for his expertise in e-learning development and teaches classes and seminars at leading universities, in many government facilities, commercial firms, and educational institutions. He speaks at several industry conferences each year. He is on a mission to improve the quality of e-learning with practical approaches that work.

Easier Multi-Language Captivate 5 Application Simulations—Captions

The Big Idea
What

This idea provides tips for creating Captivate 5 simulations that need to be delivered in more than one language. It specifically focuses on efficiently changing the captions for each language.

Why

This process is a lot more efficient than using the Captivate 5 Recording Settings dialog box and rerecording the project over again in each language.

Use It!
How

When you create a simulation in Captivate 5, you can choose from one of several available languages as one of the options under the *Settings* button in the recording dialog box. If you need to deliver your simulation in more than one language, you can rerecord the same steps in each language. This is not too bad if your simulations are short, but inefficient if you have many simulations to record or if the simulations are longer.

There is a more efficient way to create simulations in multiple languages that will ensure that each language version will show the exact same simulation with no variations except for the language.

Let's see how to create a Captivate demonstration that shows learners how to open the Symbol dialog box in Word. We want to produce the demonstration in English, French, and Spanish. Before recording the steps in Captivate:

1. Open and prepare Word so that it is ready for recording. For instance, size the Word app to the height and width you wish.

Figure 5.54. Select Language

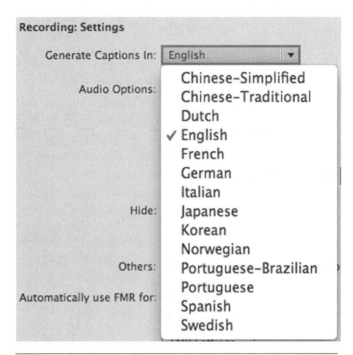

Source: Joseph Ganci

Open the Symbol dialog box and make sure it's located where you wish it to appear during the simulation.

2. Reset everything in the application you wish to simulate to an initial state so that you can begin the simulation capture. In this case, close the Symbol box.

Now you are ready to create the demonstration. When you have completed it, save the Captivate movie to a file, for instance *wordSymbol.cptx.*

Creating Multi-Language Versions—Captions

1. Copy the Captivate movie for each language, for instance, wordSymbol_English.cptx, wordSymbol_Spanish.cptx and wordSymbol_French.cptx.

2. Now you are ready to create the non-English versions. Let's start with the French version. Open the French version, wordSymbol_French.cptx. As part of the capture process, Captivate automatically created caption boxes in English as a default.

3. Choose File>Export>Project Captions and Closed Captions. Save the export file and allow Captivate to automatically open the resulting Word document. It will be named the same as your Captivate file except the extension will be doc instead of cptx.

4. The Word document will open and will show a table like the one below. Notice the Updated Text Caption Data column. This is where you will be making changes.

Slide ID	Item ID	Original Text Caption Data	Updated Text Caption Data	Slide
10102	10116	Select the **Insert** menu	Select the **Insert** menu	1
10117	10130	Select the **Symbol** . . . menu item	Select the **Symbol** . . . menu item	3
10131	10136	The **Symbol** dialog opens	The **Symbol** dialog opens	5
10137	10157	Click the **Insert** button	Click the **Insert** button	6
10150	10172	Click the **Close** button	Click the **Close** button	7

5. **Don't** make any changes in any column except the one with the header *Updated Text Caption Data.* In that column, change the text to the desired French version. This is a Word document, so use any and all tools available to you to make life as simple as possible, for instance copy and paste, search and replace, etc. Here's the same Word table after we've made changes to the fourth column.

Slide ID	Item ID	Original Text Caption Data	Updated Text Caption Data	Slide
10102	10116	Select the **Insert** menu	Sélectionnez le menu **Insert**	1
10117	10130	Select the **Symbol** . . . menu item	Sélectionnez le menu **Symbol** . . .	3
10131	10136	The **Symbol** dialog opens	La boîte de dialogue **Symbol** s'ouvre	5
10137	10157	Click the **Insert** button	Cliquez sur le bouton **Insert**	6
10150	10172	Click the **Close** button	Cliquez sur le bouton **Close**	7

Note that you can only input text into these cells. If you include images, for instance, they will be ignored when this file is imported into Captivate.

6. Save the caption Word document and return to your Captivate source file. Choose File>Import>Project Captions and Closed Captions and import the Word document you just saved that contains the updated captions.

7. All the captions will change to reflect the changes you made in the Word document. Save your Captivate source file.

8. Repeat this process for other language version files.

You now have a separate Captivate file for each language and each file has captions in the desired language.

Technologies used: Captivate 5, Microsoft Word

Adopt or Adapt

This idea is adaptable for all Captivate projects that use captions and need to be produced in multiple languages.

Attribution

Submitted by Joseph Ganci, president, Dazzler Technologies Corp., Asburn, Virginia, USA

Contact: jganci@dazzletech.com or www. dazzletech.com

Since 1983, Joseph Ganci has been involved in every aspect of multimedia and learning development. Joe holds a degree in computer science and has written and continues to write many books and articles about e-learning. He is widely considered a guru for his expertise in e-learning development and teaches classes and seminars at leading universities, in many government facilities, commercial firms, and educational institutions. He speaks at several industry conferences each year. He is on a mission to improve the quality of e-learning with practical approaches that work.

Easier Multi-Language Captivate 5
Simulations—Narration

The Big Idea

What

This idea provides tips for creating Captivate 5 simulations you need to deliver in more than one language. It specifically focuses on efficiently changing the narration for each language.

Why

This idea will help assure that your Captivate simulations are consistent across languages.

Use It!

How

If you need to deliver a simulation in more than one language, you can rerecord the same steps in each language. This is not too bad if your simulations are short, but inefficient if you have many simulations to record or if the simulations are longer.

There is a more efficient way to record simulations in multiple languages that will ensure that each language version will show the exact same simulation with no variations except for the language used.

Let's use as an example a Captivate demonstration that shows someone how to open the Symbol dialog box in Word. We want to produce it in English, French, and Spanish. There are two ways to create narration. The first is to record yourself at the computer while running through the capture process. The second is to import audio files, one for each slide, after the capture process is complete.

Before recording the steps in Captivate:

1. Open and prepare Word so that it is ready for recording. For instance, size the Word app to the height and width you wish. Open the Symbol dialog box and make sure it's located where you wish it to appear during the simulation.

2. Reset everything in the application you wish to simulate to an initial state so that you can begin the simulation capture. In this case, close the Symbol box.

Now you are ready to create the demonstration with narration in English. When you have completed it, save the Captivate movie to a file, for instance *wordSymbol.cptx*.

Creating Multi-Language Versions—Narration

1. Copy the Captivate movie for each language, for instance wordSymbol_English.cptx, wordSymbol_Spanish.cptx, and wordSymbol_French.cptx.

2. Now you are ready to create the non-English versions. Let's start with the French version. Open the French version, wordSymbol_French.cptx.

3. Let's assume that we have recorded narration during the capture process and there are seven slides in the demonstration. Open the English version of the demonstration, wordSymbol_English.cptx.

4. Choose Audio>Audio Management and note that Captivate has automatically called the narration audio clips Narration01 through Narration07. Open the Library and you will see the same list there.

5. Save the English version and open the French version, wordSymbol_French.cptx. Go to the Edit tab and make sure you can see the Library (Window>Library).

6. Click on the Library option Open Library above the library objects list. Choose the wordSymbol_English.cptx file. A separate window will open, showing the library for the English version cptx file.

7. Shift-click the narration audio files so that you select all of them (or as many as you wish) and drag them to the library for the current file. Place them under the Audio category to keep things neat. Save your file.

8. Choose all the audio objects that you just imported in the library and choose the Export option, either by right-clicking and choosing Export to Folder or by choosing the Export icon above the list.

9. Save the audio files to a folder. Open each in a separate audio editor or edit it directly in Captivate's audio editor and record the correct narration in French. Save your narration files to the same locations.

10. In Captivate, either in Audio Management or in the Library, choose the audio you wish to change and choose Update. If all of your files are in the same location as where they had been exported, the older audio will be replaced with the new audio.

11. Repeat this process for other language version files.

You now have a separate Captivate file for each language and each file has the narration in the desired language.

Technologies used: Captivate 5, audio editing tool of choice

Adopt or Adapt

This idea is useful for making sure that you have consistent Captivate simulations across languages.

Attribution

Submitted by Joseph Ganci, president, Dazzler Technologies Corp., Asburn, Virginia, USA

Contact: jganci@dazzletech.com or www. dazzletech.com

Since 1983, Joseph Ganci has been involved in every aspect of multimedia and learning development. Joe holds a degree in computer science and has written and continues to write many books and articles about e-learning. He is widely considered a guru for his expertise in e-learning development and teaches classes and seminars at leading universities, in many government facilities, commercial firms, and educational institutions. He speaks at several industry conferences each year. He is on a mission to improve the quality of e-learning with practical approaches that work.

Easier Reformatting of Captivate 5 Captions

The Big Idea

What

This idea provides tips for efficient reformatting of Captivate 5 simulations.

Why

This process makes it easy to do multiple formatting changes to your captions easily.

Use It!

How

You can take advantage of Captivate's ability to export captions to Word to reformat captions faster and more easily. Because all captions are placed in a table column, you can choose the column and make a change to all the captions at the same time, very quickly.

1. First output your captions to a Word document by choosing File>Export>Project Captions and Closed Captions. Save the export file and allow Captivate to automatically open the resulting Word document. It will be named the same as your Captivate file except the extension will be *doc* instead of *cptx*.

2. The Word document will open and will show a table like the one on the next page. Notice the *Updated Text Caption Data* column. This is where you will be making changes.

Slide ID	Item ID	Original Text Caption Data	Updated Text Caption Data	Slide
10102	10116	Select the **Insert** menu	Select the **Insert** menu	1
10117	10130	Select the **Symbol** . . . menu item	Select the **Symbol** . . . menu item	3
10131	10136	The **Symbol** dialog opens	The **Symbol** dialog opens	5
10137	10157	Click the **Insert** button	Click the **Insert** button	6
10150	10172	Click the **Close** button	Click the **Close** button	7

Don't make any changes in any column except the one with the header *Updated Text Caption Data*.

3. You can change individual caption formatting, or change all the captions at once. Let's do the latter. Choose the column in Word.

Slide ID	Item ID	Original Text Caption Data	Updated Text Caption Data	Slide
10102	10116	Select the **Insert** menu	Select the **Insert** menu	1
10117	10130	Select the **Symbol** . . . menu item	Select the **Symbol** . . . menu item	3
10131	10136	The **Symbol** dialog opens	The **Symbol** dialog opens	5
10137	10157	Click the **Insert** button	Click the **Insert** button	6
10150	10172	Click the **Close** button	Click the **Close** button	7

You may change several attributes of the text:

- The font

- The foreground color

- The background color

- The justification (right, left, center)

You can also perform other tasks:

- Number the captions as you would a list.

- Add bullets to each caption all at once.

- Add a table within each cell. (Not recommended, as results will vary.)

- Perform any other tasks that affect the text.

Here's an example of changes we've made the text in the *Updated Text Caption Data* column. We've changed several attributes. These are all preserved.

Slide ID	Item ID	Original Text Caption Data	Updated Text Caption Data	Slide
10102	10116	Select the **Insert** menu	Select the **Insert** menu item	1
10117	10130	Select the **Symbol**. . . menu item	1. Select the Symbol. . . menu item	3
10131	10136	The **Symbol** dialog opens	2. The Symbol dialog opens	5
10137	10157	Click the **Insert** button	3. Click the Insert button	6
10150	10172	Click the **Close** button	4. Click the Close button	7

Note that if you insert images or other non-text objects in the cells, they will not be imported.

4. Save the caption Word document and return to your Captivate source file. Choose File>Import>Project Captions and Closed Captions and import the Word document you just saved that contains the updated captions.

5. All the captions will change to reflect the changes you made in the Word document. Save your Captivate source file.

Technologies used: Captivate 5, Word

Adopt or Adapt

This idea is useful for making efficient changes to the captions in your Captivate simulations.

Attribution

Submitted by Joseph Ganci, president, Dazzler Technologies Corp., Asburn, Virginia, USA

Contact: jganci@dazzletech.com or www. dazzletech.com

Since 1983, Joseph Ganci has been involved in every aspect of multimedia and learning development. Joe holds a degree in computer science and has written and continues to write many books and articles about e-learning. He is widely considered a guru for his expertise in e-learning development and teaches classes and seminars at leading universities, in many government facilities, commercial firms, and educational institutions. He speaks at several industry conferences each year. He is on a mission to improve the quality of e-learning with practical approaches that work.

Creating a Slide Replay Button in Captivate 5

The Big Idea

What

This idea presents a workaround for making a slide replay button work in Captivate 5.

Why

This allows the learner to review audio or video slide content again if you do not include the playback bar.

Use It!

How

The playback bar in Captivate gives users control. If you include the playback bar, learners can rewind an entire movie, go back or forward a slide, and perform other actions. If you don't want to include the playback bar, you may still want to allow the learner to replay the slide. For example, the learner may want to listen to the audio or view a video again.

You can create a replay button so the learner can click it and replay the current slide. However, when the user clicks the replay button, there is no option for replaying the current slide. If the learner uses the Jump to Slide option, he or she will not see the current slide as an option.

The trick is to create a slide with no content that appears *before* the slide to be replayed (shown in Figure 5.55) that plays extremely quickly and advances to the next slide (the one to be replayed). You can then set the replay button to navigate or jump to the previous slide, which will quickly move to the desired slide.

This idea is simpler and avoids the use of an extra slide but does require using an advanced technique, variables, and actions. Don't worry

Figure 5.55. Place Empty Slide Before Slide to Be Replayed

Source: Joseph Ganci

too much about learning the more advanced technique; just follow these steps:

1. Place a text button on the stage (insert>Standard Objects > Button). Label it Replay.

2. In the Properties Action panel, drop down the On Success menu and choose Execute Advanced Actions. Click the folder icon below that.

3. Type "replay" in the Action Name field.

4. Double-click the first line of the empty list.

5. Drop the Standard Actions menu and choose Assign.

6. To the right, drop down Select Variable and choose cpCmndGotoSlide.

7. To the right of that, drop down the variable menu and choose variable.

8. It now changes to Select Variable. Drop down the list and choose rdInfoCurrentSlide.

9. Double-click the blank line below and drop down Select Action. Choose the first command, Continue.

10. Click the Save button, then Close.

11. The Replay script can now be used anywhere in your movie. In fact, you can simply copy and paste this button anywhere and it will allow learners to replay the slide they are currently viewing.

Technologies used: Captivate 5

Adopt or Adapt

A replay button allows learners to review dynamic slide content again if you do not include a playback bar.

Attribution

Submitted by Joseph Ganci, president, Dazzler Technologies Corp., Asburn, Virginia, USA

Contact: jganci@dazzletech.com or www. dazzletech.com

Since 1983, Joseph Ganci has been involved in every aspect of multimedia and learning development. Joe holds a degree in computer science and has written and continues to write many books and articles about e-learning. He is widely considered a guru for his expertise in e-learning development and teaches classes and seminars at leading universities, in many government facilities, commercial firms, and educational institutions. He speaks at several industry conferences each year. He is on a mission to improve the quality of e-learning with practical approaches that work.

Using System Variables in Captivate 5

The Big Idea

What

This idea explains how to work with system variables in Captivate 5.

Why

Variables allow you to customize events in your project. Although some developers worry that they will be hard to work with, in reality, you can start working with variables quite easily.

Use It!

How

Variables can be extremely useful in Captivate projects. Variables hold data for use in the project. Instructors can use variables to personalize the course (Welcome back, George!), keep track of changing events (The time is 10:15 A.M.), and more.

There are two types of variables, system and user. Each variable has a *name*, which identifies the variable using an English descriptor (the name should always be descriptive) and a *value*, which is the current content of the variable. A variable can only hold *one* value at any given time. If a new value is placed in a variable, the old value is destroyed.

System variables are included in Captivate and are often quite useful. Using them can help you avoid a lot of needless work. There are sixty-three system variables. To see the list of system variables, choose Project> Variables . . . and then choose System from the Type dropdown. Each system variable has a description to help you understand its use.

Captivate places system variables in categories. Related variables are in the same category. The chart on the next page shows the variable categories.

Variable Category	Types of Variables in the Category
Movie Control	This includes commands you can send to Captivate by setting values. For instance, you can set the system's volume level or mute it entirely during a learner's session. You can open and close the closed captioned box or pause and resume the learner's session.
Movie Information	This includes information regarding the currently running movie. You can use the variables in this category to find out the current slide number, label, or type. You can check how many seconds have passed since the learner has started the lesson, and much more.
Movie Metadata	This includes information normally stored in metadata files, such as copyright and description of the lesson.
System Information	This includes information related to date and time.
Quizzing	This includes information coming from a quiz that the learner is currently taking.

Ganci shares one simple use of a system variable in order to show the basics of working with them.

If you want to show the current time on the screen you can use the system variable cpInfoCurrentTime. This can come in handy for simulating software or an instrument panel that always shows the current time. Here's how to show the value of this variable on the screen.

1. Insert a text caption on the screen such as:

   The time is currently

2. Now look at the Properties panel in the Format section. There you'll see two buttons next to Insert. Select the button on the right (Figure 5.56).

Figure 5.56. Insert Button

Source: Joseph Ganci

Figure 5.57. Insert Variable Dialog Box

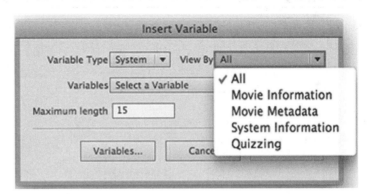

Source: Joseph Ganci

3. Click the button and an Insert Variable dialog box will appear (Figure 5.57). Choose System in the Variable Type dropdown. If you know the category in which the variable you want appears, choose it because it will give you a shorter list from which to choose. If you don't, select View by All and you'll get the full list.

4. To insert the time from the list of variables, choose cpInfoCurrent-Time and click OK. On the stage you will now see

   The time is currently $$cpInfoCurrentTime$$

   The two dollar signs on either side of the variable name tell Captivate to replace the dollar signs and the variable name with the variable's *value* (the current time). Preview or publish your file and you'll see that the current time is now being shown and is continually updated as long as the text caption is shown on the screen. (See Figure 5.58.)

If you want the time to appear on every slide, put the text caption on your master slides!

Technologies used: Captivate 5

Figure 5.58. Screen Output

The current time is 9:13.

Source: Joseph Ganci

Adopt or Adapt

This idea can be adapted to work with the other Captivate system variables.

Attribution

Submitted by Joseph Ganci, president, Dazzler Technologies Corp., Asburn, Virginia, USA

Contact: jganci@dazzletech.com or www. dazzletech.com

Since 1983, Joseph Ganci has been involved in every aspect of multimedia and learning development. Joe holds a degree in computer science and has written and continues to write many books and articles about e-learning. He is widely considered a guru for his expertise in e-learning development and teaches classes and seminars at leading universities, in many government facilities, commercial firms, and educational institutions. He speaks at several industry conferences each year. He is on a mission to improve the quality of e-learning with practical approaches that work.

Adding a Non-Articulate Flash File as a Tab in Articulate Presenter

The Big Idea

What

You can embed Articulate Engage and Quizmaker files as tabs on the Articulate Presenter player. This idea shows how you can do the same thing with a Flash .swf file that is *not* an Articulate Engage or Quizmaker file.

Why

This idea lets you utilize non-Articulate .swf files as a tab in the Articulate Presenter player. This provides a great deal of flexibility in what can be used as a tab in the player.

Use It!

How

If you want an Articulate Engage or Quizmaker file to be available from anywhere in an Articulate Presenter presentation, you can embed it in the Articulate Presenter player. For example, you may decide to produce an Engage Glossary Interaction and embed it as a tab so that the learner can go to it from any place in the presentation.

But what if you have a non-Articulate .swf file that you want to embed as a tab in the Articulate Presenter player? Well, as it turns out, you *can* add an outside .swf file as a tab with a minor workaround. A Flash file example is shown in Figure 5.59.

Kelsall explains how to make this work.

1. While inside Articulate Presenter, embed an existing Engage interaction as a tab (Figure 5.60). (Articulate tab in PowerPoint> Engage Interaction (select Player Tabs)>Add Existing . . .). It can

Figure 5.59. Flash .swf File to Embed

Source: Jade Kelsall

Figure 5.60. Add an Engage Interaction as a Tab

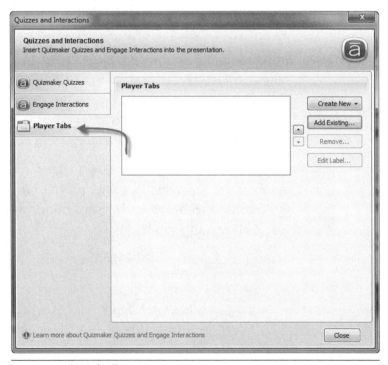

Source: Jade Kelsall

be *any* Engage interaction. (Don't worry, it won't be staying in the presentation.) I use a dummy Engage interaction that has no content for this purpose.

2. When it has finished embedding, click the Edit Label. . . button and type in a label (such as Game or Glossary). This is the label that will appear in the player as a tab.

3. Publish the presentation. Make sure that you have *not* chosen Slide Only View in your Player Template because in Slide Only View, the player tabs are not visible.

4. When the presentation finishes publishing, select Open Folder in the Publish Successful dialog box, as shown in Figure 5.61. Then open the data folder in the published files. Inside the data folder, open the .swf folder and look for a folder that starts with engage_. If you have multiple Engage interactions embedded into your presentation, there will be one of these folders for each of them. The player tab interaction will be the one that starts engage_a.

5. The engage_ folder contains all the files that relate to the Engage player tab. Find the engage.swf file in this folder. This is the "dummy" Engage interaction that you want to replace with your desired .swf file (Figure 5.62).

6. Take the .swf file that you want to display as a tab and insert it into the same folder. Delete the "dummy" engage.swf folder. Rename the .swf file that you want to display as a tab as engage.swf.

Figure 5.61. Select Open Folder in Publish Successful Dialog Box

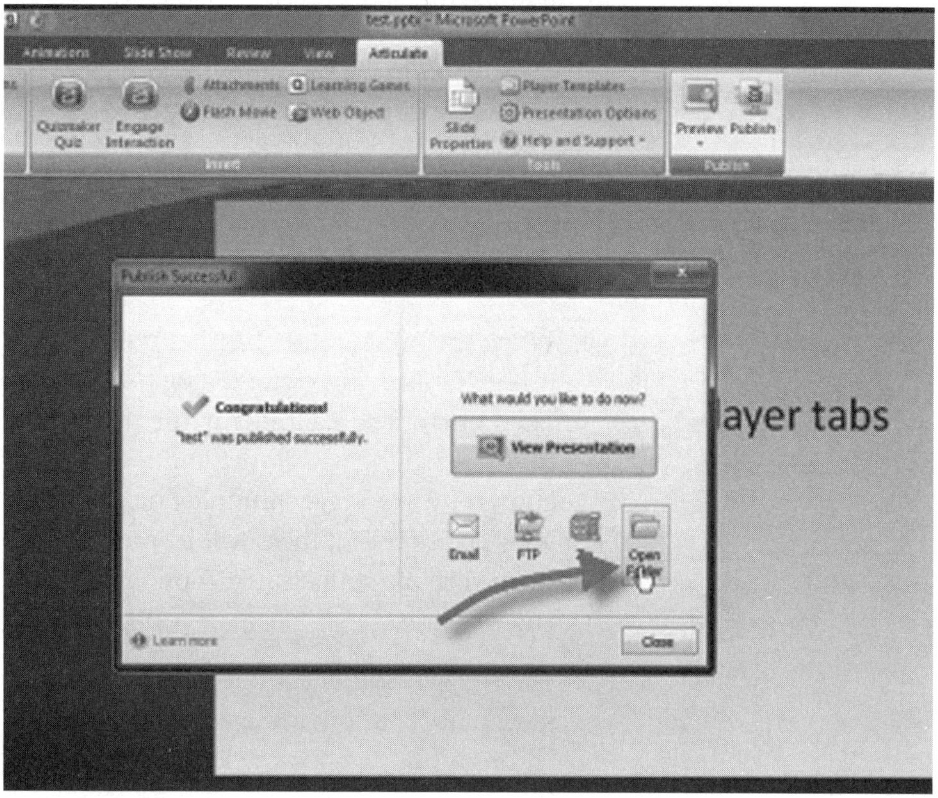

Source: Jade Kelsall

7. Preview the presentation and click on the tab to see your desired .swf file open.

Technologies used: Articulate Presenter and Engage, Flash .swf file

Figure 5.62. Engage.swf File to Be Replaced

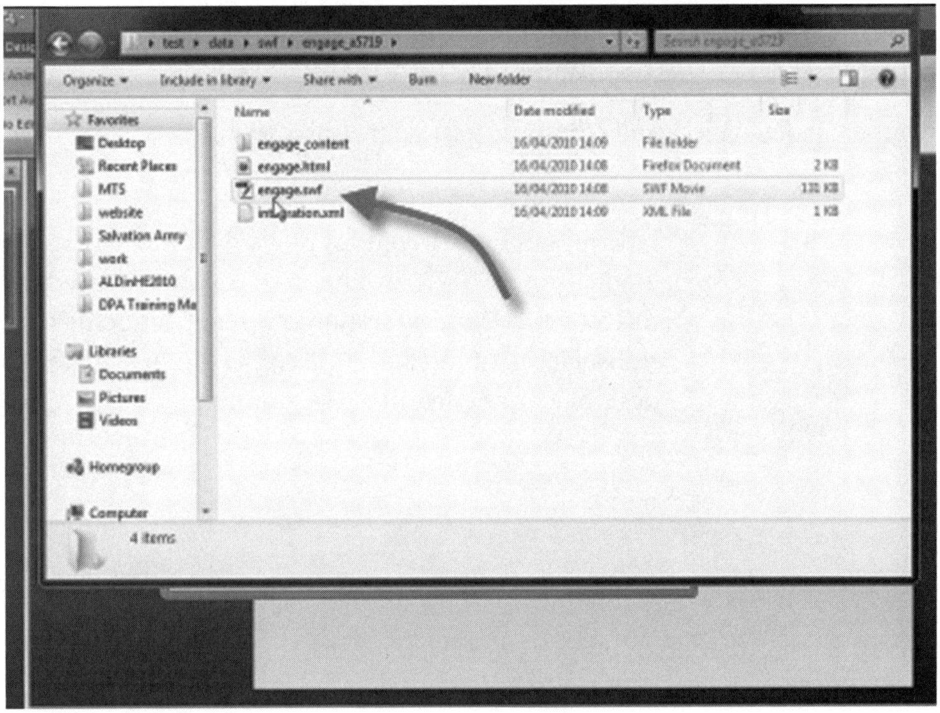

Source: Jade Kelsall

Adopt or Adapt

There are numerous Flash .swf files that might be useful to embed as a tab in an Articulate presentation—glossaries, contact information, credits, a practice element, and so on. If you cannot create what you want in Engage or Quizmaker, you can create it in Flash or in another tool that produces .swf files and embed it as a tab in the Articulate Presenter tab using this process.

Attribution

Submitted by Jade Kelsall, e-learning support assistant, Skills@Library, University of Leeds, Leeds, Providence, West Yorkshire, UK

Contact: jade@jadekelsall.com or http://jadekelsall.com/blog/

Jade Kelsall has worked for Skills@Library at the University of Leeds since graduating in 2007, and her role involves the design and development of interactive e-learning resources to help students to improve their academic skills. Her main area of expertise is the Articulate Studio package. She also does freelance e-learning development.

Linking from Engage to Specific Presenter Slides

The Big Idea

What

This idea shows how to use an Articulate Engage interaction as a menu or introduction to specific Articulate Presenter slides.

Why

This lets you use Engage as a menu or to provide concise information that can be expanded upon on linked Presenter slides.

Use It!

How

A post in the Articulate discussion forums asked how to link from Engage to a particular slide in PowerPoint. In order to do this you'd normally have to use ActionScript code that told the Articulate player to go to a specific slide. And the result wasn't that good.

Moxon, from a workaround developed by Articulate engineer Gerry Palmer, describes how to link to whichever Presenter slide you want from Engage, without the programming or mess. Here are the steps:

1. Create the Engage interaction and add a hyperlink on a word (select some text and press the Hyperlink button). (See Figure 5.63.)

2. In the Hyperlink dialog box, select URL as the type of hyperlink and add the following code with the last number indicating which slide in PowerPoint you want to link to: asfunction:_level44.play-Slide,5, as shown in Figure 5.64.

   Note that the hyperlink in the example is linking to slide 5. If you want the link to go to slide 4, then replace the 5 at the end with a 4.

Figure 5.63. Create Hyperlink in Engage

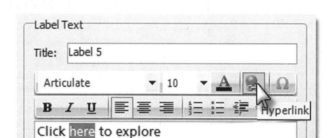

Source: Dave Moxon

Figure 5.64. Select URL and Add Code as Slide Number

Source: Dave Moxon

Note also that the http:// we have at the beginning of a regular link is not used here.

3. Next, click OK.

4. Publish the interaction to the related Presenter project.

5. Find the Engage slide in the project and you will see a Properties button. Select Allow user to leave interaction: anytime.

6. Now publish your PowerPoint presentation with Articulate Presenter and the hyperlinks in Engage will link to slides in your presentation (in this example to slide 5).

Moxon provides a few caveats about this workaround.

- The link will not change automatically if you add extra slides to PowerPoint and the correct slide to link to is no longer the slide you entered. You will need to edit the hyperlink by opening the interaction again in Engage and then republishing to Articulate Presenter. Therefore, it might be a good idea to create your links from Engage to PowerPoint at the very end of the process, just before publishing.

- The workaround is *unsupported* by Articulate so Articulate Support cannot answer questions about it.

Technologies used: Articulate Presenter, Articulate Engage

Adopt or Adapt

This idea works when you want to use an Engage interaction for navigation or allow learners to obtain more information by going to a specific Presenter slide.

Attribution

Submitted by Dave Moxon, product specialist, Articulate, Chateauroux, France

Contact: dmoxon@articulate.com or http://daveperso.com

Also involved: Gerry Palmer, engineer, Articulate

David Moxon joined Articulate as a support engineer in 2007 and is now Product Specialist for Europe. After fifteen years of running his English language school in France, David decided to incorporate e-learning to create a "blended" approach. He experimented with different software and chose Articulate Studio. "The results were outstanding. While I used the traditional teaching for conversation, students tested their comprehension skills online. And they loved it!" He adds it was really his students who chose Articulate for him. David graduated from Cambridge University, Cambridge, England, in 1985 with a degree in economics and philosophy.

Adding PDFs to Articulate Presenter Projects

The Big Idea

What

This idea shows different methods for adding PDF files to Articulate Presenter projects and provides detailed steps for adding PDF files as WebObjects.

Why

The Portable Document Format (PDF) is a useful and popular way to share documents. There are numerous ways to use them inside Articulate Presenter projects, but working with PDFs as WebObjects has some unique benefits.

Use It!

How

There are three typical ways to add PDF files to Articulate Presenter projects.

1. Add the PDF as an attachment. To do this, click the Attachments button on the Articulate tab in PowerPoint. In the Attachments dialog box (Figure 5.65), input a title, method of linking, and browse to the PDF files to include.

2. Add hyperlinks to desired PDF files on a PowerPoint slide. You can either hyperlink directly to a file you have added as an attachment using the format data/downloads/thenameofyourdocument. pdf (where thenameofyourdocument.pdf is the name of the PDF document you want to embed) or simply hyperlink to thenameofyourdocument.pdf and copy the file to your published files folder after you have published your project.

3. Use an online service such as Scribd (www.scribd.com/) to upload your PDF and then view through the Presenter player via a WebObject. To do this using Scribd, go to www.articulate.com/support/presenter09/kb/?p=1617.

Figure 5.65. Attachments Dialog Box

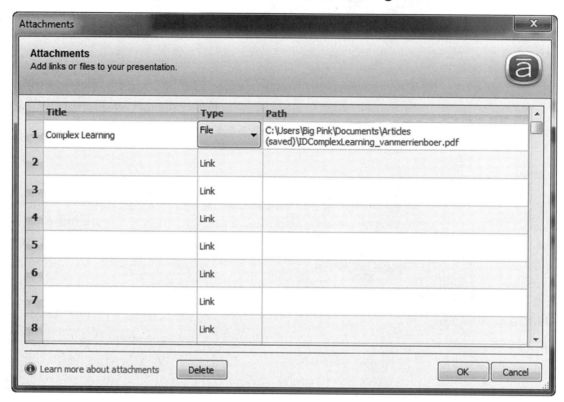

Source: Dave Moxon

Here's an alternative way of displaying PDFs directly inside of a Presenter slide that does not rely on uploading to a third-party site. WebObjects allow you to point to external HTML sites on the Internet and incorporate them into your Presenter slides or embed a local HTML page that you have created (see Figure 5.66). Doing it this way gives you the ability to zoom in on the PDF or print it directly.

Moxon explains the steps for adding PDF files as WebObjects:

1. Create a folder for your WebObject.

2. Use your favorite HTML editor or Notepad and paste the following code:

    <html>

    <head>

Figure 5.66. PDF Inside Presenter Player Using a WebObject

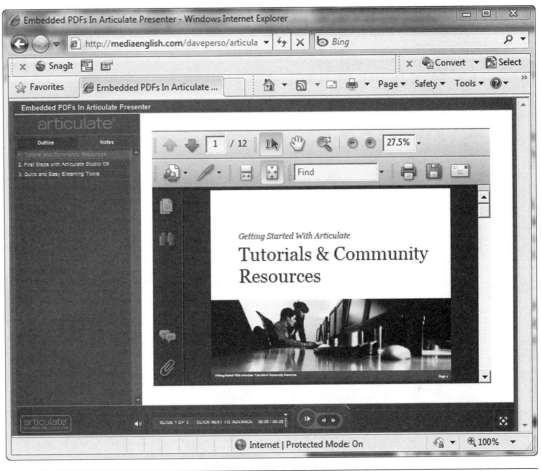

Source: Dave Moxon

</head>

<body>

<embed src="thenameofyourdocument.pdf" width="100%" height="98%">

</body>

</html>

Note that thenameofyourdocument.pdf is the name of the PDF document you want to embed. The name you have in the code *must* match the PDF you wish to embed. Note that "curly" quotes will NOT work in this code. They must be "straight" quotes.

The size variables width="100%" height="98%" can be changed, but setting 100% for width and 98% for height allows the WebObject to display without an unnecessary scroll bar appearing to the right of the WebObject in Presenter '09. It also allows you to open the presentation to fill your screen and have the PDF fill up the WebObject window (which is not the case if you specify sizes in pixels).

3. Save the document you have created as an HTML file and call it index.html. If you are using Notepad, save it as a text file and then rename it to index.html. Make sure that the file is *not* named index.html.txt, as this will not work.

4. Copy the PDF you want to embed into the same folder as the index.html file.

5. In Articulate Presenter, create a new slide, select the WebObject button from the Articulate tab and navigate to the folder you created with the HTML and PDF file. Presenter will detect the index.html file you have in the folder and automatically pull in the PDF file in the same folder.

Articulate Presenter loads these files automatically, so you don't need to worry about where the files are. (But if you are interested, after publishing, look in the data folder and you'll see a folder beginning with the name webobject for each WebObject you add to your presentation. In each of those folders, you'll find your PDF files and index.html files.)

6. If you want to embed several PDFs in your presentation, you'll need to create a separate folder for each PDF.

7. When your project is complete, publish it.

Moxon provides some caveats for using this technique:

- PDFs added this way will not display in Preview or offline. To view, the project must first be uploaded to the web or a course management system.

- While the PDFs that are added as WebObjects correctly display in Internet Explorer 8, Firefox 3, and Google Chrome, you may find that some browsers are not compatible. Check before you distribute!

- The PDFs that are added as WebObjects do not display on a Mac, even when viewed on Safari. This seems to be a Mac problem caused by the way the operating system handles PDF files in general.

- WebObjects do not display on Android devoices.

Technologies used: Articulate Presenter, HTML, PDF files

Adopt or Adapt

There are many reasons why you would include PDF files in a Presenter project. Pick the method for adding them that makes the most sense for your situation. For example, if you want them to be available from anywhere in the presentation, adding PDF files as attachments makes the most sense. But if, for instance, you want learners to read PDF documents at specific points within the project, adding PDF files as WebObjects lets you place them exactly where you want them to be read.

Attribution

Submitted by Dave Moxon, product specialist, Articulate, Chateauroux, France

Contact: dmoxon@articulate.com or http://daveperso.com

David Moxon joined Articulate as a support engineer in 2007 and is now product specialist for Europe. After fifteen years of running his English language school in France, David decided to incorporate e-learning to create a "blended" approach. He experimented with different software and chose Articulate Studio. "The results were outstanding. While I used the traditional teaching for conversation, students tested their comprehension skills online. And they loved it!" He adds it was really his students who chose Articulate for him. David graduated from Cambridge University, Cambridge, England, in 1985 with a degree in economics and philosophy.

Embed Articulate Quizmaker Quizzes (or Articulate Engage Interactions) into Adobe Presenter Presentations

The Big Idea

What

This idea shows how to place Articulate Quizmaker quizzes and Articulate Engage interactions into Adobe Presenter projects.

Why

Adobe Presenter is a commonly used tool for creating narrated PowerPoint slides for the web, but the quiz facility in Adobe Presenter is limited. Quizmaker is *much* more full-featured. It lets you create all sorts of interactive quizzes and surveys. And Engage interactions let you display content in unique ways. So you may want to embed Quizmaker quizzes and surveys and Engage interactions in your Adobe Presenter presentations.

Use It!

How

Clothier developed the following process for embedding Quizmaker quizzes and surveys and Engage interactions in Adobe Presenter.

1. Create the Quizmaker quiz using Articulate Quizmaker.

2. Publish it (Figure 5.67) using the "Web" option. Find the quiz.swf file (you'll need to use it in Step 4).

3. Open the PowerPoint slides that contain your project and choose the slide you want to add the quiz to.

4. In the Adobe Presenter add-in menu (PowerPoint 2003 or 2007) choose Insert Flash and insert the quiz.swf file (Figure 5.68) from the published Quizmaker quiz.

Figure 5.67. Publish Quiz Using "Web" Option

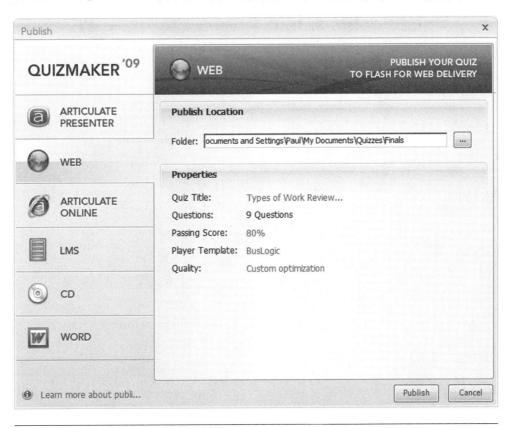

Source: Paul Clothier

5. Resize the inserted .swf to the dimensions you want by dragging the resize handles.

6. Choose Publish in the Adobe Presenter add-in menu and publish to "My Computer." (The preview will show this slide with a spinning "loading" icon because it cannot yet locate all the Flash content.)

7. Locate the published Adobe Presenter files. Go into the /data/resources folder and you should see a file named something like embedded_flash_1.swf. Delete this file.

8. Copy everything in the Quizmaker output files into the /data/resources directory in the Adobe Presenter project.

Figure 5.68. Insert Flash Quiz.swf File

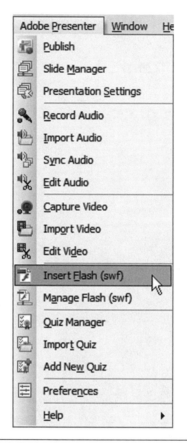

Source: Paul Clothier

9. Move one directory level up into the /data directory and open the viewer.xml file in a text editor. (Clothier highly recommends the free Notepad++ editor.)

10. Locate the line that says:

    "embeddedContent url="./resources/embedded_flash_1.swf" container="mediaContainer.flash1.content" (*Note:* this is on one line but may wrap to a second line if too long.)

Figure 5.69. Replace embedded_flash_1.swf with quiz.swf

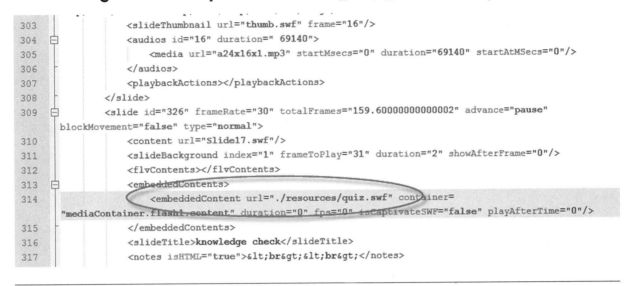

```
303        <slideThumbnail url="thumb.swf" frame="16"/>
304        <audios id="16" duration=" 69140">
305            <media url="a24x16x1.mp3" startMsecs="0" duration="69140" startAtMSecs="0"/>
306        </audios>
307        <playbackActions></playbackActions>
308    </slide>
309    <slide id="326" frameRate="30" totalFrames="159.60000000000002" advance="pause"
    blockMovement="false" type="normal">
310        <content url="Slide17.swf"/>
311        <slideBackground index="1" frameToPlay="31" duration="2" showAfterFrame="0"/>
312        <flvContents></flvContents>
313        <embeddedContents>
314            <embeddedContent url="./resources/quiz.swf" container=
    "mediaContainer.flash1.content" duration="0" fps="0" isCaptivateSWF="false" playAfterTime="0"/>
315        </embeddedContents>
316        <slideTitle>knowledge check</slideTitle>
317        <notes isHTML="true">&lt;br&gt;&lt;br&gt;</notes>
```

Source: Paul Clothier

and replace (Figure 5.69) the text *embedded_flash_1.swf* with *quiz .swf* so you have:

> "<embeddedContent url="./resources/quiz.swf"
> container="mediaContainer.flash1.content"

11. Save the viewer.xml file.

12. Move up one directory level and you should see the index.htm file for your published Adobe Presenter files.

13. Double click the index.htm file to open your published Adobe Presenter project.

14. Test the files. Your Quizmaker quiz should be visible and operational on the appropriate slide, as in Figure 5.70!

You can use exactly the same steps to embed Engage interactions into your Adobe Presenter projects. Instead of using quiz.swf, you will use engage .swf. So in Step 10 you will replace the text *embedded_flash_1.swf* with *engage.swf.*

Figure 5.70. Quizmaker Quiz Inserted on Slide

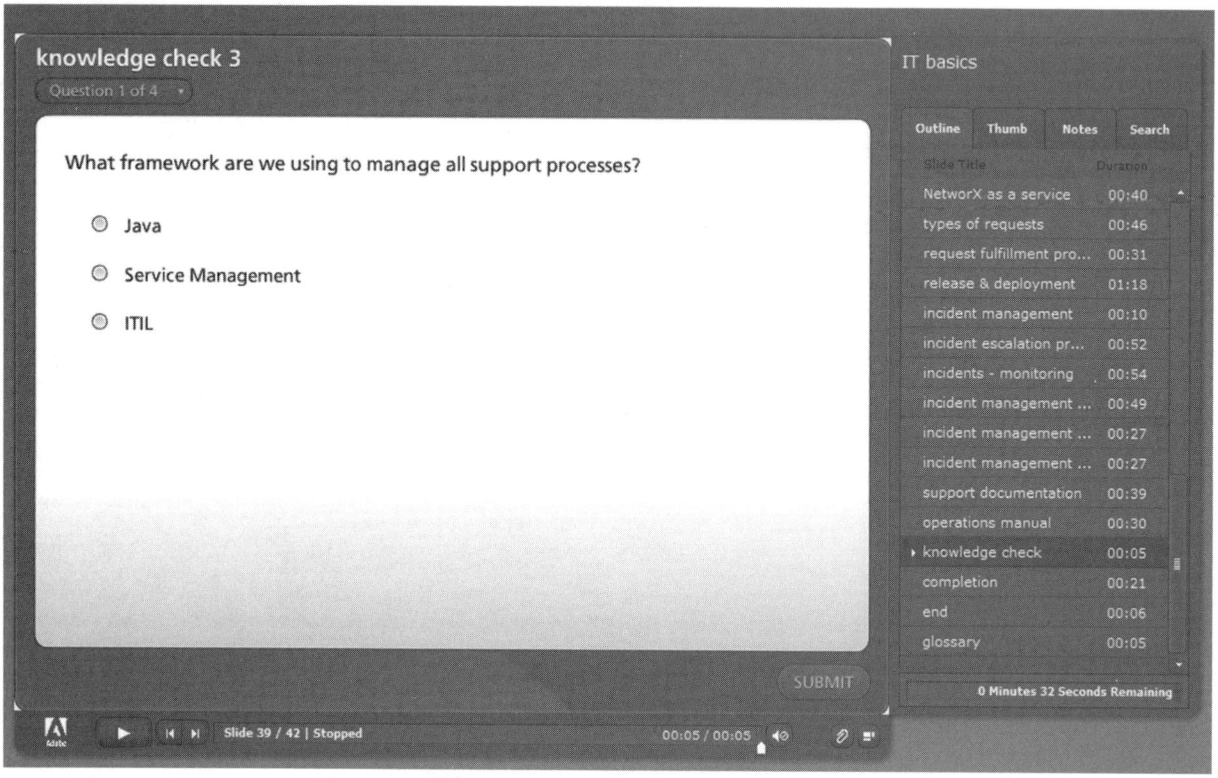

Source: Paul Clothier

Technologies used: Adobe Presenter, PowerPoint, simple programming find and replace

Adopt or Adapt

This idea can be adopted for any Adobe Presenter projects when you want to include an Articulate Quizmaker quiz or an Articulate Engage interaction. The same steps could be used to embed other types of Flash content into Adobe Presenter projects.

Attribution

Submitted by Paul Clothier, principal, TapLearn, Sausalito, California, USA

Contact: paulc@taplearn.com or www.taplearn.com

Paul Clothier is a learning specialist, e-learning and mobile learning developer, speaker, and writer who has been in the technology training and learning field for over twenty-five years. A published author, his articles on e-learning and mobile learning have been featured in numerous learning and training magazines. He has a special interest in mobile learning and instructional design for small screens. Paul is the principal of TapLearn, a mobile learning consultancy.

f you are new to using technology for learning, some terms in this book may be unfamiliar to you. This glossary will help you make sense of some of the most commonly used terms. In addition (in the realm of "shameless plug"), my first book, *Making Sense of Online Learning*, written with Amy Sitze, should be very helpful to people new to this field as well because it was written just for you.

Term	*Definition*
asynchronous	As it relates to online learning, events that are not time-coordinated. People use the materials (and possibly communicate with each other) at different times. Examples include email, threaded discussion, most higher education online courses, and self-paced online courses.
assessments	Materials and processes used to determine whether the learner has met the learning objectives and can perform the necessary skills.
authoring and development tools	Also called applications or software, used to create electronic information and instruction.

blended learning   A combination of learning methods (including, but not limited to, online and face-to-face instruction). Employ the best features of each delivery method—for example, the immediate feedback that happens in classroom learning and the exploration that's possible in self-paced online learning.

blog   Short for "web log." Contains personal journal entries posted in chrono-logical order to a web page. Typically updated on a regular basis and require no programming skills. Some blog hosts provide a web page interface that allows users to simply type a text entry into a form and click on the submit button to publish blog entries.

collaboration   Working together to achieve a common goal.

e-learning   Instruction that uses electronic, networked technologies.

Facebook   Social networking website that allows users to post status updates and pictures and read their "friends'" status updates and pictures.

feedback   Typically means written or verbal evaluation of a learner's action or response to help the learner improve. Feedback is usually programmed into self-paced e-learning so the learner knows whether the choice selected is correct and, if not, why not.

Flash   An Adobe authoring tool typically used to develop animations, simula-tions, and games (and more).

interaction   Learner actions that impact the flow of content or information. Typical interaction types include:

Content interactions involve what the learner does that affects content delivery, including low-level interaction, such as selecting which link to click, or higher levels of interaction, such as answering questions and making decisions in a scenario.

Social interactions involve sharing information, getting help, and providing help to another. May involve posting and responding to what others post (such as on a discussion forum, Facebook, or Twitter), but can also involve using additional technologies such as a webcam and VoIP.

job aid	An electronic or print document that describes how to perform step-by-step tasks. (Other types of job aids are developed, but step-by-step tasks are the very common.)
learning management system (LMS)	Application that handles administrative tasks such as creating course catalogs, registering users, tracking users within courses, recording data (such as test scores) about learners, and providing reports about users.
mobile learning	Learning content and job support accessible on mobile devices, especially smart phones.
mp3	MPEG-1 Audio Layer 3, an audio encoding format with up to 10-to-1 data compression.
mp4	MPEG-4 Part 14, a compressed file type used for video and audio files.
multimedia	Combination of digital media, such as text, images, sound, and video, into an integrated presentation where the combination affords more than the elements alone.
podcast	Audio or video files made available on the Internet for download. Often released periodically and downloaded through web syndication.
plug-in or plugin	Browser extension program used to play supplementary file types. Include Flash, Windows Media Player, and PDF.
simulation	Allow the learner to interact with the content in a realistic way.
	Software simulations let learners interact with and gain feedback on online versions of software applications. Often divided into demos (where the learner watches how the task is performed) and hands-on simulations (where the learner interacts with the content to perform some of the tasks).
	Process or procedure simulations let learners interact with and gain feedback from online versions of a process or procedure.
	Soft skill simulations let learners interact with and gain feedback from online versions of human interactions.
social media	Internet technologies for sharing and discussing information and providing support.

synchronous	As it relates to online learning, events that are time-coordinated or simultaneous. Learners are "attending" and using the materials at the same time, even though they may be in different locations. Examples include chat, online classroom, and web conferencing.
transfer	The degree to which instructional efforts impact job performance.
Twitter	Social networking website that lets users send and read "tweets (short, maximum 140-character messages).
virtual classroom application	Web applications, such as Connect or WebEx, that allow learners to meet synchronously to present, share information, and work together. Typically used for webinars and synchronous classroom sessions.
VoIP (Voice over Internet Protocol)	Uses the Internet as the telephone transmission technology (rather than phone lines).
web conferencing	A method for meeting synchronously over the Internet, using web conferencing applications. May involve sharing slides, desktop applications, polling, talking (by the presenter, participants, or both), synchronous text discussions, and more.
wiki	Collaboratively maintained web information. Allows users to collaboratively add and update content, using a web browser, without web programming.

Patti Shank, Ph.D., CPT, is the president of Learning Peaks LLC, an internationally recognized instructional design consulting firm that provides learning and performance consulting and training and performance support solutions. Clients include government, NGOs, corporations, nonprofits, higher education, content experts, and educational organizations, including Adobe, Oracle, Fidelity Information Systems, The Denver Hospice, Morgan Stanley, Hunter Douglas, Kaiser Permanente, The University of Colorado Health Sciences Center, and California State University.

Patti is well known for her independent and systems-oriented approaches to training, learning, and technology and is listed in *Who's Who in Instructional Technology*. She's an often-requested speaker at training and instructional technology conferences, is quoted frequently in training publications, and has contributed numerous chapters to training and instructional technology books. She is the co-author of *Making Sense of Online Learning* (Pfeiffer, 2004), editor of *The Online Learning Idea Book, Volume 1* (Pfeiffer, 2007), co-editor of *The e-Learning Handbook* (Pfeiffer, 2008), and co-author of *Essential Articulate Studio '09* (Jones & Bartlett, 2009). She was an award-winning contributing editor for *Online Learning Magazine*, and her articles are found in eLearning Guild publications, Adobe's *Resource Center*, *Training* magazine's *Online Learning News and*

Reviews, and *Training Directors' Forum e-net*, Magna Publication's *Online Classroom*, and elsewhere.

Patti completed her Ph.D. at the University of Colorado–Denver, and her interests include interaction design, tools and technologies for interaction, the pragmatics of real-world instructional design, and instructional authoring. Her research on new online learners won an EDMEDIA (2002) best research paper award. She is passionate and outspoken about the results needed from instructional design and instruction and engaged in improving instructional design practices and instructional outcomes. Patti can be reached through her website: www.learningpeaks.com/ and via Twitter: @pattishank.

In addition to work, some of Patti's favorite things include black licorice, hiking, mystery novels, buying cooking and electronic gadgets (and complaining because they don't work as expected), dancing to the tunes in her head, YouTube and TED videos, hanging out with friends and family, laughing, and new ideas.